Contents

Acknowledgements

I am especially grateful to Christopher Long, who first gave magazine space to the 'Action Column'; to Mark Ausenda and Rachel Horner who published most of these pieces in *World Magazine*; and to Richard Girling of *The Sunday Times Magazine* who commissioned me in the spring of '88 to complete a series of five 'Great British Adventures' which appear here in lengthened form. I would also like to record my gratitude to Mark Thackera of Olympus Cameras (UK), who periodically provided the technical back-up which made many of the photographs possible. Finally, many thanks to the instructors, guides and friends who, faced with myself as pupil, must at times have wondered whether it would be easier to teach plankton to play the piano. If I can do it, anyone can.

Dedication

For my Mother and Father,
who always let me learn the hard way.

Nick Crane's
ACTION SPORTS

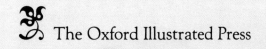
The Oxford Illustrated Press

© 1989, Nick Crane

ISBN 0 946609 95 0

Published by:
The Oxford Illustrated Press Limited, Haynes Publishing Group,
Sparkford, Nr Yeovil, Somerset BA22 7JJ, England.

Haynes Publications Inc, 861 Lawrence Drive, Newbury Park,
California 91320, USA.

Printed in England by:
J.H. Haynes & Co Limited, Sparkford, Nr Yeovil, Somerset.

British Library Cataloguing in Publication Data:

Library of Congress Catalog Card Number:

Photos by Nick Crane unless otherwise stated

Cover photos, clockwise from top left: freefall parachuting with
the Red Devils (photo: Graham Robertson/Parachute Regiment
Freefall Team); hot air ballooning over Wales (photo: Thunder
and Colt); paragliding in the Peak District (photo: David Higgs);
white water canoeing on the River Dart (photo: Rob Stratton);
mountainbiking in Morocco; sub-aqua diving in the Red Sea
(photo: Terry Gibson).

Introduction

Risk takers have been playing these games since the beginnings of time. The 'new challenge' has always appealed to adventurous minds; by daring to step over the line, risk-takers leave the crowd behind and enlarge their own world.

The trick with risks is to isolate the potential dangers and then remove them by treating each as a problem with only one solution: the safe one. From the outside—to those standing on the far side of the line—the game still looks 'risky', but to the risk-taker who now has a measure of the difficulties, the game is a personal test of skill, rather than nerve. None of these sports *ought* to be dangerous; if they are, you're doing something wrong.

Risk-taking saves time. And time is irreplaceable. Some of us sense this more than others. The best antidote for a stressful working life may not be a week flat-out on a beach; prostrating the mind merely leaves it vacant for occupation by the home stresses which flew out with the other personal luggage. Pick instead a new challenge, something that is exciting, stretching, absorbing, new, and you not only escape entirely from that other life, but return to it on a flood-tide of confidence and strength that carries you clean over the pitfalls which once seemed part of the daily grind.

Action sports offer an escape with a very steep learning curve. In one week—or even in one weekend—you can learn more about yourself than you did all year. Inner fears and phobias evaporate in the burn of concentration demanded by learning to fly,

dive, ride or climb. The pride earned through jumping from an aeroplane at 12,000 feet, or learning to roll a canoe, will stay with you for life. Then there are the aesthetic spin-offs: the psychic calm which comes with rock-climbing; the elemental intensity found among the ancient skills of woodlore; the unearthly colours of caves; the eternal moment of liberation felt—and kept—during that first flight beneath the wing of a glider. All these sports have a thrill-quotient, be it dashing waves, free-falling through the air at 120mph or galloping through a forest of flaming aspen—but thrills are just a part of the story. Many of these sports double as types of travel. Horses, bicycles, sea canoes, walking boots, skis, hot-air balloons can be used as vehicles for truly *exotic* journeys; journeys on which you can look at landscapes (and yourself) from a new angle. And all of these are 'soft' vehicles; ones which allow you to move through, and feel for, the countryside, the mountains and wildernesses.

The sports in this book cover the complete range of physical and mental skills; they can be done from your own doorstep or from any one of the hundreds of foreign locations. The sports demand as little as the cost of a pair of boots to as

much as it costs to buy a flying machine. Some of them are very accessible (I have a friend who goes paragliding in his lunch-break) while others require travelling-time and complex equipment.

Individuality now seems to be a hard-won right. In a world where we are being forced to conform to style-types, or career-moulds, or regional identities or family stereotypes, all to a background of pressure on work, personal space and 'green' space, more than ever we need to be able to describe (at least to ourselves) who exactly we *are*. The truth is that we are each no more than the sum of our own experiences. The more experiences we have, the richer we become, and the more we have to share.

Nick Crane,
London,
May 1989.

Action: *River Rafting*

When a bullet fired from a crazed mountainman slams into Drew in James Dickey's book Deliverance—filmed later by John Boorman—the impact is enough to knock his partner Ed from their two-man canoe into the throat of a cataract. Drew's body is snatched away, but Ed, very much alive, finds himself fighting a force of overwhelming power. He has several seconds to learn how a river works, or die.

It was this particular river-image that I was doing my best to ignore as our frail inflatable was swept towards the Parakka-kurkkio—one of Sweden's bigger rapids. I was sitting at the front of the raft, one leg braced beneath a rope. In my hands I gripped a stubby wooden paddle.

The floor of the raft began to bend with the muscle-flex of the river surface. Choppy waves splashed my knees. I snatched a glance backwards: Micke, now standing, was levering his whole body against the two great steering blades. He grinned. The bow of the boat slapped the water, sending spray stinging across our faces. A muted boom, glowing louder, steadily filled the air. Ahead, something strange had happened to the river's perspective: instead of tapering into the distance, or curling round another bend in the trees, a hundred metres ahead, it disappeared. Downwards.

'Paddle back!' Six paddles plunged into the churning River Kalix. I wrenched so hard that flutes of icy water leapt over my legs. The tortured roar of water smashing on rock all but drowned the oarsman's urgent call to backpaddle harder. The boat was picking up speed. I dug the paddle as if I was scrambling for cover during a shell-attack. In a breathtaking surge the raft slid down a smooth scoop and reared on its stern over the following crest.

We tipped over the brink.

Raft design has not changed much since South American aboriginals made the journey which was later to be replicated by Thor Heyerdahl in his 4,300-mile drift from Peru to the Pacific Islands on his raft *Kon Tiki*. Heyerdahl and his crew of five sat on a raft of lashed-together balsa logs; modern rafters sit on rubber tubes of air. It is because rafts are such robust, buoyant platforms that they can carry many times their own weight through waters whose turbulence would capsize any other boat. For over two thousand years rafts have occupied a specialised niche in the world of water-borne vessels. Modern models are built using nylon-Hypalon fabric and composed of independently-inflated air-bags; if one punctures, the raft remains afloat.

Great rivers such as the Blue Nile, Zaire and Colorado have been explored by raft. The risks are not inconsiderable. When Christina Dodwell and a BBC film crew joined an American team attempting a first descent of the remote Wahgi River in Papua New Guinea she told me: 'It was mind-blowingly frightening, but that was the exhilarating thing. It was on the third

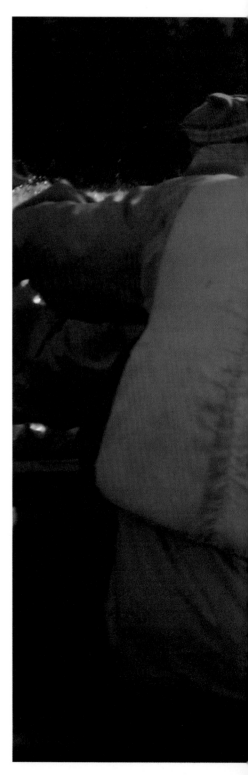

The thunder of water being smashed to smithereens drowns all other sounds once a raft tips over the brink of a rapid: the river seems locked in a struggle of unbelievable violence. Trapped between banks and stretched over a rack of tilting bedrock, waves wrestle for space with shoulder-charges and slams, toppling backwards against the current as if concussed, or rearing up in towering defiance. And amid this sucking, spitting, heaving collision the slabs of water will part to reveal a terrifying hole whose whirlpool edges revolve like a giant grindstone, big enough to swallow a boat. Rocks flash by, spray stinging faces, arms digging, digging, but all that you can remember at the bottom of the rapid, when you're laughing with your friends and looking down at the water lapping at your knees in the half-filled boat, is the sound of the thunder. (The photograph was taken on the Parakkakurkio rapid on the Kalix river).

day that my boat turned over. The boatman had only flipped three times in 12 years. Once you've swum for your life, it's never as frightening again. The BBC cameraman nearly drowned and had to be kept in a dark room for two weeks with ruptured ear-drums. The local tribesmen who found him told him they called the river "Eater of Men".'

On rafts have floated the fantasies of many a growing imagination. When Tom Sawyer, Huck Finn and Joe Harper nicked a log-raft on the Mississippi and poled themselves into the stream piratically crying 'Hellum-a-lee—hard a-port!' they couldn't have known that a century later over a million Americans a year would be making river trips.

The transition from adventure fantasy to commercial reality began in 1962, when a couple of Californian students floated down the Grand Canyon on a raft built from wood and old innertubes. One of the students, George Wendt, became hooked, and in 1967 founded OARS, an outfit that charged people a few dollars to drift downstream with a guide. Sobek, the international offshoot of OARS, now runs river trips as far afield as Chile's Bio-Bio, and down the Euphrates in Turkey.

River-running, or white water rafting is, like skiing, a thrilling sport set in spectacular surroundings. It combines teamwork, danger and excitement. But it is also a unique method of reaching areas of wild country that are otherwise difficult or impossible to reach.

There are not many deep, fast rivers in Europe and the few there are have often been dammed for hydro-electric schemes and therefore been made un-navigable. However Lapland, Europe's last

wilderness, is one area with rivers big enough to justify blowing-up a rubber raft. I flew with friend-photographer Peter Inglis to northern Sweden. Peter had seen an advertisement for a rafting 'experience' two days earlier, and on a whim had booked us in. We would be a crew of seven, with a local boatman at the steering oars.

We were met at the airport by Ulla Mannela—one of the river guides—and she drove us through the forest to a large wooden building in a clearing beside the water. There we met our companions. We looked an unlikely crew: somehow, the Lapps were going to have to create a cohesive team from a bank manager, a journalist, a tank-designer from the Ministry of Defence, a photographer, a teacher, an accountant and a secretary from the City. A quick glance revealed a probable age span of 18 to 55, and a weight range from 8 to 15 stone. The human dynamics were bound to be interesting: how would we all cope, cooped up together for two weeks on a little rubber bubble? Would anyone crack when the going got tough? I thought of Maurice and Maralyn Bailey, alone on their 4½-foot inflatable in the Atlantic for 118 days.

The trip was organised by the company Jukkasjärvi Hembygdsgård, who base themselves in a collection of Lappish chalets on the banks of the River Torne, in Sweden's far north. Northern Sweden is the land of the Lapps; nomads who eke a living from the edge of the world by farming and herding reindeer. There are others here too: mining families whose ancestors made the long journey north from southern Sweden and Denmark at the turn of the century to look for precious metals. They travelled along the rivers, sledging the frozen

surfaces in winter when ice formed a smooth, hard roadway, and boating them in summer in slender high-prowed vessels which could survive the many rapids. Many of the falls were too dangerous for the fragile wooden hulls and the boats had to be man-handled through the forests on adjacent timber trackways.

In 1982, the UK company Avon asked some local boatmen in Kiruna to test one of their new rubber boats. The Lapps were so impressed by the versatility of these new river craft that they bought the test boats, and were soon ordering more. A year later organised trips were being offered on Avon inflatables down two selected rivers. The river guides of 'Jukkas' as the company is known—men and women—have all grown up with the forests and rivers of Lapland. Our small group, who were all first-timers in Lapland, would make two journeys: the first down the river Torne, the other down the Kaitum and thence into the Kalix. These rivers hurtle across the Arctic Circle from the mountains high on the Norwegian border. Born up in the mountains not far from Narvik, on the Norwegian coast, the Torne cuts a vigorous swathe through the forests of Sweden to pour into the Baltic near the Finnish border. We were to follow it for 200 kilometres through to its middle reaches.

Our boatman for the Torne, was Johann, otherwise known as 'Yokka'. He wore a floppy felt hat, an orange flower tucked in its brim and a curved bone scabbard at his waist; he looked young enough to be a pupil. With Yokka for the week was another Lapp. Mike was older, had wire-brush stubble, had recently completed his national service and would help out with the camps. He wore a spotted neckerchief,

gathered at the neck by a wooden toggle.

In a store-room at Jukkasjärvi, Yokka and Ulla issued us with yellow waterproofs, wellington boots and life-preservers. Our spare clothes were stuffed in huge blue plastic sacks and bound tightly shut. It was a short drive to the launch site, a small shingle beach tapering into the flat rain-spattered lake of a swelling in the Torne. Not a ripple marked the sheet-metal surface of the river. Squeaking, and slightly self-conscious in our rubber-plastic river uniforms we heaved the raft off the trailer and carried it to the water's edge. The clothes bags were stowed beneath a tarpaulin at the front of the raft. Food for five days (reindeer steaks, caviar spread, grog) was packed in watertight plastic crates strapped to the seats. After a stiff pose for a departing photograph, Yokka said 'Now we start the adventure.'

The Torne proved a perfect introduction to river-rafting. At night we beached the raft and camped in the forest. It was a romantic journey, with cosy evenings around crackling birchwood fires and ethereal river mists creeping across the river at dusk. Yokka taught us how to catch grayling with a spinner and let us take turns steering the raft through the smaller rapids. Mike showed us which berries we could eat without ending up in Luleå Municipal Hospital. He also taught us how to use the aluminium canoe that we towed behind the raft.

We learnt the 'feel' of the raft. Compared to a canoe, a raft is as cumbersome and unresponsive as a builders' skip on a ski slope. Steering is achieved by 'ferry gliding' the raft across the river's current: by twisting the raft through 45° and rowing against the current, the force of the water

pushing on the upstream side of the raft is enough to allow it to slide crab-wise across the river. Unlike normal rowing, the oarsman faces forward, watching for rocks, stoppers (the rearing wave at the foot of a drop), standing waves, reversals (dangerous eddies of backward-moving water that can suck the raft under a fall) and holes—all of them capable of flipping or swamping a raft. Only by paddling the raft faster or slower than the river's current is it possible to steer.

Fitted to the top of the inflated tubes is a rowing frame on which are mounted the two long steering blades. The raft's 'engine', six or so paddlers, sit down each side, one leg tucked under a strap to prevent 'man-overboards' in rough water.

At the end of the fifth day, we came to a bridge over the river. The 'Jukkas' van was waiting. Since the second week of rafting would be down the much more serious Kalix and Kaitum rivers, we were to be allowed a weekend's rest and recuperation.

I've always wanted to climb the highest mountain in Sweden. It's called Kebne-kaise, and stands at 2,117 metres, not far from the border with Norway. Ulla arranged for us to borrow a van. We drove to Nikkaluokta, then hitched a lift in a small helicopter to the Kebnekaise Fjälls-tation, a clutch of wooden chalets used as a climbing/skiing base in the heart of the mountains. The climb took ten hours, the last few metres being a teeter along a knife-edge snow arete in a blinding white-out. Earlier, I had counted the contours between the summit ridge and the glacier below. Anyone falling would not have stopped for 517 metres. We returned to the Fjällstation just before dark, cold and

RIVER RAFTING

ferry glide to use the force of the current to cross a river crabwise.
flip to turn a raft upside down.
haystack a **standing wave,** tip-ped with white water.
hole sometimes called a **hydrau-lic, souse hole** or **suck hole** and to be avoided at all costs.
paddle a spade-shaped tool used by crew-person.
puncture more serious in a rubber craft than on a bicycle but easier to find because you can see the bubbles.
rapid a bumpy bit of river, whitish, with black bits.
rooster tail a towering standing wave liable to **flip** a raft.
slot the narrowest part of a gorge or canyon.
swamped a raft which has the river on the inside as well as the outside.
waterfall a steep rapid.
wrap to fold a raft around a rock.

Micke Krekula, our oarsman on the Kalix and Kaitum rivers 'ferry glides' the raft across the current looking for the 'V' of smooth water which marks the entry point to the rapid. Behind him, the four stern paddlers (the outdoor photographer Peter Inglis is far right) backpaddle furiously to give the raft steerage way.

hungry. Next morning, back at Nikka-luokta, Mikael Krekula was waiting for us.

'Micke' would be our boatman on the Kalix and Kaitum. He is an impressive

man. Like many Swedes he had learnt more about outdoor survival in his twenty years than most westerners pick up in a lifetime. Camping, fishing, canoeing, ski-touring, mountaineering, navigation, shelter-building, cooking, companionship, were all second nature to Micke.

From the glaciers hard on Norway's Atlantic coast, the Kaitum falls east as if descending a massive staircase. Swelling in volume every kilometre, it joins the river Kalix then pours into the northern Baltic. We were joining it about a third of the way

from its icy rising. Our safety, said Micke, would depend upon our ability to work together.

'If you fall out of the raft in a rapid' Micke told us 'turn feet first so you bounce off the rocks.' In water just a few degrees above freezing, and moving fast, we would have just minutes to drag ourselves to the bank—if we weren't sucked under. 'If you do get pulled down' Micke concluded, 'they say you should pull yourself along the bottom of the river until you're clear of the current, then swim upwards. That's the

rapid: Parakkakurkkio. Landing upstream of the falls, we walked its length first, looking for the holes and rocks, then flew down in a welter of whoops and spray. Rocks flashed by, freezing slabs of water leapt inboard and we ran out over a series of huge standing waves. At the bottom, we were soaked; exhilarated; laughing with relief.

We lived on the water and slept in the forest. Each day, two hours before sunset, we pulled the raft up the river bank and pitched the tents. We were welding together as a team. Peter became the group specialist at lighting fires. The man from the MoD turned out to be a gourmet cook and the accountant, a thin man from Dublin, became the team wit. We fished for grayling in the dusk, and stalked trout in the black marsh pools after dark, cooking our catches in the fire's embers. To Micke we became 'Den Engelska Gummibatsbesattningen'— the English gumbootpaddlers.

There is a magic possessed by those northern forests that I've not felt anywhere else. If there is sound, then it is of the wind sighing in pines or the tumble of water on rock. But mostly there is a silence; a regenerative silence. The sky rules the mood, changing hour by hour as clouds shrink, stretch and shred in the upper winds, sometimes torn away completely to leave a ceiling so clean and empty that the forest seems to go on forever.

This was not the wilderness terror of Dickey, but a rich, delicious returning to real, raw values. It wasn't the ghosts of whisky-soaked murderous 'crackers' that whispered in the dark pines at night but the murmurs of Tom, Huck and Joe enjoying their bacon over an open fire on Jackson's Island. One night, fortified against the chill of an Arctic night by a bottle of Scotch, we lay back watching the Northern Lights: curtains of green neon, swelling, breaking and fusing in bizarre cosmic reflection.

On the last day we came to Saarikurkkio. 'Nowhere in Sweden,' shouted Micke above the bellow of the water 'have I seen a rapid like this.' The whole width of the Kalix was being forced through a narrow rocky cleft just a few metres wide. The force was awesome. From the raft, beached a hundred metres above the fall, we ferried the crates and bags by foot through the forest to a point on the bank beyond the rapids. To control the boat, it would have to be as light as possible. Micke spent half-an-hour scrutinising the gigantic waves from a vantage point on a nearby hill.

Calling us together, he pointed out the route down the chute. At one point a standing wave like a small haystack climbed high each side of two bottomless stoppers. The plan was to fly the raft right over the top of this standing wave.

He drifted into the main stream. Ahead the air boiled with water vapours and the thunder of thousands of tons of water being smashed to smithereens.

'Paddle back. Warm up,' commanded Micke. It was a relief to turn fear into physical effort. Suddenly the current picked us up. We were sucked forward as if by a giant magnet. 'Back, BACK!' came Micke's shout. Water lumped over my legs. I dug deep, my left arm going under with each frenzied paddle stroke. Every sense was under bombardment: bursting wave sparks filled the air like a thousand imploding televisions; ear-drums were compressed by the weight of noise; lungs hauled volumes of watered air.

The raft shot on, lifting. We tipped over a small fall. 'Forward. FORWARD HARD!' The raft flew round the edge of a black vortex sucking like a drain, then accelerated towards the standing wave. For a moment I was paddling air, then the raft tipped. I was thrown sideways, tangling with Peter's legs; hanging on for dear life.

The raft lurched level. We span past a gaping hole in the river, hurtled round its lip then flew like a projectile into the face of another standing wave. 'More forward' came Micke's urgent cry. The boat leapt. We were through, roller-coasting the crests of decreasing standing waves. Water sloshed about our knees. Peter was hugging Micke and there was a confused babble of laughter. 'Great!' shouted Micke. 'Now we have just one more rapid: the Mestoslinka. It has never been rafted. A canoeist tried, but was drowned. I think with this team, we can do it.'

And we did. Just.

theory anyway. Though I've never met anybody who's managed to do this.'

We put the boat in the water beyond the small mountain village of Killinge. The Kalix looked much wilder than the Torne, with foam-backed rocks jutting at random from the current. The river thundered brutally past our feet. When we let go of the rocks, our rubber boat was snatched into the current and tossed carelessly downstream while we fought to keep control.

Ii took two days to reach the first big

Action: *Hot-Air Ballooning*

Getting up in the air is no problem' said Bäcklin, pausing to open the propane valve. A blast of heat bathed our heads as orange fire roared upwards into the envelope.
   'It's coming down again that can be interesting,' he said, grinning.
   Bäcklin wetted his finger and held it over the side of the basket.
   'We're coming down.' He caught my questioning glance. "Yes", he explained, 'if the underneath of your finger feels cool, then the balloon is descending; if the top side of your finger feels cool, then you are going up. It is quite scientific.'

Below us, Wales curved away in all directions. Fields and forest fitted together in a uniquely-viewed mosaic. The slender thread of a road picked its way down the valley bottom and disappeared behind a bluff. Travelling at the same speed as the wind there was no sensation of motion; we hung still and silent 2,000 feet above Cwm Pennant. Our globule, filled with 77,000 cubic feet of hot air, maintained station like an orbiting planet above the greater globe below. I had an (almost) overwhelming urge to climb over the leather-bound lip of the basket and walk around outside.

The burners above our heads blasted again.

'Power lines are the biggest danger. And of course we need to land near a road so that the retrieve van can reach us easily.' Bäcklin peered downwards. (Looking over the edge of a balloon basket is rather like looking into a microscope.)

The radio cleared its throat: 'Balloon to retrieve. We'll probably come down before the lake. Over.' Far below us the message blurted into the cab of the retrieve vehicle—a Japanese pick-up. We watched the silver pip detach itself from the verge of the country road and creep down the valley towards Bala Lake. The ground began to magnify.

In just a few seconds we had lost a thousand feet.

'Can't burn here or we'll scare the horses.' Bäcklin was pointing to a pair of ant-size animals. The balloon continued to sink, soundless. The bleats of lambs wafted

up to us. A cliff approached. The basket was still going down. Unnervingly close to the cliff, we could now see ledges busy with ivy and shrubbery. The roaring burner startled a family of rabbits who shot along the grassy shelf, turned and ran back again, confused by the gigantic red disc that had suddenly eclipsed their sky.

Tree tops slithered beneath our feet. Just when it seemed inevitable that the basket would slam into the top of the cliff, we lifted, tugged from above by our warming bubble, till the basket popped over the lip of the cliff into the sunlight. We were looking down on the River Dee and the roofs of Bala town, the lake beyond grey and greasy in the last of the evening light.

'We'll land in the corner of that triangular field.'

The field looked absurdly small.

'Take off your camera. Face forward. Bend your knees. Hang on tight. AND STAY IN THE BASKET. If you get out, the basket will be lighter and so the balloon will take off again, and I will land in the lake.' Very fast, a tree rushed by. Grass zoomed towards us. A feeding trough flashed by. With a bump we grounded. The basket tipped on its side and filled with flailing arms and legs. 'OK?'

'OK.' We were down. We had been in the air for one and a half hours.

The balloon had landed precisely where Bäcklin had predicted. The wrinkled skin of the envelope lay across the field, warm breath panting from its throat and its red, sagging flank melting into the darkling

grass. People were running across the field towards us. The nose of the silver pick-up poked around a distant gateway.

Bäcklin brought me round. 'OK, out now. Hold the crown-line while I find the farmer. That's the only awkward thing about ballooning; you have to ask permission to land after you've actually done it.'

It had been a six-week wait for the weather to turn. My first flight in a hot air balloon went quicker than blinking. Mats Bäcklin, a Swedish-born designer working with Thunder and Colt, one of Britain's two balloon and airship companies, had offered to take me up. A few minutes' drive from Thunder and Colt's factory in Oswestry on the Welsh borders we unrolled the balloon and rigged the basket, propane tanks and instruments on the turf fronting the elegant Georgian facade of Sweeney Hall.

Inflating the balloon took less than ten minutes. Using a petrol-driven fan, cold air was blown into the envelope. Then the burners were ignited. Hot air was squirted into the balloon mouth. The nylon swelled, tightened and raised itself. We climbed in. The ground crew cast off the mooring line and the world fell away.

We climbed to 6,000 feet, drifting west at 15 knots. The farms on the flanks of the Berwyn Mountains dwindled into dots. The two 30-kilogram propane tanks would be enough to keep us in the air for approximately 2¹/₂ hours.

The art of ballooning lies largely in reading the wind. A height difference of just a few feet can alter a balloon's course by several degrees; you turn left or right by going up, or down. Holding his waterproof map, Bäcklin pointed down to Llanarmon Dyffryn Ceiriog. 'After leaving this village we're committed to crossing the Berwyns. There is no good place to land for 45 minutes.' He let the balloon sink so that we could examine the grass embankments of an Iron Age hillfort. Sheep freckled the hillside.

Blocking the horizon, the high ridge of the Berwyns rose to meet us and we skimmed the summit of Cadair Bronwen. Its cairn, a massive stone structure which

Utter stillness is one
of the many unique
features of balloon travel.
Moving with the winds
there is not even a breeze
to ruffle the hair of those
in the basket. The
unreality is encouraged
by the romance of
watching the world drift
by from the creaking
wicker basket of a flying
machine lifted straight
out of the pages of the
best adventure fiction.
'Lift' is created by
heating the air in the
balloon 'envelope' with a
gas burner. The pilot is
Mats Bäcklin.

I've panted by when fell-walking, dropped behind us. It looked no bigger than a single finger.

I watched the stream patterns: like the branches of a tree they gathered water from the high moor, funnelled down into little gorges and so to a scattering of tiny dwellings. (It was the hamlets of this part of Wales that put George Borrow during his wanderings of 1854 through 'Wild Wales' in mind of the villages of old Castile and La Mancha.)

For a device of such simplicity, it has taken a surprisingly long time for the balloon to evolve. Since the beginnings of time, Man must have looked at the clouds, wanting to wrap and ride those light, fluffy sky-rafts. To fly like a bird involved frenzied flapping, inconceivable aerodynamics and probable death, but to drift like a cloud across the sky seemed a subtler, calmer path to the gods. Standing in the way of this aesthetic quest was the discovery of a packageable substance lighter than air.

According to ballooning lore, as early as the 12th century BC the Chinese were using smoke-filled envelopes to lift men above the ground. But as a modern science, the date that counts is 1709, when a Brazilian priest, Bartolomeu Lourenço de Gusmão showed a model hot-air balloon to Johan V of Portugal. No account exists of the model having been developed into a full-scale manned balloon, and it was left to the French to scoop the credits later the same century.

On June 5th, 1783, two papermakers from Annonay watched a bag of hot air rise above a small fire that they had built. The two men, brothers Joseph and Étienne Montgolfier, then built a bigger model and managed to lift into flight three passengers: a sheep, a rooster and a duck. History proffered no laurels on the shoulders of these three pioneers.

One month later, the Montgolfiers floated into the record books with their *experience arostatique* above the Bois de Boulogne. Suspended beneath a balloon filled with the smoke and heat of burning wool and straw, two pilots—Jean-Françoise Pilâtre de Rozier and François Laurent, Marquis d'Arlandes—rose over 400,000 upturned faces and flew for a full 23 minutes and 9 kilometres before returning to earth.

Less than a year after the Montgolfier flight, the invention of a fabric which was resistant to the leakage of helium and

HOT AIR BALLOONING

ballast sandbags which can be thrown over the side of the balloon basket to give added lift.

Big Bender a balloon race in which the aim is to change course as acutely as possible.

rough landing in which the balloon basket passes through two hedges, a greenhouse and a wedding party before coming to rest in a field recently spread with chicken manure.

crewperson same as **ballast**.

gift-wrap a messy landing which ends in collapsing the balloon over a house, tree, car, picnickers etc.

funny the name given to a balloon envelope which is not a conventional 'bubble'. Funnies include a giant pair of jeans, a sparking plug and a light bulb.

gores the panels of which a balloon envelope is constructed.

pilot glamorous hotshot in charge of the valve.

variometer an instrument used to measure the rate of ascent or descent.

wet finger same as the variometer.

hydrogen spelled the premature death of hot air ballooning. Gas balloons were more buoyant and so could be built with smaller, more manageable envelopes. Added to that, their ability to stay in the sky was not dependent upon burning prodigious quantities of dangerously-combustible fuel.

Sport ballooning took off in 1906 when the American millionaire-publisher James Gordon Bennett initiated an annual balloon race designed to test to the limit the skills and endurance of the pilots. Most of the balloons competing in this aeronautical equivalent of the Paris–Dakar motor rally were specially built for the event. The risks were considerable: after 43 hours in the air, the winner of the 1908 race ended up in the North Sea. Four years later an American competitor was locked up after crossing by mistake into Russia. The race ran for 26 editions until the outbreak of World War II put an end to all aerial frivolities.

It was not until the 1950s when a young American called Ed Yost working for the US Navy developed the propane burner and lightweight polyurethane-coated nylon, that hot air balloons could re-emerge as safe, reliable aircraft. And eleven years after the barrage balloons were winched down, sport ballooning began in Britain. In August 1966, at Dunstable Flying Club, the British Balloon and Airship Club was formed. At the time, there were only three hot air balloons in the country; now there are over 500.

Hot air ballooning is not cheap; the price of a single four-man balloon would buy 3,000 hours on a squash court. But they *are* beautiful: the exquisite curve of hot skin sits in the sky like a bubble of molten glass; the basket is woven from Palambang wicker and trimmed in padded suede. Every fitting is the best stainless steel. The basic cost of a four-man balloon is roughly the same as that of a small saloon car. Provided you do not 'gift wrap' a tree or greenhouse, a balloon envelope will last for 400 hours of flying time.

The British Balloon and Airship Club reckon that over 50 per cent of balloons in Britain are used for advertising. 'More and more companies are discovering ballooning; it's an incredible publicity stunt. You've got a sixty-foot hoarding floating across the sky. People have to stop and look.'

It is the 'funnies' that *really* turn heads. Who could grudge a gasp if a 150-foot pair of Levis floated overhead; or a sparking plug or an ice-cream cone? The 'funnies' are very difficult to fly. Neither have balloons been ignored by the art world. Austrian fantasist André Heller was commissioned by Vienna to put the city back on Europe's cultural map. Heller's three aerostatic sculptures—Dragon Fish, Moon and Dream Lab—raised heads and eyebrows across Europe. Dream Lab was a multi-coloured tentacled sputnik affair; a cross between a sea-urchin and a juke-box.

In America, ballooning is bigger. One of the country's leading enthusiasts is Rocky Aoki, a Japanese-born ex-wrestler who became a multi-millionaire after bringing *teppan-yaki* cooking to his chain of Manhattan restaurants. Aoki's passion for adventure is obsessive. Twice he has been involved in powerboat accidents which between them resulted in a torn aorta, broken legs, and a ruptured spleen and gall bladder. His heart stopped beating. Then, in Japan, in 1981, he and two other

Americans climbed into the gondola of a 130-foot, 7½-ton helium balloon called Double Eagle V. Eighty-four hours and 31 minutes later, having thrown everything out of the ice-burdened gondola (including a $10,000 TV camera) in an attempt to keep it airborne, they slammed into a Californian mountainside and became the first men to fly a helium balloon across the Pacific.

After his 6,000-mile Pacific flight Aoki drove a 1959 Rolls-Royce Silver Wraith from Milan to Moscow. In his luggage was a hot air balloon. He planned to inflate in Red Square and offer rides to Russian officials. But this was post-Mathias Rust, (the schoolboy who was imprisoned for landing a plane in Red Square) and the Russians were not in the mood for frolicsome western aviators. Aoki was prevented from even unrolling his balloon.

Aoki is typical of what the American behavioural psychologist Dr Frank Farley defined as a 'Type T personality'; a thrill-seeker biologically committed to adventure. Type Ts favour novelty, complexity, ambiguity, conflict, intensity, uncertainty. They are upbeat, happy, optimistic. 'You're afraid to die; you're afraid to live,' Aoki told me. (It's always struck me as curious that the maddest people in the world have a habit of sounding the most sane.)

When I met Aoki in New York in 1987, he was preparing for the first international balloon competition to be held in China. For the weekend he took me up-state to fly three of his China-balloons in the 11th Annual Pennsylvania State Hot Air Balloon Championships.

Shuffling in the dawn cold, crews gunned the propane burners; the chemical billows of 25 brightly-coloured balloons rippled on the wet grass like soft blancmange. They grew in the rising light. Aoki watched. 'Aren't you coming too?' I asked Aoki. 'No,' he shouted above the roaring burners, 'I look.' As the balloons lifted one by one over the golden trees I could see Aoki's face watching with the wonder of a young boy who knows that he can blow bubbles in any sky he likes.

This was a 'hare and hounds' race: ahead of the main flock was the 'hare', a red balloon dressed as a Campbell's soup can. The soup can would fly for maybe half an hour then land and spread a marker on the ground. All the 'hounds' would try and fly over the marker, and—at the right moment—hurl a coloured streamer over the edge of the basket. The pilot who managed to land his streamer closest to the ground

marker would be the winner. It is a game of the utmost flying skill.

Conditions were difficult: a heavy autumn mist tickled the dull surface of the Delaware river and low cloud smeared the sky between the peaks each side of the valley. There was hardly any wind. There were three of us in Benihana No.2 balloon: myself, Muriel Ives, and the pilot, a Tom Sellick lookalike called Tom Baldwin, who regularly competes across the States. As we lifted off, he asked if Muriel and I were comfortable. We rose to three hundred feet.

Baldwin thought that we were too close to the hare.

'See, we need room to left or right. Get too near and we'll overshoot.'

Looking for slower-moving air, Baldwin let the balloon sink down towards the tree canopy. Another balloon, white with a blue waistband, had miscalculated badly and was now sitting on the surface of the Delaware, blasting continuously in an effort to pull free from the river's surface tension. A mile to the left, far too high, a second balloon was heading over the ridge line of the Pocono Mountains.

'Uh uh. They got *problems*', tutted Tom.

'Muriel,' I asked, 'is your husband worried about you doing this?'

'Yup,' she said, grinning.

Our basket flew through a tree.

'Pick a leaf,' suggested Baldwin.

The lower, softer wind was carrying us further to the right than the breeze a couple of hundred feet higher. Two balloons flew over the top of us. I could see the rain spotting the river. Coloured bubbles filled the valley, sparking and barking, wriggles of steam rising from the hot tops of the balloons. Soon we were further to the right

than all the other balloons. Baldwin pulled the valve and we rose, picking up speed. We drifted, timelessly, dreamily. Good canoeing country. Deer on the forest edge.

'Coming down!' We were sinking fast. Baldwin was leaning over the edge, fingering the valve. Our green streamer trailed from his left hand. He was muttering quietly. A white marker lay in a small pasture ahead. We were going to miss it by a hundred yards. But an unseen current caught the balloon and we curved left, tickling an oak tree. Baldwin swung back his arm and lobbed the streamer out of the basket. It fluttered down to land thirty feet from the marker.

We walloped into the corner of a soaking wet hay-field. Crown-line duties complete, I helped roll the dripping nylon into its carry-bag. Aoki arrived, shaking his head.

'Seventh,' he said. 'You didn't win. Only winning counts.'

Back at Thunder and Colt I was invited to join a test flight. Bäcklin wanted to show me their latest project. This was the 'baby' of company boss Per Lindstrand, another Swede. Near the huge doors of the hanger-like workshop stood a gleaming steel sphere no bigger than an average lift car. Inside were two aircraft-seats and several banks of instrument panels. Round the small, curved door were scrawled fitters' instructions: 'Floatation Collar'; 'Sea Anchor'; 'Smoke Beacon'.

This small metal ball was to attempt the first hot-air trans-Atlantic flight. In one of the seats would be Per Lindstrand; in the other Richard Branson—Britain's answer to Rocky Aoki. The Virgin Trans-Atlantic Challenge was going to be every bit as awesome as Aoki's Pacific flight, with the added difficulty that, being a hot-air balloon, the Virgin team would be reliant on fuel to keep them aloft. Outside temperatures at 30,000 feet would fall to minus 50 degrees centigrade. The inside of the 2.1 million cubic-foot balloon would fill with falling snow as the water-vapour condensed. Goran Almé, another of Thunder and Colt's Swedish designers, had yet to make critical technical judgements: until he had estimated the warming effect of solar and infra-red radiation he could not fix the optimum volume of the envelope, nor estimate the total fuel requirement.

So my last flight was with Almé and Bäcklin and the 'Christmas tree'—a spiky branch of radiation-measuring sensors that Almé wanted to lower from the basket at varying altitudes above Shropshire. Bäcklin

The vast balloon of the Virgin Atlantic Flyer poised for take off at Sugarloaf, Maine, on 2 July, 1987. As pilots Richard Branson and Per Lindstrand took off, one of the fuel tanks broke free and crashed to the ground. The balloon rose at a rate of 1,000 feet a minute, to an altitude of 27,000 feet. 31 hours, 41 minutes later the Virgin Atlantic Flyer touched down in northern Ireland. It was the first crossing of the Atlantic by hot air balloon (photo: Virgin Atlantic Flyer).

piloted. Thirty minutes after dawn we lifted off, rising like a rocket through layers of chilly air and clouds until at 10,000 feet, Almé lowered his Christmas tree and huddled above the LCDs of his Micrologger computer. Over the edge the ground had gone. We hung between the blue and the white.

Two months later Branson and Lindstrand successfully crossed from America to Britain in the Virgin Atlantic Flyer. Aoki made three flights in China and is still trying to fly in Russia. Nobody has flown a hot air balloon across the Pacific . . . yet.

The 'hare and hounds' race: competitors chase a lead balloon across the countryside, altering direction by searching for different wind currents at various altitudes. An altitude change of just a few feet can alter a course by several degrees. The winner of a 'hare and hounds' is the pilot who drops a streamer closest to a marker laid on the ground by the 'hare'. These two balloons have just taken off at the start of the 11th Annual Pennsylvania State Hot Air Championships.

Action: *Dinghy Sailing*

Looking across the calm pool of Mylor Harbour it was hard to believe that the forecast of Force 5–7 winds (gusting to Force 8) could be correct. From the foreshore to the mouth of the creek a fleet of pleasure boats ranging in size from sea-going ketches to pocket-sized pram dinghies nodded slumberously at their mooring buoys. An inch under 17 feet long, our own boat, a Laser 16, waited in the shallows with Tim Penaluna, an instructor from the Cornwall Activity Centre who was going to accompany me on this journey into the secret reaches of the world's third largest natural harbour.

Dinghies are the smallest conventional sailing craft and are ideal for exploring tidal rivers and sheltered coasts. 'Dinghy' itself is derived from *denga*, the Hindu word for the sailing boats used to ferry goods and people along the rivers of India. Merchantmen trading with India adopted the word *denga* to describe the small boats carried on the decks of their own ships.

Messing about in boats has been a peculiarly British hobby; we have many rivers and lakes, and a convoluted shoreline that lends itself to local exploration. Sailing boats were never cheap; traditionally they were built to a 'clinker' design which involved the overlapping of thin planks held together by thousands of copper nails. The small-boat revolution was sparked in the early sixties by a sailing enthusiast called Barry Bucknall.

Bucknall borrowed from canoe-design the idea of building a hull from panels of plywood held together with resin and strips of fibre-glass tape. The result was a lightweight hull that was quick and cheap to make. The slab-sides, and angles rather than curves, made it one of the ugliest boats ever to float, but it was practical. The *Daily Mirror* spotted the promotional potential, and Bucknall's boat became the 'Mirror Dinghy', bringing to a part of the population a sport which had always been financially (and socially) out of reach. Mirror dinghies could be kept in a garage and strapped to a car-roof. They were easy to launch. Over 68,000 Mirror dinghies have been sold. Mirror Dinghy number 55,448 was carried to a height of 4,910 metres in the Bolivian Andes and sailed on Lake Huallatani. It set an altitude sailing record.

Although Mirrors were inexpensive (you could buy them in kit form in 1963 for £63 11s), they were still well beyond the reach of *my* pocket money. When I was fourteen years old I saw a book in Norfolk County Library called, I think, *Build your own Boat*. It was by Percy Blandford. I sent off for plans. Using a mahogany bed-head for the transom and marine-ply from the local wood yard I built my own six-foot sailing dinghy. Like the Mirror, it was a 'pram' dinghy, with a truncated, rather than a pointed, prow. In many ways a real perambulator would have been more seaworthy. The mast and boom were made from the shaved trunks of poplar trees which I raided from the garden whilst on her sewing machine, my mother made a sail from nylon bought in a ships' chandlers in Norwich.

My tiny dinghy sailed off the coast of Cornwall, off the Norfolk coast and on various of the Norfolk Broads. Like a small, armour-plated landing craft, my little pram would plough uninterrupted through seaweed, rocks, reeds and frailer craft like canoes. Being only six feet long, it had its limitations, one of which was that it sank if more than two people climbed on board. It was also impossible to sail into the wind, despite the retractable lee-boards my father added in later years. Above all it was heavy. This was due to the inch-thick mahogany that formed too high a proportion of the hull. When I grew out of

it, it was sold to a trawler skipper at Yarmouth for use as a tender.

My father had his own boat: a lightweight fibreglass 14-footer which used to sail on the lazy rivers of East Anglia. It was so fast and light that we were often half way up the opposite bank before we could turn it round. *Petronella* was a nightmare: as perpetual crewman, my memories are of frantic tacking and continual bailing. Disasters were frequent. To prevent all the equipment floating away while the boat was upside down, my father had secured sponge, thermos, bailers, spanner, lunch box and some plastic bags by lengths of string, so that you often found yourself trying to swim through a self-weaving net. *Petronella* came to an unseemly end one afternoon when she was sailed at full throttle into an overhanging tree on the River Yare. Her mast snapped in two. She spent the rest of her life gathering moss and various other brands of creeping green microbiology at the bottom of the garden.

The Laser that I was about to board in Cornwall came from a family of day-boats made in Banbury, Oxfordshire and designed by Bruce Kirby, who later went on to design the 12-metre Canadian entry for the America's Cup. Lasers are widely used by British sailing schools, being fast yet stable. They are also spacious, and manage to be an easy-to-sail family day-craft while retaining the lines and performance of a truly competitive boat. It is a boat in which you can have all the fun of water-over-the-gunwhale sailing without the swimming.

We floated away from Mylor beach and nosed silently through the other boats towards the uncluttered channel beyond the

Stretching the seams on Carrick Roads; Tim Penaluna risks a ducking by letting me take the helm as we skip across the waves driven by a gusty Atlantic breeze. There are few things more thrilling than the moment when crew, boat and wind work suddenly with each other; sailing is one of those adaptable sports which manage to combine excitement with sensitive travel (photo: David Reed).

The Laser is a solid but fast day-boat, capable of planing over the waves or pottering around in creeks. A custom-made 'tent' can be erected over the boom, providing sleeping space for two. On the transom is a small well, designed to accommodate a cooking stove. The outboard motor can stay in place while the boat is being sailed and is handy for 'cheating' your way into harbour at the end of the day. This is Mylor Harbour, just outside Falmouth, in Cornwall (photo: David Reed).

breakwater. Our sails sagged listlessly. Penaluna, the skipper, sat at the helm, watching the masthead burgee swivel illogically through all the points of the compass. 'Penaluna' is a name as Cornish as the granite cliffs of the Lizard; his dark ringlets and beard gave the misleading impression that he was a pirate, but in fact he used to be a Customs and Excise officer.

As we edged level with Penarrow Point, a shadow of ruffled water raced from the wooded shore and slammed into the sails. Kicked by 151 square feet of taut nylon the Laser leapt forward, heeling steeply as the keel dug for purchase. Toes hooked through the straps; I leaned out as far as I dare, the back of my head tapping the water as I watched the huge bow wave streaming past the hull. Now we were flying. We heaved another inch out of the sheets. The bow lifted from the water and began to plane over a surface that could have been as hard and slippery as ice.

For an hour we dashed to and fro between mile-wide shores, taking turns at the tiller, to skim before the gale beneath a sky of seamless blue. My enthusiasm for speed was only checked when I noticed that we were sailing so far over that the boat was filling with water. 'Bear away a bit,' offered Penaluna politely.

As we changed course for the north I could look backwards past Pendennis Point to the open sea. If you were to sail in a straight line south from here, you would next touch land at the small port of Ribadesella, in northern Spain.

The south-westerly blew us straight towards the 'neck' of Carrick Roads. Ahead of us were the spreading tentacles of hidden creeks that cut half way across Cornwall. A catamaran knifed past, high on one hull. In front of us a shag bobbed to the surface with a fish twitching in its tweezer-like beak. We were aiming for a narrow gap in the pillows of wooded hills. Deflected off the surrounding heights, the wind began to eddy and veer, as if it were unsure whether to help us on our journey from the sea. We passed to port of a black marker buoy.

'That's Turnaware Point' Penaluna said, nodding towards a knuckle of land that guarded the mouth of the river. 'There's a huge bar running out from the Point. People go the wrong side of the buoy and get stuck. It's embarassing to see.'

Beyond the buoy we gybed and ran the Laser in to Channals Creek. Safely moored, we followed a footpath beside an iron fence up the hill to the gardens of Trelissick House. From the edge of the ha-ha that once prevented cows from straying onto the tennis court we could look down on the entire length of Carrick Roads, out to the sea, and even to the hills above the Helford River ten miles away. It was an expansive panorama; quite different to the confined tunnel of river that burrowed northwards behind the house.

Channals Creek was already drying out when we returned to the boat, and we had an energetic ten minutes manhandling the Laser down to the receding water. For a moment it looked as if we would be marooned. The creek was used to film the original version of 'Treasure Island'.

In a faltering breeze, we sailed into the throat of the river, then slipped beneath the towering bow of a laid-up tanker, our sails as white as paper against her rusting walls. The tanker was called, 'Methane Princess'. Tied up beside this rotting monument to the bulk conveyance of marsh-gas was a prim little ship decorated with brass and mahogany called Jezebel. 'Belongs to a millionaire' said Penaluna. 'Nobody knows who owns it now, but it used to be Robert Stigwood's.'

A soft, continuous sigh, like the wistful letting-out of breath, carried from the impenetrable banks of trees that now hemmed us in to a channel that offered no choice but to continue, or to return towards the sea. What wind there was came straight over our stern. The tiller flopped idly against my palm.

We drew level with a pontoon which reached out from Smuggler's Cottage. We tied up. Presently another boat arrived, a pleasure steamer, the MV Heather. Off it stepped Peter Newman. He was born at Smuggler's Cottage in the last year of the Second World War. The beach we were standing on was chosen by General Eisenhower for one of the many secret embarkation points prior to the Normandy landings. Using concrete blocks known as 'chocolate boxes', the Americans built a wide ramp for the landing craft. Few of the men who left this leafy twist of river on 4 June 1944 can have guessed how horrifying their destination—Omaha Beach—would be. Now the chocolate boxes have been lifted; Newman broke them up and used them to build his rockeries.

A friend of his, "Smokey" Penrose arrived on his boat just as we were leaving. A peaked-white hat rested above his nut-brown face. 'I was on the tugs,' he explained. 'In 1942. They were coal-burners then. Because I was small like a whippet I used to be the one to go into the coal bunker. I'd come out as black as night. They all called me "Smokey".' He tipped the cap back off his forehead.

'I remember all the Yankee barges here. The LSTs, the LCTs, the Mulberries in Helford River, all getting ready for D-Day.'

He paused. 'Must have been 1944, or '45, when I was on the *Stanton H. King*. We were bow tug for one of the American Liberty ships which had just arrived at Falmouth Docks. The pilot rang full astern and the engineer put it full ahead. Nearly dragged the stern tug under. 'Course the line parted. She ran straight up the slipway at full speed and broke her back.'

I could have listened to Smokey's 'I remember' stories till the tide went out.

Reluctantly we left Smuggler's Cottage, sailing round the bend in the river to skirt Maggoty Bank. At Malpas Point we swung into the Tresillian River. So tight were the trees, and so low was their canopy, that there was nowhere to land a boat. We could have been up the Amazon. The water, now a caramel colour, moved sluggishly with us. In places the centreboard grazed the bottom. Just as the tide was turning we reached a clearing on the left bank. There were two or three houses. We tied the boat to a mooring line and splashed ashore. St Clement seemed to have gone to sleep. Outside Condurra Cottage a sign read: 'On this spot, between September 3rd–13th 1752 Absolutely Nothing Happened'. Next to it was a typed list of all the birds spotted during the previous month on the Tresillian. I counted 46 species. Doves were chortling to themselves on the thatched roofs beside the old church, but we saw no-one; it was as if the village was abandoned.

With night approaching we caught the departing tide, and by 8 pm had made the mouth of the River Fal. Half a mile into the river, where the banks turn gently left, we steered into a sheltered creek. We had just finished rigging a 'tent' over the Laser when a rubber boat arrived to collect Penaluna. He would spend the night ashore. 'I have my family', he said, grinning.

Alone but for the calls of unseen birds I sat staring at the still banks, waiting for darkness. Nothing moved. I imagined hundreds of pairs of eyes watching through the leaves: Montagnards, unknown tribes, a black-eyed Buddha called Mr Kurtz were all in there, breathing softly; waiting. By the light of a gas lamp I crept inside my sleeping bag and fell asleep reading Cyrus L. Day's *Knots and Splices*.

It was the piercing screech of a wading bird that woke me. The first thing I noticed was that the dinghy was neither floating nor level. I found the torch; it was 4 am. I unzipped the side hatch in the 'tent' and stood precariously on the seat. Rolling

DINGHY SAILING

avast as in 'Avast there me 'earties'. This is an order from the helmsman to stop an activity. Not common dinghy parlance.

baggwrinkle the strands of a rope, plaited to form a pad to prevent chafing on rigging or sails.

beneaped a dinghy that has run aground and which will not refloat on the next tide, because the next tide has decreased in range.

bilge the bit of the boat where the curved side meets the flatter bottom. A wet place, favoured by sweet wrappers and old sponges.

capsize a heroic (sometimes dangerous) form of accident.

gybe (ryhmes with 'vibe') to change from one tack to the other by moving the back of the boat (**stern**) through the wind. Gybing can cause the boom to swing sharply across the boat, striking the head of the crew. A **bad gybe** is one which renders a crewperson unconscious.

lee-o shouted by helmsman (sometimes in panic) to indicate that he is about to turn the boat around (**going about**).

painter not a decorator but the rope, line, or frayed piece of string used to tie the dinghy to the shore, or to pull it off mud-banks.

run-aground an undignified accident, nearly always regarded as being the fault of the crewperson for keeping inadequate lookout.

tiller the stick which the helmsperson holds, which is attached to the **rudder**, which steers the boat.

away in all directions were moonlit billows of bubbling, dribbling mud. Muted burps and gurgles filled the chilly air. The Laser was resting nose-down, on the edge of a slimy chasm. It looked as if I was stranded in a sea of chocolate mousse. I put the kettle on for tea.

When I woke next, the tide had come in and my tea was cold; Mill Creek was filled. Penaluna returned.

The patchy breeze had held from the south-west and we had to tack interminably, gaining a few yards with every reach. We watched landmarks—a dead tree, moored boat—trickle by with agonising slowness. The wind seemed to be

defying us to reach the sea. The black buoy off Turnaware Point sat at the exit of the river like a full-stop. But at the bulge in the river opposite Channals Creek we found more room to manoeuvre, and in one long reach sneaked past the buoy and burst into the light and space of Carrick Roads. The sails cracked into life and we heeled under the blast of an uninterrupted Force 5.

We set course for St Just in Roseland and St Mawes. There is a sheltered creek at St Just. We crept into the still water, slipping between moored boats whose halyards shivered against their metal masts filling the air with the delicate tinkling of wind chimes. I waded ashore. Climbing above the water are the gardens of St Just church. In the 1920s H.V. Morton, in his book *In Search of England*, wrote that he had 'blundered into a Garden of Eden that cannot be described in pen or paint. There is a degree of beauty that flies so high that no net of words or snare of colour can hope to capture it, and of this order is the beauty of St Just in Roseland'. The churchyard tumbles down a steep slope, a maze of slim paths that twist through ferns and flowers, white gravestones and secret pools. Beyond the arched wooden lych gate is the spring that for centuries has provided the water for baptisms and sailors' kegs.

Our final port was St Mawes, whose south-facing aspect is a suntrap and whose white cottages cascade down to the boats like a Greek fishing village. Having beached the Laser, Penaluna and I leg-stretched along the waterfront road. A cannon boomed as the first of a small fleet of Cornish racing yawls heeled through the harbour mouth. Rosy-cheeked Jo Greaves was leaning against the wooden paling in front of Pink Cottage. She was watching the end of the race:

'You know it's easy to spend a day doing nothing here (I believed her). There's so much to see, and of course you have to watch everything through to the end.' (How true.)

'We ought to get back to Mylor.' Penaluna led the way back to our boat. Catching an eddy of wind we skipped through the harbour and out into the waves that were tossing in from the Atlantic.

As I hung over the side, stomach muscles screaming and spray from the choppy sea exploding over the foredeck, I caught a glimpse of Penaluna, locked at the crazily tilting helm, one hand on the tiller, eyes on the horizon and his waterlogged beard creased by a big Cornish smile.

Action: *Cattle Driving*

Louis Ballast invented the cheeseburger in Denver in 1944. The capital of Colorado is still growing. The glass stalks that have sprouted from downtown Denver over the past six years have all but swallowed the old D & F Tower—a brick-built campanile-style building copied from St Mark's Square in Venice. Over three hundred feet up, in room 1722 of the Westin Hotel, I could look past the illuminated moon of the D & F clockface to the mountain wall that fringes the city limits.

Colorado—the state that claims an area six times that of Switzerland and a thousand mountains over two miles high—is the ultimate hiking-climbing-rafting-skiing-riding-wildlife-thinking-dreaming paradise. Hidden among those ranks of hills lay Lost Valley, the 'dude ranch' to which I was headed.

Before enrolling as a cowboy I took two days to introduce myself to the American West. On buses and feet I visited collections of Indian artefacts (The Denver Art Museum) and day-tripped out to Buffalo Bill's grave. The man who brought his Wild West Show to Queen Victoria at Windsor Castle now lies encased in concrete, safe from those who still believe that his true resting place should be in neighbouring Wyoming.

Lost Valley ranch lies two hours' drive west of Denver at the end of a long dirt road that picks a corkscrew route through conifers and ravines.

It was in 1885 that Bill Graham rode his horse from the gold-mining town of Cripple Creek up the Platte River to the point where the water funnels through a deep canyon. Turning uphill, he crested a ridge above what is now known as Wildcat Gulch, and saw for the first time a hidden valley—a valley that had been known to generations of Ute Indians, but which had yet to be visited by white men.

On all sides, the valley was hemmed in by mountain slopes, but beside the small creek in the valley bottom stretched a necklace of bright pastures. Riding at once to the nearby town of Golden, Graham had filed his claim then returned to build his timber ranch house. He used to drive the cattle he raised on the valley's grass over to Cripple Creek, where he sold them to the gold miners.

One hundred years on, Lost Valley still rings to the sound of horseshoes being hammered on anvils. And each spring and fall the air is heavy with the lowing of Herefords and Aberdeen Angus. Guests—or 'dudes'—come to stay at the ranch for anything from a weekend to two weeks. ('Dude' actually comes from a German word for 'fool' and was adopted in the 1880s by Americans as a slang term for a towny. So to be called a 'cool dude'—often taken by the recipient as flattery—is not actually terribly polite.) During the two round-up weeks (normally the beginning of June and end of September), dudes can help the regular cowboys (wranglers) search for and bring in the cattle; for the rest of the year there is a continual programme of adventurous trail riding through the forests and peaks of the eastern Rockies.

When I arrived at Lost Valley I was greeted by Bob Foster Jnr—six-foot plus in high-heeled boots and stetson. Foster's father, 'Big Bob', bought the ranch in 1960 and installed the kinds of comforts needed to ease the lot of today's holiday cowboy: there are tennis courts, a swimming pool, jacuzzis, and luxury private cabins. There are over 150 'quarter-horses'. The quarter-horse breed is descended from the Spanish stock of the *conquistadores* which were crossed with thoroughbreds from England in the mid 1700s. The result is a horse which is fast, intelligent and agile; ideal for rounding-up cattle over difficult terrain. Bob showed me to a log cabin.

'Ride as much as you like; eat as much as you like; relax. There's easy rides leaving at ten tomorrow, and a couple of all-days at nine. Rise at five if you want to help the wranglers feed the horses.'

I woke next morning to see a low sun slanting across the corral. The rising dust was punctuated by the snorts of horses and musical reassurances of the wranglers. 'Easy now Comanche. Ho Captain, don' *lean* on me son-of-a-gun, jus' look at that sunrise Poco! God Bless America!'

The wranglers make sure that you are matched to a horse that suits your experience. Ernie Frey, a denimed, spurred, undergraduate taking a break from his studies in Texas, asked how much riding I'd done.

'Two hours,' I replied, expecting to be paired with the equine equivalent of a pedal-car.

'You a fast learner Nick?'

'I think so.'

'Here, you have Hawken. He knows the way home.'

Five minutes' riding from the ranch and eight horses splashed through a creek and into the pasture. A red-tailed hawk detached from a tree-top. The horses broke into a lope and the brittle air filled with the percussive sound of hooves on hard turf. Hawken, with whom I'd earlier had a brief dispute, thundered towards the distant trees.

Western reins are held in one hand so that the other is free for roping steers—or in my case for hanging on like grim death to the saddle horn. Steering is achieved by laying the reins on one or other side of the horse's neck. It is quite straightforward.

At the pasture edge we slowed to a trot. A coyote crossing the valley froze in mid stride, head turned. Having successfully forded a deep creek without getting ducked, I tagged along at the back of the queue through waterside shrubbery to the start of the trail up Wildcat Gulch.

Ponderosa pine climbed each side of a trail ribbed with roots and rock. Quarter-horses are sure-footed, and

The Wild West lives on through the traditions and skills inherited by 'wranglers' who still spend their working days rounding up cattle from the isolated pastures dotted through the Rocky Mountains. As a 'dude' it is possible to join a round-up, riding (if you want) from dawn till dusk, on trails that climb mountain passes to 10,000 feet, ford rivers or wind through heart-stoppingly beautiful valleys of blowing willows and golden aspen. (This photograph is of Hawken's saddle).

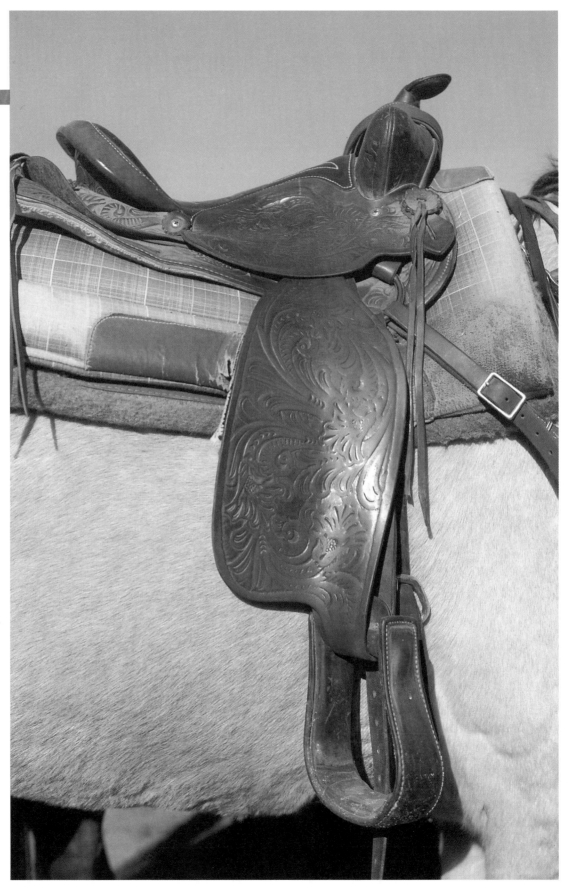

A round-up in front of the Rockies (actually in Jackson County, Colorado). These cowboys are the real thing. American quarter-horses have the agility and turn of speed of a sheep-dog, are sure-footed and (generally) well-mannered. Imagine how the West would change if jeeps and helicopters took over from the horse.

Hawken, who knew this trail like the back of his feeding trough, picked his way upwards with the agility of a mountain goat. Our task was to round up four cows that had slipped through the horses of the previous day's sortie.

At 10,000 feet we crested the pass then began a slippery descent to the South Platte. The trail passed stands of aspen, their leaves turned to a burning gold before being stripped off the branches by the fall winds.

It took thirty minutes for the horses to tread down the mountain to the narrow valley where the South Platte tumbled quickly over boulders fringed by yellow willow. Our wrangler for the day, Randy Kelly, led us down to the water's edge so that the horses could drink.

'We'll sweep the mountainside. If you see cows, holler. Don't go too high. It gets kind of vertical up there.' Randy was the sort of horseman that Louis L'Amour would have had riding a long-legged zebra dun down the dusty main street of Deadwood Gulch a few minutes ahead of a bullet-riddled stagecoach. Randy and four of the others disappeared along the valley trail in a stutter of dust.

I teamed up with Barry Sweeney, Second Vice President of America's biggest auto parts company, and Andy Kitco, who owns a business in San Diego which specialises in grinding the blades for meat-cutting machines. We turned up the slope, scattering grit. Sweeney wore a bright red bandana and in anticipation of a dusty day had switched his contact lenses for glasses, which somewhat spoiled the effect. Kitco, like many dudes, was clad from neck to boot in appropriately-scruffed denim. He wore a stetson as big as a steering wheel. Everyone, dudes and wranglers alike, wore tan riding boots, high heeled, of tooled Texan leather. My own round-up wear was rather more prosaic: a pair of thin cotton walking trousers, running shoes and no hat. Already I could feel the inside of my legs

chafing raw on the western saddle; Hawken had stamped on my unprotected foot and broken what felt like five toes; my head, exposed to the high-noon sun, felt as if it was being barbecued.

For twenty minutes we scrambled through ravines and over fallen trees, Hawken ready to tackle gradients that would have been hard for a human being. We met two bat-eared deer, a squirrel and a mountain bluebird. The sky kept its perpetual blue, the breeze syrupy with pine resin. We didn't see a single cow.

We rode up the mountainside until we reached the foot of the cliff. The slope that we were on was so steep that I was convinced Hawken would slip and fall head over hooves. We descended leaning back from the saddles, the horses sliding sledge-style down to the river.

'Try the other side, uh,' said Kitco. He led the way down the bank. The horses picked their way through water deep enough to brush their bellies. They seemed to know what they were doing. I could feel Hawken's hooves slithering on invisible boulders. Cool water travelled osmotically up my trousers. On the far side, we explored a jungle of small willows. No cows.

'I'm headed back to the other side.' Kitco called, and left. Under a vertical sun, Sweeney and I fell into a languid conversation about the resale price maintenance of automotive parts. We forded the river again. Kitco was nowhere to be seen. Neither were the other riders. Hawken was leaning for home.

It was early afternoon, and the ranch was still three hours away. We turned for home, stepping slowly up the long switchbacks towards the pass. Through the tree-line the trail dipped past clumps of wiry mountain grass. One thousand feet below us the gorge wall stood like a gravestone over the now-shadowed river. This end of day contentment was spoiled by the tapping of hooves of the rest of the group. Leading the posse was Kelly. He was irate.

'Where d'you guys go jus' tearing off

Lost Valley ranch: just two hours outside Denver, Colorado, these lapboard cabins cluster round the central corral, half of which is used to contain cattle already brought in from the mountains, while the other half is used for mustering dudes' horses at the beginning and end of each day.

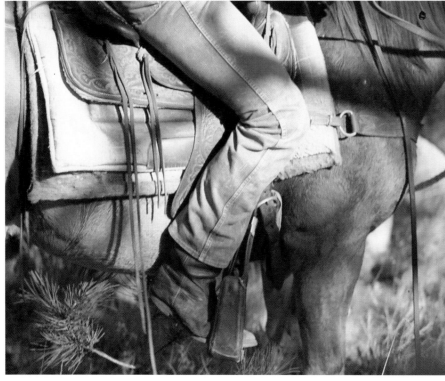

Randy Kelly. Like all wranglers, Randy is blessed with more than ordinary reserves of patience. This picture was taken early in the morning as Kelly checked the horses for shoeing prior to saddling up for the day's rides.

Horse-riding in the Rockies conjures up many endearing images; here the denimmed leg (denims are the one type of trouser we are told in the U.K. *never* to wear because the thick seams wear holes in your thighs) of a wrangler rests against the burnished leather of a western saddle, dappled by sunlight which flickers through a stand of Ponderosa pine. The leg belongs to Terry Fasol.

without telling me. We've been looking all over for you. Didn't know whether you were in front or behind. Never git outta contact with me again.' Wow. Hawken looked hideously smug.

That night, back at the ranch, 'Little Bob' outlined his plan for the recapture of the remaining cattle. Over one hundred were by now locked safely in the corral. But eight were still out in the mountains. 'It's a bit like searching for a needle in a haystack—only this haystack occupies 26,000 acres,' he said with relish.

The *Lost Valley Brand*, a daily ranch newsletter, appeared on the dinner tables. The editor (Little Bob) opened the newsletter by welcoming the latest guests to arrive at the ranch: from Colorado Springs had come Dave Guevara, and from Littleton Co, Docia Love and her daughter. After dinner wranglers and dudes square-danced the night away to tunes like 'Salty Dog Rag' and 'Cotton Eye Joe'. Company directors from California, a fine art restorer from London and a carpenter from Essex whirled and yodelled as Rudy and Dolores Parks called the steps.

'The more guests get fired up, the more I enjoy it' enthused Little Bob. 'Coming here is more than horses and mountains. There's no TV, video or telephones in the rooms; only ranch noise. The lack of man-made forms and lines . . . my Dad calls it 'the quietness'. We're the only private land in the middle of a 40,000-acre National Forest; land God made. It revitalises. Most people who come here are office-bound; here they're physically exercising . . . picking up manure, riding, hiking . . . they go home physically tired but mentally and spiritually refreshed. People come here and spend a week on an animal which can't communicate . . . they have to communicate through other methods. They learn.'

Early the following morning, wranglers Mike Smith and Terry Fasol called together the riders who wanted to take on an 'all day'. Bow-legged and burnt, I felt ready for an all-day all right—in bed. Kitco, regarding the staggering apparition of a bandy, peely-skinned Englishman at 6 am looked at the cloudless sky and said.

'Boy! Your pale ass gonna *BURN*.'

Kitco's wife Dianne, who was perhaps the best of the dude riders that week, presented me with a beautiful, blue bandana. (I tied it around my neck, like the wranglers did, but must have used an illegitimate knot because the bandana had gone by the evening.)

Fasol and Smith divided the dudes (there were about 15 of us) into two groups. From a pasture called Webster's Park, one group took the upper trail, the other plunged into the valley trees. High on a ridge, we spotted our quarries browsing through a meadow a thousand feet below.

Fasol pulled a CB from its holster and called up Smith: 'Cowboy 1 this is Cowboy 2. We have two units down by the Wigwam River. Two units at Wigwam. Do we get them?'

From somewhere out in the forest crackled the voice of Smith: 'Bring um in!'

By the time we had dropped to the valley

CATTLE DRIVING

bunch quitter a horse liable to take off at high speed in an unexpected direction.
chaps leather leggings worn to prevent chafing of the inner thigh; not to be confused with 'chaps', as in 'Hello there chaps' unless you are talking to your trousers.
cantle binder the back part of a saddle; this term is never used.
corral car park for horses.
dude a townie playing at cowboys.
gilet padded waistcoat favoured by **dudes.**
hard run gallop.
kack saddle.
lope canter.
saddle horn the raised peg on the front of a western saddle, used for hanging coats, holding on to while the horse tries to throw you off, or, more properly as a bollard around which to wrap the rope when **jerking a steer.**
skiving reducing unworked leather to a uniform thickness prior to turning it into a saddle, or whatever.
wrangler derivation of the Spanish word *caverango*, meaning the herder of saddle horses (this is true).

the cows had sensibly taken to cover. Fasol spread the eight of us out at thirty-yard intervals and we began a series of long sweeps through the valley forest. It took sixty minutes of uncomfortable riding through dense brush and confusing ravines before we made contact with the cows.

The brushwood suddenly splintered as two cows with calves made a break for the Wigwam. They careered through the undergrowth then splashed through water and up the far bank. The chase was on: horses burst from sleepy walk to supercharged gallop. Kitco crossed the creek and urged his horse up a grass gangplank to the top of a rock outcrop. Vincent Demana, a lovely man from Springfield, Ohio, who wore a hilarious felt hat with a crown like the nose-cone of the Space Shuttle, yelped 'Yo' and leapt into a tangle of brush. A cow flashed by in front of me. Glory at last! Hawken hardly needed a nudge. We scrambled over fallen trees and galloped along the river bank, overtaking the cow which was now ambling along the trail looking for a gap in the closing net of horses. I had an overwhelming urge to do something heroic, like leap from my horse and wrestle the cow to the ground. But my contact lenses were so smeared with dust that I could hardly tell whether I was chasing a cow or another horse.

Fasol loped past on his brown and white pinto, calling his troops to order: 'Don't get in front, keep left, keep right, keep behind. We need a semi-circle behind them. Push then move forward slowly!' With Fasol choreographing both the cattle and his unruly cowboys, we made a noisy passage to the valley floor. Outflanked, tired of the chase, the cows began the long plod home.

As the sun dripped below Buffalo Peak and the last dashes of aspen lost their flame, I slipped down from Hawken to walk with him back to Lost Valley.

Action: *Microlighting*

Had Daedalus been using a microlight aircraft instead of a bunch of feathers held together with cord and wax, his pre-flight exortations to his son Icarus would not have dealt with the dangers of flying too close to the sun, but on such specifics as checking the cylinder head temperatures of his Rotax 462 liquid-cooled engine and avoiding the air-lanes above Knossos. You can imagine Daedalus' last instructions: 'Icarus, bank not at angles greater than 30° nor dive at speeds in excess of 89 mph lest you end up in the wine-dark drink.'

Only too mindful of Icarus' sorry end, I pedalled up the hill towards Popham airfield. I'm least brave in the air. Or on water. It was a bright midsummer morning and the woods beside the road rustled with the slither, pip, crick and call of wind and myriad animals. Popham airfield sits on top of a hill in Hampshire, halfway between Basingstoke and Winchester. I'd been told to look out for a gateway on the left. I lifted the bike over the gate and bumped along a cinder track, past a water-tower and limp wind-sock, and down a hammock-dip in the hill to the two airfield buildings, languid beneath their peeling camouflage paint.

On the mown grass in front of the buildings stood miniature, insect-like flying machines. Conversation wafted from an open window. A low drone filled the warm air. Past the water-tower dropped a 'flying wing'. It swooped onto the grass and trundled towards the hangar.

Popham is the home of Mac and Paula Smith's 'Airborne Aviation Ltd', one of several microlight schools in the country. One of the three instructors is thirty-year-old Steve Laver, a flier since he was nineteen, and like many microlight enthusiasts, a graduate from the world of hang-gliding.

'We'll go up in the red one. It's a 'flexwing'. Very light. Easy to fly. Very manoeuvrable' he said. The microlight was parked in the sun, the curved fabric wing cocked coyly to one side and shading the struts on which are mounted the engine, two-bladed wooden propeller, wheels and dual seat. It looked incredibly rudimentary; as if someone had got one of those sit-on lawnmowers tangled in the washing line. Laver explained that, far from being one of Heath Robinson's cast-offs, this machine was a uniquely versatile aeroplane. It could land and take off from bumpy fields no bigger than a football pitch; it was cheap (by normal flying standards); it could carry two people; it could be kept in the garage at home, towed on a trailer to a field and 'rigged' in 15 minutes—and it was tremendous fun. On the dashboard were several dials: an altimeter, engine temperature gauges, rev counter, compass and air-speed indicator. The only flying controls were a foot-throttle and the control-bar that moved the flexible wing.

'The main function of power is to control height, not speed. To fly at a constant height, you find the right revs for weather conditions and aircraft weight. For turning,

Despite their use of the latest materials, microlight aircraft cannot fail to conjure up that sepia era of stringbag flying machines and seat-of-the-pants travel. Here is a machine which can take off from small grass strips or pastures, can be stowed in a garage or towed behind a car and yet is plane-enough to cross continents. Long-distance flights include Richard Meredith-Hardy's from London to Cape Town, and Eve Jackson's from the UK to Australia. A serious objection to microlights is their intrusive sound and presence in skies that are already getting crowded; they do have many practical applications, such as surveying and aerial photography. The pilot is Steve Laver, seen here flying along the London to Winchester railway line near Micheldever.

The other type of microlight. Unlike the 'flexwing' in the previous photograph (which is in effect a motorised hang-glider), the 'three axis' microlight seen here with its owner Phil Crossman (a computer specialist) is a scaled down conventional aircraft. It has a joystick, rudder pedals and so on. You sit side-by-side in a small cockpit. Tamer than the flexwing.

move the bar to the left, and you'll bank to the right—and vice versa. The tank holds about 9½ gallons; enough for 3–4 hours, say 200 miles. It'll climb at around 1,200 feet a minute.'

Twenty minutes later, I was being strapped onto the rear seat of a Gemini Flash 2. Through the slot in the front of my full-face helmet, I watched Laver ease himself into the narrow cockpit. He leaned back between my legs. Just behind my head, the engine fired. The rev counter twitched into life. Laver's voice came over the helmet intercom, running through pre-flight checks. 'OK?' he finally asked. 'Yes!' I bawled back, unnecessarily loud.

I still didn't believe that we were actually going to leave the ground.

Opening the throttle, the tiny craft rocked across the grass towards the end of the field. It felt like riding pillion on a scramble bike. By the water-tower, we turned. The motor kicked. We accelerated down the strip. At 30 mph I was beginning to enjoy it: three wheels drummed the hard turf; the grass whizzed by and wind whipped our clothes. It was like riding a go-kart.

Then the thing took off. The world I knew dematerialised. My stomach yo-yoed on a piece of elastic somewhere between the crazily tilting fields of Hampshire and the microlight, which seemed to be ascending like an express elevator.

We collided with something hard and the whole plane leapt up then down like a car hitting a speed-hump at 40 mph. 'Thermal' said Laver's disembodied voice.

I felt the plane levelling out, and opened my eyes. Beneath my left knee slid the toy-like buildings of a farm. The roar of wind and motor, heart-stopping thermal bumps and sliding dimensions were causing me confusion, excitement and abject terror.

'Good, isn't it!' said a voice in my helmet. 'We'll go up another thousand. How are

you feeling?'

'Great,' I lied through closed eyes. Had my knee-caps not been separated by Laver's reclining body, they would have been knocking chips off each other.

The plane tipped on its side. Expecting to fall out, I grabbed the seat-edge. We were leaning over space as the ground revolved below.

'That's Basingstoke over there.' Below us drifted a pattern of fields, and in the far distance the grey blocks of Basingstoke. 'And that's the Isle of Wight. The light-coloured strip is the Solent.' I twisted my head. The view was incredible. To the north-east arrowed the M3, a glistening thread pointing to London, separating a patchwork of barley and hay squares stitched together by hedges and streams and byroads.

'Helicopter!' Laver's arm pointed to a khaki military blob scuttling over the hedges far below us. 'And another.' He pointed to the left as a smaller helicopter crossed our bows a mile away. 'And there's another Flash joining the circuit.'

'It's a bit crowded up here isn't it?'

'You get used to it. Your eyes adapt to

MICROLIGHTING

control bar similar to handlebars on a bicycle.

flexwing a bendy aeroplane which looks like a hang-glider balanced on a lawn-mower.

g-force force exerted during a tight turn; tends to leave stomach on wrong side of backbone.

heavy landing microlight stops moving when it is six-feet underground.

money commodity required in quantity; can be spent on micro-lighting, or set on fire, whichever provides the greatest pleasure.

prop not something to lean on; often made from piranha pine.

pull-start piece of string with handle, used to start microlight engine.

trial flight your first warning.

trike the lawn-mower part of a flexwing microlight which the pilot (and passenger) sit on.

spotting small moving objects.' Way below us the silver delta wing of the other microlight crept over the dark stain of Micheldever wood. The voice in the helmet interrupted:

'I'll show you a tight turn. You'll feel the G-force.'

'Thanks. I'd like that.'

The plane seemed to stand on its wingtip. We lay sideways over an interchange on the A33. Gravity pushed me solidly into the seat. Experimentally, I tried unclenching my muscles, and was pleasantly surprised to find it comfortable. It even felt safe. This was becoming fun.

We twisted and turned, then followed at 2,000 feet the road I'd cycled along two hours earlier. Finally, reluctantly, we zoomed down at 65 mph, rode the thermal 'bumps' over the pale cornfields behind the airstrip, and turned behind the water-tower. The motor quietened. Over Laver's shoulder I watched the grass strip waver from side to side as he juggled with the cross-wind. The nose dipped, the grass rushed up and we flattened out to kiss the ground as light as a falling feather.

By the time I'd peeled myself off the Flash 2's seat, Laver was away with the next trainee.

Microlighting is a fast-growing sport. It took off at the end of the seventies when hang-glider pilots began to explore methods of self—rather than wind-willed flight. Some—like Will Knowles (another Popham instructor)—fitted chain-saw engines to their hang-gliders ('It took me 45 minutes to climb 1,000 feet, but I was *flying!*'). There were accidents, culminating in 9 deaths during 1982. The Civil Aviation Authority put its foot down, and with the British Microlight Aircraft Association devised a thorough policing of microlight designs and pilot training. Every microlight now requires CAA certification. Already there are over 2,000 qualified microlight pilots in Britain.

The hobby of microlighting is not in the same cost bracket as say train-spotting; it is even more expensive than hot-air ballooning. Some schools—such as Airborne Aviation—offer a five-day intensive course which will take the complete novice through to a first solo flight. An air-experience flight for a reasonable fee will help you decide whether wheeling with the birds is your kind of thrill. Some at Popham have diluted the costs of microlighting by clubbing together and forming a syndicate (two is the ideal number); others like the Parachute Regiment's Malcolm Clucas were bought secondhand.

Microlight language is becoming complicated. West Germans call them 'ultralights', while the Italians, pointing at Leonardo de Vinci's ornithopter drawings, call microlights 'Leonardinis' John Olsson, editor of *Pilots International* magazine, sees microlights as having more than a recreational role to play: 'The military are interested, and Britain is the biggest microlight producer after America.' At the Rochdale factory of Mainair Sports, manufacturer of the Gemini Flash, machines are being built at a rate of three a week.

The hang-glider-derived 'flexwing' (or 'weightshift') microlight, with its characteristic moveable delta wing and three-wheeled trike has now been joined by the '3-axis' microlight. 3-axis machines are in essence lightweight re-inventions of the aeroplane, with stick and rudder controls. Using the latest lightweight alloys and fabrics, builders are managing to produce 3-axis planes that weigh less than the 150 kg maximum stipulated for microlights by the CAA.

One of the most popular 3-axis microlights is the Gemini Thruster which came initially from Australia. Phil Crossman, a Popham regular, bought one of the first to be made available in the UK, and is now addicted to his 'tail-dragger': 'It's a better aircraft, more stable, better in wind but a bit thirsty. You can fly it in worse conditions than a flexwing could manage.' He took me up and wove through the air like a swallow at dusk. Unlike the flexwing you sit *inside* the 3-axis plane, side-by-side with the pilot, with a windscreen to keep you cosy. It was much more comfortable than the open-air Flash 2, but less exciting. The 3-axis is less exerting to fly than a flexwing, but is much more complex and bulky when 'de-rigged', so is not as genuinely transportable as a flexwing.

The arrival of a new form of travel always precipitates a hot rush of pioneering adventures. Microlights fitted with wheels, skis and floats (made from canoes) were used for aerial observation in the 'Iceland Breakthrough' expedition led by Paul Vander-Molen. Eve Jackson piloted one from England to Australia—and an old Etonian, 28-year-old Richard Meredith-Hardy bought a Gemini Flash and covered 10,700 miles between London's Docklands and Cape Town in 330 flying hours. More recently, David Young and Christina Dodwell flew a Pegasus XL microlight from Koutaba in Cameroon, through Nigeria, Niger, Mali, Mauritania and Senegal, finally touching down at the Atlantic port of Dakar. For the takers of challenges, the next microlight prize has to be the first crossing of the Atlantic.

Action: *Sub-Aqua Diving*

On the evening of Sunday 28 February 1886, a few miles off the North Welsh coast, the lookout on the Missouri was straining into a blinding gale of sleet and snow. Like most of the 64 crew, he was looking forward to the snug bars and warm beer of his home port, Liverpool. In the hold was a mixed cargo: 395 head of cattle, 3,000 bales of cotton, 4,000 sacks of flour, palm oil, tallow, general provisions that included bacon, walnut logs, bales of leather, drawing chalk, a Canadian-made bellows organ . . . and three stowaways.

The ship's master was 45-year-old Captain Reuben Poland. Born in Sussex, he had gained his Master's certificate at the age of 27, and this was his fourth Atlantic crossing in the *Missouri* since Christmas. British-built *Missouri* was 425 foot 6 inches long; she had four masts and a 600 horsepower steam engine. She was only five years old.

Early that Sunday *Missouri* had rounded Fastnet Rock, off the southern tip of Ireland, and begun the final leg of her voyage. The coastguard high on the Old Head of Kinsale reported the great ship pushing north-eastwards towards St George's Channel. At 8 pm Captain Poland took a bearing on the Tuskar Rock and ordered a change of course to NE by E ³/₄ E. To allow for the moderate gale blowing up from ESE he allowed another point for leeway. The *Missouri* was on course for disaster; Poland had under-estimated the leeward pull of the tide.

At 11 pm sleet and snow began to flicker through the rigging and sudden squalls began to whip icy spray over the deck.

By 3.30 am on the Monday morning the lookout was finding it so difficult to see that the Captain reduced the *Missouri's* speed by half. Conditions were wretched. Somewhere off the starboard bow was the treacherously rocky coast of North Wales.

At 4.15 am, uneasy with his heading, Poland changed the ship's course slightly to the north and ordered a depth sounding. He was too late.

Before the lead could be cast a gun flash lit the sky. It was the North Stack coastguard. Through the driving white-out the Captain was horrified to glimpse the rising outline of a cliff.

With a rending of iron on rock and her propeller thrashing full speed astern, the 5,000-ton *Missouri* struck Holy Island.

One hundred and one years later, under the expert guidance of Stewart Tattersall, of Chester School of Diving at Dee Sports, I was sinking through the green waters of Port Dafarch towards the seabed resting-place of the *Missouri*.

It was my first sea-dive and it had taken Tattersall many patient hours to prepare me for this moment. A leader, with a repertoire of adventurous anecdotes that range from the jungles of Borneo to the Red Sea, Tattersall made his way through the Parachute Regiment and SAS before becoming a swimming teacher and then a diving instructor. He has the knack of overcoming pupil's fears for them.

As he finned deeper and greener, the bubbles from his regulator drifted past my mask like wobbling blobs of mercury. My own regulator hissed reassuringly as I sucked in; roared as I vented out. Two small brown fish patterned so delicately they looked hand-painted, paused to watch our downward progress, then flicked away.

This was the last day of my one-week diving course. Never in my wildest dreams had I imagined that six days after first pulling on an aqualung, I would be diving on a real wreck.

The sub-aquatic world has always struck me as a particularly perilous and unsuitable environment for air-breathing bipeds. Like Jules Verne's Monsieur Arronax in *20,000 Leagues Under the Sea*, I expected to freeze with condensed fear inside my diving suit while Captain Nemo—alias Tattersall—fought off sharks with a pocket knife or wrestled with giant squids. The difference between Arronax and me was that the good French professor (thinly disguised as Verne himself) could, at the twist of a quill, write himself out of nasty predicaments.

So when I turned up at Chester School of Diving, all the pre-conceived dreads were piling high. Encouraging from the start, Tattersall told me that the most important thing to remember was that 'sub-aqua is fun'. I was only slightly relieved.

The P.A.D.I. (Professional Association of Diving Instructors) open-water diving course lasts six days full-time, being a series of swimming pool sessions, out-of-the-water lessons and five open water dives. The course can also be taken in evenings and weekends over a longer period of time. The P.A.D.I. certificate allows you to dive in most parts of the world.

Today's sub-aqua equipment is a far cry from the port-holed dome helmet, lead boots and trailing air-lines used by Arronax and Nemo. People have been free-diving to surprising depths for many centuries: sponge and coral divers were operating on the sea-bed 2,000 years ago. But it wasn't until 1943 that a young French Naval officer called Jacques Cousteau, and his companion Emile Gagnan, devised a breathing system that supplied air on demand from a tank of compressed air carried on the diver's back. They called it the *aqualung*; the Americans adopted the word 'scuba' (Self Contained Underwater Breathing Apparatus).

On my first day I went to a Chester swimming pool and, together with two other students, Phil Johnson, a

With sub-aqua gear (and training) you can sink, weightless, into an otherwise hidden world. Fish hang inquisitively in front of your face mask and there are colours of a depth and purity that never translate to the air-world above. Here, Stuart Tattersall is instructing me in the use of the 'octopus rig'.

Liverpudlian who used to work in an abattoir, and Henry Pritchard, ex-Royal Welsh Fusiliers and burger-seller, was instructed in the important discipline of 'kitting up' and in the role of one's diving partner—or 'buddy'. Before I left London, I'd asked a lapsed surfing-diving Queenslander why they always dived in pairs. 'Obvious mate,' he replied, 'when the shark attacks, there's a 50% chance he'll eat ya buddy!'

Having been taught the sign language used by divers to communicate underwater, I wriggled into the gear. Encumbered by my 'ABLJ' (Adjustable Buoyancy Life Jacket) and full air cylinder, weight-belt and fins, I waddled to the water with the mask and mouthpiece jammed on my head. My face felt like a compressed pork-pie. Following Tattersall's demonstration, I stepped clear of the pool-side in the prescribed exaggerated scissor-stride and collided with the great, waiting blue.

When the froth cleared, I found myself suspended beneath the surface of the water, weightless, like an astronaut. What had felt like a suit of armour filled with porridge above the water, now allowed me to spin and turn, even somersault. I could swim like a fish! Glide like a bird! I had to restrain myself from pulling out my mouthpiece and whooping.

During the week's pool sessions we were taught how to use the inflatable life-jacket to achieve 'neutral buoyancy'—where the mere filling of your lungs lifts you upwards, and breathing out allows you to gently sink; how to clear a flooded mask; how to equalise air pressure in the ears; how to use a snorkel and how to execute emergency procedures such as sharing your buddy's air supply, and swimming 30 feet with no air at all. It all seemed remarkably straightforward; not at all frightening. Soon I was more comfortable in the water than out.

My first open-water dive came on Day 2 of the course. Somewhere north of Chester, in a water-filled quarry called 'Harry's Patch', I slithered down a muddy bank and beneath the murky waters. The difference between swimming-pool water and real water is that the latter is full of 'bits'; some so microscopically small that you only see them when they appear like falling stars in a shivering lance of underwater sunlight; other 'bits' are bigger, with fins and gills. The fish hang still, as if suspended on invisible threads, or dart like missiles across your mask. Weeds wave from the bottom,

34

SUB AQUA DIVING

bends decompression sickness, caused by staying too long, too deep.

buddy diving companion on whom your life might depend.

dead man fingers wobbly vegetables on sea floor, or diver's condition caused by overtight watch strap.

narks nitrogen narcosis; potentially dangerous condition likely to strike at depths of 100 feet or so, the symptoms including intoxication and irrational behaviour, such as handing one's breathing regulator to passing fish. Previously known as **rapture of the deep**.

octopus extra breathing regulator and hose on diving equipment, for use in emergency. Not to be confused with **octopus**, as in eight-armed cephalopod.

shark any fish longer than nine inches.

wreck sunken ship, or aged **buddy**.

and stroke your belly in a continual, slithery caress. It's a very busy place, underwater.

Beneath the surface of Harry's Patch I had a major problem with inflating feet. To achieve 'neutral buoyancy' you squirt compressed air from your tank into your sealed dry suit. (Since the water pressure at depth compresses the suit, you feel as if you are 'shrink-wrapped' in cling-film; the inrush of air prises the rubber off your body, so that you feel as if your own skin is inflating. It is a tickly, rather fun sensation.) Becoming neutrally buoyant was not difficult; my problems began when I tilted my body into a nose-dive: all the air in the suit rushed upwards and inflated my rubber legs so that I hung like an upside-down exclamation mark beneath a pair of enormously distended feet. The only way of getting the air to travel back along the suit was by turning the other way up. This proved physically complicated, but I managed it by a simultaneous body twist and forward-roll. Now facing upwards, all the air rushed through the suit,

momentarily inflated my shoulders, then exuded through the seal between the rubber and my neck in a gigantic watery fart. I sank like a stone and began the business of achieving neutral buoyancy again. I spent the afternoon in Harry's Patch either standing on my head or plummeting feet-first beneath a cloud of bubbles.

The problem, it turned out, was my neck, which was too scraggy for the suit to form a seal. I was given a smaller suit.

Two days later we made a 'drift dive' below the River Dee. In drift diving you move in the horizontal plane rather than the vertical, being swept down river, or in the grip of undersea currents. Tattersall enthused: 'I went through the Swellies recently, in the Menai Straits. The tide was running. The current was so strong that the only place to rest underwater was behind a big rock on the sea bed.' On that occasion he had swum with a buoy attached to a long line, so that the surface boat could follow his progress.

The water at the edge of the Dee was as black as ink. We bobbed out into the current, released the air from our suits and sank slowly to the gravel bottom. Moving with the solid weight of the river I watched stones and sand-banks flash by. Arms tucked in, I felt as streamlined as a dolphin, using the smooth curves of my body to steer round river bends. It was like flying an aircraft very fast and very low: subtle inflections with my fins would slip me over a boulder or send me soaring across the bed to meet the far bank. Too soon Tattersall indicated that we should cut to the bank. I was amazed to see how far we had gone in five minutes: it was a long walk back.

Our final freshwater dive resembled an out-take from an Indiana Jones film. Up among the peaks of the North Wales mountains, Tattersall knew of a deep pool. It was an abandoned slate quarry. It had, he said, 'an interesting approach'. You had to dress into diving gear, and clad in bottle and weight belt, climb the mountainside, then lower yourself by rope down a rock face into the water. The water, he said, was freezing.

It was raining lightly when we arrived at the top of the Horseshoe Pass. What, I wondered, would the unexpecting fell-walker think if he were to come face-to-face with five frogmen, masks on heads, lead-waisted and flippers flapping, climbing a mountain.

Fortunately we met no fell-walkers. The descent by rope to the pool was dramatic and the water as clear as glass. On three sides, sheer rock walls rose above the water; below the water the same walls shot down to an inverted stone cone. It was like swimming into the heart of a volcano. Parked at about 30 feet was a Ford Capri. It was upright, and with a minor wriggle it was possible to sit in the driving seat, though with an air-bottle on my back gear-changes were clumsy.

Here we practised underwater navigation. One by one, we finned across the pool for about 20 feet on a compass bearing. At the far side, we adjusted the wrist compass by 180° to try and swim on the new bearing. In theory we should have returned exactly to our start point. It is harder than it seems: you find yourself pulled by invisible currents, or swerving to avoid boulders. Even one degree of error can be critical in low-visibility water.

The following day—the last of the course—we drove up to the Isle of Anglesey. On the beach at Port Dafarch, Tattersall, my 'buddy' for the dive, zipped me into the rubber dry-suit. Sealed at the wrists and neck, and worn over a fibre-pile 'woolly bear', these suits keep you toasting warm, even in British waters. Round my waist was 28 lb of lead and on my back an 83-cubic-foot air cylinder filled to 207 'bars'.

With the inflatable anchored below the ragged cliff that had claimed the *Missouri*, we perched on the boat's gunwhale and rolled backwards, away from the wind and waves, noise and boats and people, sinking down through a silent world in slow, dreamy strokes. Ten, twenty feet, thirty feet we fell, to land as light as feathers in a forest of fronds that waved gently in the undersea breeze. On a patch of sand a somniculous starfish made to move one of his five limbs, couldn't decide which, and went back to sleep.

Following Tattersall, I finned through

Diving through the looking glass: British water may have a rich collection of wrecks to explore, but for coral and marine life you must swim further. This is a moray eel, off Ras Muhamed in the Red Sea, (photo Terry Gibson).

the slippy fingers of weed and down a rock slope. Ahead, a towering triangle rose from the sea-floor. Swimming into its arch, Tattersall rolled sideways and tapped the structure with his knife.

An unmistakable metallic clonk, like a muffled bell, carried through the water. It was the *Missouri*. We swam on. The ship's ribs lay over the rocks like a broken whale.

Here were great plates with rivet holes big enough to take a thumb, and dark metal caves, now the home of crabs that waved their pincers at us in irritation. Parts of her were encrusted with pale marine concretions; in other places I could run my finger over the brown iron and raise a pollen cloud of rust.

I thought of *Missouri* on her last voyage, charging through the Atlantic swell, hold noisy with the bellowing of uncomfortable cattle, fo'c'sle smoky with pipes, of salty hands on cards and rope. And of her sudden—unnecessary—end. If her course had taken her just 1^1/$_2$ miles further west she'd have cleared Anglesey and been in the Mersey before the next dusk. Actually, as calamities go, it wasn't as disastrous as it could have been: everybody had been saved—including some of the cattle—though they'd only fetched £1 a head at market.

And Captain Reuben Poland? He had his certificate suspended for six months then went on to weather another 8 years on the East Indies run. He survived another stranding, and in 1894 retired a Knight of the Cross.

A tap on my shoulder. It was Tattersall. He was pointing upwards. We'd been down for 50 minutes. Time had evaporated; it could have been a handful of seconds. The *Missouri* fell away as we rose up through brightening water. Expanding air poured from our lungs and suits, chasing us in a million warm and tickly bubbles so that it felt as if we were floating to the surface of a champagne glass.

Like corks from a bottle, we popped into the daylight. It's nearly impossible to make any facial expressions with a rubber mouthpiece between your teeth, but as I swivelled round to face Tattersall and give the 'OK' signal, I managed a very big, very happy, and surprisingly confident grin.

Action: *Caving*

When one of Britain's leading cave explorers offered to take me a mile inside his local mountain, I fetched from my bookshelf the 1926 volume of *The Boys Own Manual. On page 53, between 'Learning to Skate'* by Sid G. Hedges and *'A Perfect Lady: The Tale of a Ferret', I found what I was looking for: a report upon the activities of the Sidcot School Speleological Society. 'Suitably clad in garments that a seller of cast-off clothes would have spurned, we lit candles for our journey through the darkness', wrote A. Sercombe Griffin.*

Following the River Axe deep into the subterranean caverns of Wookey Hole, Sercombe Griffin and his boys squeezed past curtains of stalacmites, shed clothing to wriggle through streams of icy water, and shinned up ropes. Reassured that the geo-physical pleasures promised by crawling through small underground holes would prevent an attack of claustrophobic funk, I took the train for Wales.

I met Farr at his white-painted stone cottage which sits on the edge of the Usk Valley less than a bow's shot from the Norman castle at Tretower. The horizon beyond the castle's round tower is blocked by Llangattock Mountain. At 1,000 feet you can see the contour track—the 'Old Tramway'—that girdles the mountain's dark scarp and marks the line of the old horse-drawn railway along which the quarried limestone was dragged to the iron-furnaces of Nantyglo.

'That mountain's hollow. Riddled. We've only scraped the surface. There are miles of caves yet to find. The entrances are in the old quarries along the Tramway.'

Farr was born in Cwmdu, a twenty-minute walk up the valley, and has spent much of his life burrowing under the limestone hills that frame a quilt of sheep pastures, darks woods and solid farms. His eyes flick from crag to crag like a pinball looking for a hole.

'The caves follow the rock beds through the mountain to Clydach Gorge on the far side. When it's all explored it could be the single biggest cave system in the British Isles.'

When he was ten, Farr was taken by his father to Eglwys Faen—the 'stone church'—where Llangattock's ousted Royalist priest once held secret services, and where on Midsummer's Eve one can still hear a choir of ghosts. 'It was brilliant. The best moment of my life. In the same year I was taken down the main passage of Agen Allwedd.'

Deep beneath the moors, where the slow 'plip . . . plop . . . plip' of drops in pools echoes through the earth's night-black arteries, the young Farr had been introduced to a mysterious and largely undiscovered world.

Weekends and evenings during his teens were spent walking the mountains searching for the tell-tale draught that would indicate a hidden cave-entrance. On Llangynidr mountain, on a winter's day so sharp the ground was white with frost, Farr stumbled upon the clue he had been looking for: a patch of frost melted by warm air seeping up through the grass. Ripping the turf away with his hands he quickly had a hole big enough to squeeze through and, returning a week later with two schoolmates, began an exploration that led to the discovery of the 1,200-metre cave, Ogof Cynnes.

Having trained as a sub-aqua diver while studying geography at Swansea University, Farr joined the select—and competitive—fraternity of cave-divers. For most mortals, underwater swimming, underground and in the dark, with a limited air supply, strong currents and body-trapping squeezes, is not an obvious leisure activity. It is quite dangerous. But it is the cave-divers who are able to push

through flooded sections of tunnel and cavern to the new, untrodden sections of cave. Crowbars (and occasionally explosives) are used to break through 'boulder chokes', and one of Farr's neighbours has even laid a railway into a cave in order to shift surplus debris.

'What cavers like is a big, black space. To be a cave explorer nowadays you need to be a rock climber, surveyor, engineer, photographer and a sub-aqua diver. Cave-diving is extremely easy until it goes wrong.'

There have been near-misses and tragedies. On his first cave dive, into Dan Yr Ogof in the Swansea Valley, Farr was hauled semi-conscious from the water after swimming for 28 metres with no air. A valve on his breathing apparatus had jammed. Three years later, pushing with Roger Solari into the unexplored depths of Agen Allwedd, Solari became tangled in his guide-line and drowned. Farr's autobiography *The Great Caving Adventure* reveals a nerve-shredding catalogue of exploration that has taken him from Mexico, to the U.S.A., to Iran. Twice Farr has broken the British cave-diving depth record, swimming to 45 metres in Wookey Hole in 1977, then to 60 metres in the same cave five years later. In August 1982 he set a world record in the Bahamas by swimming 1,158 metres into the Conch Blue Hole.

The hidden feats of this compact Welshman—teacher, physical education instructor, explorer—seemed far removed from the pretty garden and young son Morgan gurgling in the late-summer warmth of Tretower. He said: 'We'll go down 'Aggie.'

'Aggie?'

'Agen Allwedd.'

'What's down there? Stalactites? Pretty crystals?' I asked hopefully. 'Rocks like Liquorice Allsorts?'

'Mud.'

Dressed in one-piece overalls, wellington boots, and helmets fitted with lamps, we marched along the hard dry turf of the 'Tramway' high on Llangattock mountain

Caving is a most peculiar activity. A body with the pliancy of overcooked spaghetti is essential if you are not going to get stuck. A cavity near the entrance to Agen Allwedd (photo: Martyn Farr).

In the Trident Passage of Agen Allwed, a caver reviews his progress, considers the meaning of life and tries to be thinner. Most cavers have wide, flat torsos and thin heads, a natural genetic adaptation which helps them squeeze through crevices (photo: Martyn Farr).

while the sun laughed overhead. Two ornithologists following the nature trail regarded us with the wordless curiosity.

The entrance to Agen Allwedd is protected by a rusty grille, locked to keep out the passers-by who have a habit of wandering in and becoming lost, and to protect the slumbers of hundreds of Lesser Horseshoe bats who hibernate in the cave during the winter.

Crawling away from the daylight, I was reminded that my history as a troglodyte included an attempt to sleep in a dung-filled Tibetan cave during a snowstorm, and a climb to a high ledge in a Northern Spanish cavern, where I had become stuck.

It was incredibly dark. For a moment I switched off my headlamp, and my body seemed to soak into the darkness so that my breathing hung in the air like a soundtrack. We splashed down a flooded tunnel; heads dipped to clear great warts of rock hanging from the roof. Evaporation dripped from limestone that glistened in the beam of our lights. I wondered what it must have been like for a ten year old: 'A real adventure. I had a little bicycle light, like a station-master's lamp, and a Boy Scouts' "tam" stuffed with cardboard to protect my head when crawling.'

Instructions echoed back to me: 'Low bit here . . . Watch your head . . . Easy going now.'

The passage twisted and turned. The temperature in a cave remains at a constant 9° centigrade all the year round. Chilled when we started, I was now boiling with exertion. Farr's orange overalls contorted and slithered, his body like a fast-moving piece of plasticine as he squeezed through a 20-foot-high slot little more than a foot wide. Struggling along in the rear, boots full of water, I became firmly jammed in the slot and only extricated myself by swivelling on my hips until I was upside down.

'Awkward bit now!' came the encouraging call. The passage disappeared into a rock wall. At the bottom was a mouse-hole through which were disappearing the soles of Farr's wellington boots.

Flat on my face, with the rock pressing on my back, I squirmed forward. The stream was washing round my chin and into the neck of my overalls, where it diverted below the waist to flow equally down each trouser leg and into my boots. Pulling, kicking and grunting, my elbows colliding with every stone and feet wedging against the roof, I edged forward. Two 'squeezes' later we came to a cascade of rubble.

'This is the first boulder choke' announced Farr. The top of his helmet vanished into the floor of the tunnel. Following his example, I tried to descend the crevice feet first, not realising that it would develop into a kind of right-angled downward spiral. I found myself trying to

bend my legs backwards and head forwards while executing a 90° twist to the solar plexus. Reversing an articulated lorry down a coal-mine would have been more straightforward.

Beyond the boulder choke the passage opened into a black cavern big enough to garage a fleet of buses. 'This is 'Baron's Chamber'. It's named after the first man through the choke. Must have been marvellous: treading a cavern like this, knowing no-one had been here before. We've got the Southern Stream Passage next. You could ride a bike down that.'

Forty feet above the cavern floor we scrambled round a narrow muddy ledge. Calcite winked across the roof. On a mudbank cellanite crystals sparkled like scattered stars.

The Southern Stream Passage opened into a final chamber: the 'Music Hall', its vastness was almost too much for our powerful headlamps to penetrate. An undulating floor and walls tapered into the blackness. On a rock in the centre of the Hall stood a metal music stand; on it a copy of 'Dafyyd y Garreg Wen'; 'Give me my harp my companion for so long. Let it once more add its voice to my song'. Somewhere beneath the strata upon which we sat tinkled a stream.

Leaving the cave would have been anti-climatic had we not fallen into conversation about Llangattock's hidden passages.

'I'm always looking. You have to try every opening.'

We'd come through the boulder choke and were nearing the squeezes when Farr glanced upwards and noticed a dark fissure in the roof.

In a blink he was scrambling 20 feet up a slimy rock wall and delicately bridging a leg-stretching gap to reach a mighty chockstone wedged in the cavern roof. He disappeared. Rocks clattered down as his waving beam of light faded. Fifteen minutes later he reappeared at the chockstone.

'What's up there?' I called.

'Looks good. I got 15 feet but there's an exposed step. Amazing! That just shows how much you can miss. Hundreds of people have walked under here and never looked up. It could go further!'

In the absence of a rope to aid his return down the rock-face he undressed and abseiled down his overalls.

The moment that makes it all worth while. After wriggling through tunnels and tapering cracks, you emerge into the splendid main passage of Agen Allwedd. The dripping darkness, the abstract contours of the passages, and the stillness all contrive to create the sensation that you are worming your way through the distorted tubes of a giant, petrified beast. In this subterranean world you lose sense of scale and feel as small as an ant; a microbe (photo: Martyn Farr).

As we walked back along the Old Tramway and the late afternoon sun settled on the confetti-like sprinkling of Crickhowell's houses in the valley below, it occurred to me that to the cave-exploring qualities already listed I should add perhaps the most important of all: ingenuity.

Action: *Horse Riding*

t's goan a be 'ot' said Frank Pointer, leaning on his old black bicycle. Frank lives in a tiny cottage by the drive of Warren Farm, which is where the tarmac ends and stones start if you are about to embark upon a traverse of Britain's oldest trackway.

A pile of discarded clothes lay on the thick verge. Steven removed an agonised expression from his face and dropped a jersey onto the pile. Steven is a producer for the BBC TV programme that once encouraged me to make a nuclear reactor out of cotton reels and egg boxes. He was going through a phase of fanatical practicality. We once had plans for crossing Iceland together on horseback.

'We'll travel light', he declared. Dolly looked up, grass sprouting from her mouth, then sneezed. My clean sky-blue shirt—which had a stitched Texan doodle across the shoulders—suddenly looked as if it had taken the full force of an exploding pressure-cooker full of spinach. Through her veil of hair Dolly regarded the results with an expression which gave the (false) impression that she was capable of being bashful.

Steven and I had not met these horses before, and Linda Inns, from whom we had hired them for the weekend, suggested that the more experienced of the pair of us ride Velvet, who at 16.1 hands was noticeably the larger of the two. We mounted. Steven is six feet tall, dark, straight-backed, and would pass as a Hussar but for the habit of wearing a 'Blue Peter' badge. I gently nudged Dolly up the hill. We were off.

'Bye', called Frank. 'Ope yur doan git a puncture.'

Apart from desultory rustles in the hedgerows and an ecstatic skylark, we were on our own. Ahead lay 43 miles of remote downland. We had two days, a whole weekend, in which to complete our journey. There would be a few farms and barns, and the odd cottage, but little other sign of habitation along the Ridgeway itself. As we climbed from the valley towards a clear skyline, an untidy cinematic montage: Clint Eastwood, desert sunrises and Tian Zhuangzhuang's 'Horse Thief', played across the sky. The soundtrack to 'Big

Country' bowled over the prairie and there was a bit of Ry Cooder too. Steven said I looked like an absent-minded stick-insect on a Thelwell horse.

Dolly's hooves clopped keenly up the chalk; behind I could hear Steven urging Velvet to keep up. Velvet had already asserted herself as the plodder in the party. We had only got as far as Roden Downs when Steven suggested that we swap horses. He said that he would be able to make Dolly go faster, and that this might encourage Velvet to lift her pace from the 2½ miles an hour we had averaged so far. Ten minutes later a man walking a dog surprised Dolly, who turned and fled, followed by Velvet. We lost a hard-won 25 yards.

Curiosity diverted us down the backslope of the Downs to East Ilsley where a woman throwing bread to the ducks in the village pond directed us to J.W.T. Hibbert's store. I emerged from the store bearing paper bags full of picnic supplies to find that Mrs Phylis Edith Hibbert (J.W.T.'s aunt) had brought out a washing-up bowl full of water for the horses. She was describing to Steven how the village boys used to earn pennies by holding the farmers' horses while they went into the pub. There were fortnightly sheep fairs held in the village until 1934.

'There used to be 13 pubs here' she concluded. 'Now there are only three.' Mrs Hibbert's husband 'Chips' was busy chopping firewood. Selling it in small

bundles, he had raised £400 for the church. 'He's 82', said Phylis, matter-of-factly.

On the way back to the Ridgeway we passed East Ilsley Football Club, a small dilapidated building apparently clad in silver foil and nearly overwhelmed by stinging nettles. Red poppy heads waved at the edges of the oat fields. Below East Hendred Down the geometric grid of Harwell Atomic Energy Research Establishment basked in the warm summer haze. For the first time, we crossed the 200-metre contour; to our right the Vale of White Horse lay as a smooth green sea.

'Scutchamer Knob' I read to Steven from one of my guide books. 'Possibly it was once an Anglo Saxon barrow. Later it was used for village fairs.' We took turns to hold the horses while the other disappeared into the trees to climb the Knob, which was about ten feet high and not as impressive as I'd hoped. When Steven returned, he snorted 'Scutchamer Knob! More like Scutchamer's Little Curvy Ridge'.

Shortly after leaving the Knob we came upon Alison and Alan. They were wearing clean cotton shorts and large rucksacks and we had difficulty overtaking them. 'We're training for the Pennine Way', said Alan. He prodded the perfect turf and added: 'But this isn't very good. It's not boggy enough.'

Velvet's relaxed attitude to forward motion was beginning to suit my mood. The pedantic roll of her hips and the rhythmic clump of hoof on earth had a metronomic regularity that could be disturbed by nothing, least of all her rider. By contrast the sprightly but illogical Dolly would alternately be leaning for the horizon or coming to a dead-stop at the sight of terrifying 'beasts' like agricultural rollers or

Picnicking with Dolly on the Ridgeway. Horses, together with bicycles and feet are to me the most rewarding means of land travel. You move slowly enough to take in the smells and sounds, the details of the hedgerows. Every clod and stone is felt, however momentary, and the journey has a texture that is absent from fleetier forms of transport. Dolly stole my sandwich the moment the camera was put away.

Steven Andrew (left), a legend in his own saddle and my companion on the 'First Horse Traverse of the Ridgeway by a Man Wearing a Beret and Blue Peter Badge Expedition'. This is Avebury Down, at the western end of the Ridgeway. The expedition nearly came to grief in the car park of a pub called 'The George'. We made the 40-mile journey in two days.

bits of old tin. When the afternoon filled with the echoey drone of a Lancaster bomber, Dolly didn't even blink.

We turned off the Ridgeway and rode to Fawley because Thomas Hardy used the village in *Jude the Obscure*. 'Jude' was brought up here, and the church, schoolhouse, village green and bowl-shaped field where Jude scared crows for Farmer Troutham can all be found. I've never understood why Fawley becomes 'Marygreen' in the book.

We had booked into Courthill Youth

Hostel for the night. Steven had never been in a youth hostel before.

The warden, a young man with one ear-ring called Craig Thomas, signed us in and said that Wantage Silver Band were going to play outside the hostel that evening. 'It's not quite what I expected', said Steven quietly. 'There seems to be a great lack of youths, and a tremendous number of old men in shorts. And I've just seen two nuns.'

The hostel has been built on land reclaimed from an old rubbish dump. It looks across the Vale of White Horse with a view that seems to go on for ever. The accommodation is arranged in a square of rescued field barns. We were sleeping in an old cow byre that had been converted into a mini-dormitory for four. Sharing our room was George Collier, a keen cyclist and member of the Harrow and Wembley Hostel Group. For the first time that day, Steven seemed out of his depth.

On a grass platform in front of the hostel, the band struck up 'Bright Eyes' and then 'The Floral Dance', followed by the 'Eine Kleine Oompah', 'Captain Beaky', 'Neopolitan Serenade' and 'The Luftwaffe March'. Afterwards, the B flat bass tuba player, Alan Tomkins, organised a sack race for the children. Steven's sack only reached his knees. In the three-legged race he tied my ankle to his with a strip of stocking, but the nylon snapped and we were disqualified. When my arms gave way in the wheelbarrow race, Steven pushed me for ten yards on my face, but we still came last. Later, a man from Wantage came up with the 'Marygreen' explanation:

'It was Hardy's mother', he said. 'She was born in Fawley.'

At five o'clock the next morning we tip-toed from the hostel. With the sun flat on our backs and the grass drenched in dew, we trotted westwards along the lip of the scarp. Crowhole Bottom, then Devil's

pink dog-roses. Birds that would have flown on sight of man or vehicle seemed not to mind the passing of a horse; I could have reached out and tickled the brick-red breast of one chaffinch.

Wayland's Smithy is a neolithic burial chamber, built about 4,800 years ago. There is a legend that passing travellers who leave a piece of silver on the lintel of the tomb and who look the other way for a few minutes, will return to find their horse newly shod. We had no silver, and the most likely consequence of turning our backs on Dolly and Velvet, was a long walk home.

We entered an empty land. No wind stirred the air. We rode in silence for mile after mile, seeing nobody. The view that had occupied us all morning was now hidden by hedges and a foreground of bulging hill-slope. My numnah having slipped off for the hundredth time, Steven departed into the undergrowth armed with nothing more than his Swiss army knife—and emerged with a length of baler twine which he looped over the saddle and numnah and tied with an enormous, very technical knot.

'Learnt this off a survival expert', he said proudly.

On Liddington Hill we reached the highest point of the ride: 896 feet above sea-level. Steven spotted a yellow hammer, then a lapwing. Midday found us walking beside the horses along a shaded path that runs along the crest of Round Hill Down. Grateful for the relief from a twelve-stone burden—or trying to rid herself of an itch—Velvet rubbed her face on my shoulder. Through gaps in the foliage we could see Ogbourne St George far below. We chose a track that dropped straight down the hillside. While I held the reins in the garden of 'The George' Steven disappeared inside and ordered two beers and a bucket of water. Dolly drank all the water, knocked my beer over, then bit the head off a geranium.

Leaving the village we saw the first (and only) running water along the Ridgeway. Beneath the road trickled the River Og. I wanted to dive in.

The airy gangplank of Smeathes Ridge lifted us exuberantly back to the skyline and Barbury Castle: an immense circular embankment on the crown of the hill. It was easy to imagine Iron Age hunters returning weary from the forests below, smelling the woodsmoke in the evening air and turning into the crowded enclave of wooden huts. We bought two ice creams from 'Frank's

HORSE RIDING

buzkashi the game one should offer to play upon meeting Afghan horsemen.

chukka the time occupied by a polo game.

deep going a soft surface for falling.

hard going the least suitable kind of surface for falling.

kicking sometimes practised by a horse who resents being sat on all day; also **biting**.

lacking activity a horse which is too idle to move.

jump a safe alibi for a horse looking for a means of unseating a rider.

nappy a horse who will not go forward despite instructions.

spooky a nervous horse.

volte a tight turn on the haunches; rider should still be on saddle at end of turn.

Super Whippy Soft' van and trotted into the fort.

The track curved round to the south past islands of beech trees. The heat beat down. Velvet tossed her head irritably at the flies; it was Steven's turn to wear the beret so I made a sunhat out of a knotted handkerchief. We had moved onto a part of the map empty of lanes or farms; instead, every grid square seemed speckled with the hieroglyphs of ancient man: earthworks, tumulii, barrows, ditches and dykes lay each side of our way. On a hill half a mile away sarsen stones lay scattered like giant bits of shingle.

Avebury itself swam into focus, its roofs visible amidst a group of trees on the plain below. This great Megalithic focus is surrounded by a high dyke and a circle of tall standing stones. Within this circle are two smaller circles.

Where the tracks cross on Overton Down we dismounted. My knees felt as if they had been clenching a barrel for two days; I could hardly walk. Steven claimed to be 'feeling fine', but had a noticeable limp.

Sensing that she was on the last mile, Velvet increased her speed to a cracking $3^1/2$ mph. At 6 pm we rode into the ancient rings of Avebury.

Punchbowl slipped by. Three-quarters of a mile after clattering across the tarmac of the Lambourn road we came to the brink of Sparsholt Down. In front of us the chalk track kinked left and dropped steeply out of sight, to reappear half-a-mile further on, soaring past a solitary barn to Blowingstone Hill. A hare popped up in front of us and galloped into the hedge.

The track rose to Whitehorse Hill, where we squeezed through the bridle gate to ride across sheep-cropped turf beside the smooth rampart of Uffington Castle. Dolly led the way down a chalky gully, but no matter how far we tried to distance ourselves from the abstract slashes in the greensward they refused to form a horse. 'It looks more like a decapitated emu to me', commented Steven.

Fifteen-foot hedges walled us in after Uffington. We trotted along an alley fluttering with butterflies and splashed with dandelion, buttercups, cow parsley and

Action: *Rock Climbing*

Like a lizard on a wall, the climber appeared locked into an attitude of frozen contemplation. A small cloud slid in front of the sun. The shadow chased along the brown cliff. When the shadow had passed, the climber had moved and the thin red line leading to the top of the cliff was making small chinking sounds where it passed through the shiny metal clips.

My head came level with Mark's feet. I looked up. He was grinning. He was sitting with his legs dangling over the edge of a narrow ledge. Beside him were the red spaghetti coils of rope. He was connected to the cliff by a length of blue nylon tape.

I clipped myself on to the tape, sucking and laughing in the high, thin air. I carefully turned around. In front of us expanded a landscape whose horizon appeared to recede with every second of staring. In the foreground, flat-faced rock outcrops the size of hotels rose above the evergreen stain of the trees, and behind them the prairie sloped away in leathery waves east towards the Great Plains. West rose the grey, guano-rimmed Rockies.

Where the prairie flattened in front of us the sun caught the silver sides of semi-trailers grunting over Interstate 80. Before the blacktop had been laid this had been the original route of the Union Pacific railroad. Straining up the gradient—2,000 feet in 31 miles—from Cheyenne had come the 'Big Boys': giant 4-8-8-4 steam engines pulling upwards of 3,000 tons each over the Divide to Laramie and the mountains.

'It's called the gangplank', said Mark as he fingered through the 'rack' of equipment that swayed at his waist. 'The only place where there's an easy slope into the Rockies. These cliffs are right at the top of the gangplank.' Mark stepped to the end of the ledge and turned to the rock.

I wondered whether the engine-drivers had ever looked across to the rocks that rise high above the limber pine and sage-brush on this windy pass? Had they ever wondered at their strange shapes, or wanted to stop the train and walk across and feel that cold granite? Others knew these rocks well. The Indians, Cheyenne and Arapahoe,

who would have used this vantage point to watch the wandering herds of buffalo and antelope. They called the rocks Vedauwoo, meaning 'earthborn spirit'. The climbers call them Vedauwoo too.

Vedauwoo (pronounced Vee-de-voo) is little known outside a select circle of Wyoming climbers, and I doubt that I'd ever have heard about it had I not bumped into Mark Jenkins on a street in Lhasa early in 1986. Mark had been on his way from Mount Everest towards home in Wyoming, and I had been with my cousin Richard on the first leg of a bicycle ride across Tibet and the Gobi Desert. Mark has an encouraging history of mildly-eccentric travels that include the first crossing of the Rocky Mountains by recumbent bicycle and the first traverse of Yellowstone by skis. Aside from having been chosen for the 1986 American North Face of Everest Expedition, he had also climbed the 26,000-foot Xixabangma, and made climbing trips to Alaska, Mexico and Africa. Surrounded by the tooth-pullers, bicycle menders and prostrating pilgrims of Tibet's capital the three of us had talked of Europe and the American West as if we would never see them again.

'When you're finished bicycling, you should come and visit,' Mark had said, 'I'll take you climbing.'

Sixteen months later I arrived at Mark's home in Wyoming's university town of Laramie—a grid-pattern town of tree-lined streets; the railroad at one end of Grand Avenue and the hills at the other. The Rockies lie just down the road to the west; Vedauwoo is twenty minutes east. On my first morning, we drove east.

'How much do you train for climbing?' I asked.

'Not much' he replied. 'I have friends who do 50 pull-ups, but that's not exceptional. Rock-climbing is basically gymnastics; upper-body stuff, but you don't need to be strong. Technique is far more important.'

'How did you get started?'

'When I was seventeen, at High School. A teacher called 'Coach' Kopischka opened up Vedauwoo, wrote the guide-book, taught us all to climb. In those days all I had was heavy hiking boots and heavy old hemp rope. Really makes you appreciate modern gear.'

We followed the trail through the pines to the foot of the rocks, where we dumped the packs of gear. I had been lent a pair of lightweight climbing shoes, canvas topped, with a tightly-moulded rubber sole. 'If they don't hurt when you put them on, they're too big,' Mark explained. The shoes are meant to be tight so that your foot feels every wrinkle in the rock.

Aside from boots, basic gear for rock-climbing includes an 11-millimetre rope, a 'sit-harness' which buckles around your waist, a device called a 'figure-of-eight' which is used for abseiling, a 'sticht' plate which is handy for belaying, and an armoury of what the Americans call 'pieces'—aluminium wedges of varying sizes that are used for protection. The lead climber of a pair inserts the wedges in cracks as he climbs, attaching them to the rope by slings and karibiners. Should he fall, he will only drop to the same distance below the last wedge as he has climbed above it (with a bit extra for rope stretch).

'The point of the equipment' says Mark, 'is to keep you from hitting the ground. The worst thing is death, and that's very rare in rock climbing. It's a very safe sport provided you keep to the rules, tie the right knots, have good equipment and know how to use it.'

The well-dressed climber also carries a selection of 'Friends'—ingenious aluminium cams fitted with a sprung trigger that withdraws the cams allowing the 'Friend' to be inserted in cracks. When the trigger is released, the cams expand and wedge the

The concentration, balance and fluidity of good rock climbing makes it a wonderful panacea for the stress of city life. Here, Mark Jenkins jams his way up an off-width crack on one of Vedauwoo's harder climbs. He is belayed by another climber who is wedged into the shadowed crack beneath the overhang.

A full 'rack' of Friends, nuts and chocks, together with the chalk bag used on climbs where even the sweat on finger-tips is enough to critically reduce friction.

device firmly in the rock.

We started on a long crack called 'Slat', a route which obliges the use of 'hand-jams', so called because you expand your hand inside the rock until it sticks fast, forming a secure anchor upon which to pull yourself upwards. Others will claim that 'hand-jam' refers to the condition of your knuckles after climbing a crack like 'Slat'.

Next we moved to 'Coldfingers', 'a good one' Mark told me, 'to demonstrate friction technique.'

'Coldfingers' goes up the centre of a steep, featureless wall, whose only redeeming feature is the roughness of its surface. 'You're going to be smearing and edging' Mark called down as I felt the rope tug tight at my waist. He could have added 'sweating'. There were no handholds or footholds; just patterns of minute excrescences onto which the sole of a boot could be ground, or flat of hand pressed. In a few places, there were button-size pimples just big enough to accommodate a carefully-balanced boot-edge. The urge to hug the rock is overwhelming.

'Keep out! Stand out from the rock so that you're vertical. Toes inward. Smear those feet onto the rock.' With no hint of holes or holds for even a single finger, I

tried to move as smoothly as treacle, incredulous that my boots and hands had enough 'stick' to stay on the rock.

Subsequent climbs introduced me to the pleasures of lay-backing, bridging, arm-bars, abseils, heel-hooks, toe-jams and the butt-jam.

My final climb at Vedauwoo was 'The Mantle Route'.

'It's a 5:9', Mark told me as he pulled in the rope. 'That means you probably won't

The rock of Vedauwoo, high on the natural ramp between the Great Plains and the Rocky Mountains is granite: old, tough rock which originally bubbled from the earth's core as molten lava then cooled into great, smooth-faced billows separated by cracks that vary from finger-nail to shoulder width. The rock is so abrasive that most climbers bind their hands with protective tape.

get up it. But it'll be interesting for you to try. The hard bit's right at the beginning. You've got to step left out of the crack onto the face. It looks blank, but when you get close you'll see places. They're too small to hold your weight for more than a second or two so you have to keep moving.'

I ran through the pre-climb checks: climbing harness tight round my waist; rope knot tight; karibiner gate closed and locked. I was ready.

'Climbing.'

The first moves are easy, upwards into a crack that tapers to nothing. Here is a place to rest. I can look left across the wall, bulging and nearly vertical. Near the top of the bulge is an obvious line for my feet. An inch from my nose, the feldspar crystals and lichen overlay an intricate matrix of grey-brown granite that looks like the surface of a far-off planet or the inside of a head.

A perfect illustration of how not to climb: this climber is nervous, out of balance and wearing footwear designed for level running tracks.

Not far from my ear is a triangular chip shaped like the Matterhorn. It is no bigger than a fingernail. This will be my main 'handhold'. I pinch it with the fingers of my left hand. It really is tiny. Diagonally above me, well out of reach, I can see a hold—a 'chickenhead'—big enough for two hands at once. All I can see for my left hand is a rounded swelling maybe five feet away. But if my shoes will stick to the top of the bulge it may be possible to move sideways, holding myself to the rock with the 'Matterhorn'. As I left the sanctuary of that crack, it seemed inconceivable that I would stay in contact with the cliff.

'Believe, believe!' I could hear Mark in my head. The 'Matterhorn' passed my head, feet didn't slip, the swelling fitted into the cup of my hand. (*Keep moving, keep moving*.) Upward, right foot finding grip on an unseen chip, left hand pushing me up from that swelling. Nothing for my right hand; (now I *have* to fall). Toes on the left foot are skating, searching, finding. Three right fingers hook a flake. Ease upwards (*gently, gently*). That huge handhold is in reach. Shall I lunge for it? No—try and get closer; a sharp move will pull my feet off the rock. My fingertips creep up the weathered rock, stretching, every crystal felt, until they can curl and grip. Almost nothing that hand has ever embraced felt as good as this.

The right hand follows. Now it is impossible to fall. I can find nothing for my feet, and so pull myself up on my arms. First my face, then chest rise level with the 'chickenhead'. Now I have to reverse my hands, still rising, so that instead of pulling I'm pushing. My arms straighten. Now I can pull a leg up; get a heel on the 'Chickenhead' and push up till I'm standing.

The rest is easy.

Action: *Nordic Skiing*

Waiting in the swirling spindrift was the fur-wrapped shadow of a Lapp. He stood perfectly still, all but obliterated by the blizzard that thundered and steamed at the meeting place of the valleys. As the taxi rolled to a halt I asked the driver, Anders, whether we had reached our destination, Nikkaluokta.

'Yes', he said.

'And,' I asked, pointing towards the figure in the snow, 'is that John Högling?'

'Yes', he said, again.

I scurried across to Högling and shouted a greeting. He nodded and helped me into a sledge attached to the back of a snow scooter. Facing backwards, legs wedged beneath a rope and a tarpaulin up to my neck to keep off the worst of the weather, I gripped tightly as the sledge snatched free of the ice, and careered away from a waving Anders. Towed at breakneck speed by the scooter, the sledge bucketed through the ravaged winter bones of some birch trees before plunging into a snow-filled stream-bed and leaping over a cornice, snow and ice spraying everywhere; it was like doing the Cresta Run in a dustbin.

Into the simpler winds of the Ladtjojåkka valley the white-out thinned to reveal a rising horizon of bulky mountains. Snow fell inboard as we glanced off snowbanks; slush arced past as we barged across a frozen lake. We roller-coasted below the truncated flank of Tarfalapakte, then up towards the cluster of huts that is the Kebnekaise *fjällstation*. Högling had covered the 19 kilometres in 45 minutes.

Outside one of the huts the others were waiting. There was time for a quick coffee, exchange of names, and then it was outside again to clip into skis, pull on the packs and set off for Singi Hut, 15 kilometres further west.

Lotti Meurling kicks-and-glides along the Kungsleden trail near Kaitumjaure at the tail-end of an Arctic winter. In her pack are provisions for a week, including sleeping bag, spare clothes, a snow-shovel, bivouac bag, medical kit, map and compass, and a large steel thermos flask full of blåbärsoppa.

One by one, the seven Swedes swept smoothly away from the *fjällstation,* their skis hissing down the gentle slope. I followed, accelerating to a remarkable speed, which I sustained for several yards before striking a tree that catapulted me into a snowdrift.

Most of the morning was occupied with a pleasantly gentle ascent. Following the tracks in front and chanting 'kick-and-glide, kick-and-glide, kick-and-glide' to myself, the time and kilometres drifted by.

The group I was with came from Stockholm: my cousin Peter Meurling and wife Lotti, my other cousin Kate Meurling, Tord, Bengt, Per Åke and Kaj. Like most Swedes, they had been cross-country skiing since childhood, and like most Englishmen I have always found balancing on slippery planks an elusive art. Where my cousins could glide gracefully in a seemingly effortless rhythm, I lumbered along like a broken locomotive in search of a collision. Scandinavians invented skiing; wooden skis dating back 4,000 to 5,000 years have been discovered in bogs in Sweden and Finland.

The plan was to make a seven-day trek through the mountains that form the border with Norway and Sweden. We would be skiing through the least-populated part of Swedish Lapland, a virtually untouched wilderness five times the size of Wales, with a total population slightly smaller than that of the English county town of Norwich. During this time we wouldn't see a road, and would be carrying all our food, sleeping gear and survival equipment on our backs.

With the wind now driving veils of stinging ice up the valley, we stopped in the lee of a large rock, excavated a seat using snow shovels, unrolled our insulated mats and nibbled a quick lunch. I fell asleep.

A lone skier (Kaj Hollmann) paints perfect curves across the western flank of Unna Aurekasj. At moments like this the blizzards and biting winds, the labour of the climb and the occasional weakening of the spirit are blown away in the sheer ecstasy of flying down the unmarked snow of an Arctic mountain.

Shortly before dark, we arrived at Singi Hut to find it drifted up to the windows by blown snow. Pushing through the door, tasks were quickly divided: some to bring in snow and melt it for cooking, others to chop wood for the stove, Peter to cook. These huts are administered by the STF—*Svenska Turistföreningen*—and like youth hostels, they have a resident warden. All of them are fitted out with wooden bunk beds, benches and tables and a wood stove.

We were greeted next morning by a surprise sun, and air cold enough to frost tonsils. Earlier in the month, Peter had

written to me describing the weather at this time of year as being 'usually stable: either good or bad, but not both. Good means −5° to −15° centigrade, sunshine and no wind; bad means high winds with snow'. It was a completely accurate forecast.

Changes of weather mean changes of wax for the skis. There are five or so different colour-coded waxes, ranging from blue for hard icy tracks to orange for old wet snow. It has never been known for any two skiers to agree on which wax to use on a given day. The method of applying the wax to the skis is also open to interpretation: basically you smear on the wax, then rub it in using a fibrous block, though how much you put on, and how much of the ski you cover, is always a contentious subject. 'Smearing' is made easier if the ski-bottoms are stood facing the sun for a few minutes before application.

Waxed, sun-screened and eager, we pushed off northwards following 'Kungsleden', a marked trail that runs for

some 450 kilometres southwards from Abisko to Hemavan. In summer it's a long-distance hiking trail; in winter it is a well-beaten ski-touring route, marked by red diagonal crosses. To prevent absent-minded skiers straight-lining to oblivion, any corners on the trail are marked by double crosses.

With one day behind me, I had learnt how to fall over less often. I had been Alpine skiing three times before, but this was the first time I'd used Nordic skis. They are thinner and longer than downhill skis, with bindings that allow the heel to lift. This means you can 'walk' (and 'run') the skis, but you cannot throw them into parallel turns or 'snowploughs'. The only effective way of slowing or turning while skiing downhill is to master the 'Telemark' turn: a tricky feat of balance in which the skier drops one knee and moves the leading 'steering' ski far forward then round towards the new direction. For the time being I confined myself to straight-line

Waxing skis at the start of the day. Waxing is made easier if the skis are left pointing towards the sun for a few minutes. If you choose the wrong type of wax for the snow conditions, the skis will either not grip, or will 'ball up' with sticky snow. It is part art, part science, and quickly learnt.

descents softened by prudent use of snowdrifts.

Boots suitable for ski-touring have a 'Vibram' sole and ankle protection so that you can climb with the skis on your back in places where the ground is too steep or rocky for skiing.

At the mouth of the Kuoperjåkka valley, we turned off the trail, cutting fresh tracks to reach a rocky knoll where we dumped the packs, before continuing for a side trip up the Rabots Glacier. Taking it in turns to push the trail, we skirted the crescented terminal moraine, then mounted the snout of the glacier itself. The ramparts of Kebnekaise, Sweden's highest mountain, hung from the pure blue sky above our heads, each needle pinnacle of rock clear enough to be an inch away.

This was my first steep 'uphill' on skis. It was not easy. The art of 'edging' is to stand parallel with the slope and kick the metal edge of the upper ski into the snow. You then transfer weight to the upper ski, raise the lower ski and kick it in. In steps of nine inches or so, you can make a laborious ascent. If your weight-bearing ski does not rest parallel with the hill's contours, you will slide forward or backwards, which is inconvenient in areas where there are precipices.

On less steep snow it is possible to zig-zag upwards in the fashion of a hairpin road. The problem here is the hairpin, which should be tackled by the following method: put all your weight on the outer, downhill ski, then turn your uphill ski through 180 degrees. Your feet are now beside each other, but facing in opposite directions; for non-Scandinavians, this can be excruciatingly painful. Transferring your weight to the uphill ski you then lift and swing the outer ski round until it too points in the new direction. This manoeuvre is rather harder than trying a U-turn on a Wall of Death, and it is likely to result in your receiving a mild rupture, falling over sideways, or sliding downhill with one leg in the air. For the three days it took to master the uphill turn I relied on Kaj to hold me upright, Per Åke to provide a technical commentary and Kate to catch me when I slid backwards out of control.

We got to within a hundred metres of the glacier's highpoint, then turned and swooped back down to the packs. It took two hours through air chilling by the minute to reach the next hut, at Sälka. With legs like lead after a 28-kilometre day, we pushed up the final slope to find a team of huskies settling down for the night, noses tucked into their own fur. I was glad to be sleeping indoors.

The night was clear and cold. The huskies howled and, just before midnight Lotti spotted the Northern Lights. We crowded outside, shivering in the moonlight to watch a shimmering green aurora occupy half the

The motorways of the Arctic: frozen lakes. But these motorways are clean and safe. This is Suorvajaure, and it provided us with a day's fast skiing down from the mountains to the road-head, where a Swedish bus (fitted with ski racks) whisked us back to Gällivare and the train to Stockholm. A civilised way to travel.

sky as it played games with shapes, making seaweed, caterpillars and clouds, stretching, breaking and reforming like a phantom unable to decide what form to take.

Where most of the first two days had been on marked trails, the next two were to be decidedly off-the-beaten-track. From Saälka we started northwards with an enjoyable slide over a level frozen river surface. It was warm enough for shirt-sleeves; the sun blinding on the entirely white landscape.

Leaving the security of Kungsleden we turned up a narrow valley called Lulep Suorre. It was a 380-metre climb to the col, some of it a precarious skirting of steep-sided bowls in the valley-side.

Near the top, we stopped. My plastic thermos flask had been reduced by the accidents of the first day to a handful of atoms, so I was now sharing Bengt's stainless steel two-litre flask which he kept filled with a sweet, fruity *Blåbärsoppa* (blueberry soup). I had also noted that the Swedes' plastic lunch boxes were always filled with dense-looking rye bread, which they flavoured with caviar spread, liver paste, and cheese—all packaged in sensible toothpaste tubes. My own sliced wholemeal, carried in a plastic bag from Britain, had long since disintegrated into a drift of crumbs eatable only by spoon. My jam pot had split.

The caps were hardly back on the flasks before a new wind drove thick mist up the valley. The head of the Lulep Suorre had opened suddenly to bring us to an exposed, sloping plateau. Pieces of ice like broken glass skittered before us. The wind-blasted snow-crust had turned partly to ice over which the skis rattled unnervingly.

Visibility was limited to a confusing litter of rock outcrops. There was nothing on

which to focus a compass bearing. We stopped, bowed away from the blast, trying to control the flapping map.

'If we don't find the hut, we can dig a snow-cave' shouted Peter, as casually as if he was deciding to take the bus home instead of the tube. That's another thing Swedes are good at: surviving in the open.

I was not disappointed when, after another twenty minutes on a fairly arbitrary compass bearing we hit a reindeer fence that we knew would lead to the hut at Hukejaure. Just four kilometres from the Norwegian border and 150 kilometres north of the Arctic Circle, the hut stood on a low hill overlooking a small lake. It was March 26th; we were the first Swedish ski group to reach the hut that winter. Water for cooking was hauled by bucket from a hole drilled in the centre of the lake.

During the following day, a 20-kilometre glide over the mountains to rejoin the Kungsleden, we climbed up to a pass at 1,000 metres, then, with skis strapped to our packs, we carefully kicked steps downwards, treading carefully round the

NORDIC SKIING

bird-nesting skiing through trees; hazard potential is substantial.

chattering the unnerving sound that skis make when they suddenly begin to pass over ice.

double helicopter two aerial turns through 360°. A double helicopter while bird-nesting and wearing a backpack is unlikely to be survivable.

headplant alternative method of stopping.

herringbone laborious method of skiing uphill; ski tips are apart and ski-tails together.

kick-and-glide the key to cross-country motion; when you suddenly find you can do it, it's like mastering a bicycle.

schuss to ski in a straight line down the slope; can lead to involuntarily high speeds and spectacular mistakes.

schussboomer derogatory term often directed at Englishmen who have no option but to go in straight lines at uncontrollable speeds.

telemark the fabled loose-heeled turn liable to rupture non-Scandinavians.

wax pocket the upward flex in the centre part of the ski along which you apply the wax; when body weight is transferred to the ski, the wax pocket is pressed down onto the snow, providing traction.

top of a likely avalanche slope before replacing the skis in the shelter of some rocks.

From the hut at Singi, we watched two Norwegians set off under a brilliant sky, a dog-team towing their sledge of equipment. They quickly became fly-like specks in the vast dish beneath the mountains. Ski-touring luggage is fairly heavy and bulky and there are different schools of thought regarding the best way to carry it. You can put it on your own back; you can put it on a sledge and haul it; or you can put it on a sledge and get dogs to haul it. I rather liked the Norwegian solution.

From here we would be heading south down Kungsleden for the remainder of the trek, but first a little deviation. Half an hour beyond Singi we forked right onto untouched snow, heading for the summit of 1,354-metre Unna Aurekasj. This was, as Bengt put it, 'to prove that you can ski *up* mountains as well as *down*'.

On three sides the noble peak of Unna Aurekasj is very steep, but to the west there's a gentler approach. After ploughing in a long line up calf-deep snow, zig-zagging on the steep parts, we came to a broad col and dumped the packs on a prominent rock. From here it was considerably steeper; the snow crisper. The sun twinkled in the snow like a scattering of diamonds. One by one we crested the summit ridge, skiing cautiously above the cliffs overlooking the distant thread of Kungsleden as it headed down the valley of Tjäktjavagge.

Before us stretched row upon row of pristine snowpeaks. It was as if we had been lifted on a slightly higher wave than all the rest.

To the west, the crests rolled into Norway; southwards we could see the isolated eruption of summits that formed the Sareks National Park while to the east it was hard not to roam over the knife-edge ridge of Kebnekaise. Northwards lay the Arctic.

Kaj left first, winging downwards, counting off the Telemarks as he painted a series of perfect curves across the clean white canvas of Unna Aurekasj's western flank. Bengt, Lotti, Peter, Per Åke, Tord and Kate followed, each tiny figure like a needle weaving another strand into the plait as it reached down the mountain. Finally I left the summit, creasing the slopes with an unabashed, exhilarating, perfectly straight furrow. But one day I too will be able to Telemark.

Action: *Woodlore*

Part way up the wet grass hillside Golden Fox paused and looked back through the falling mist to the smashed trees. The beech and oak lay on their sides like skeletons, their roots welded to slabs of fresh chalk that showed white as bone against the dark ground. We continued up the hill, scrambling through a tangle of bramble to reach the edge of the wood.

'Whose is this?' I asked, pointing to a hole in the damp soil around which lay feathers.

'You tell me', Golden Fox replied.

'Rabbit?' I guessed.

'Fox', he said. 'They store their food underground. Sometimes they don't do it too well. I've seen pigeon legs sticking out of the earth. It looks really odd.'

He moved a few feet into the wood.

'We'll wait a minute here.' The wood was absolutely silent. But as the sound of our footfalls and breathing drained away, a rising tide of new sounds filled the air. Loudest were the random clicks of water drops hitting the dead leaves around our feet. Bit by bit the clicks multiplied and amplified till the moist air tick-tocked like a thousand clocks. Other sounds broke in: the call of a bird, a breath of wind through bare branches, the crack of a stick, a bark, and, growing above them all, a distant bass like that of a cataract.

'To see in the woods you must unfocus your eyes; use peripheral vision. You're not going to see Bambi side-on right in front of you; you're looking for the tiniest movements; the flick of a whisker, twitch of an ear. Or the waving of a snail's antennae. Most people see nothing.'

Before he had finished speaking, a grey squirrel ran down a nearby trunk.

'On my last visit to London I saw

Building a wickiup under the supervision of Raymond Mears during the wet chill of a December night on the North Downs. This shelter took four hours to build, using dead wood collected from the ground. The roof was insulated with layers of fallen beech leaves. Although it rained all night, inside we were warm and dry (photo: Peter Inglis).

fox-droppings in Chelsea, kestrels over the Kings Road and an owl in St James. The city is full of wildlife. Can you see anything to eat?' he asked. I looked around the threadbare winter wood. Short of gnawing a bole or sucking leaves there seemed little over which to salivate.

'There. By your leg. On that old log. Jew's Ear. Peel it off the bark carefully.' From the rotting wood I detached a couple of thin flaps of a brownish fungus. It felt slightly moist, like damp skin.

'Put it in your pocket. We'll eat it later. Leave the smaller ears. Never strip all the food.' We moved a few feet to the end of a hawthorn hedge colour-brushed by deep-red berries, and snacked on apple-tasting flesh scraped from the large pips.

'Drop the pips where you eat. They'll grow into the hedge.'

And into the wood we stepped.

Seventy-six years 4 months and 18 days earlier a hungry, exhausted North American Indian had staggered into a mining town on northern California's Feather River. His tribe, the Yahi, had been driven from their lands by gold-miners and settlers. For forty years a dwindling band of Yahi had eked a precarious existence from the bluffs and woods of Deer Creek. 'Ishi'—as he became known to the whites—was not just the last of the Yahi, but the last Indian in North America to live in his natural habitat. After his capture 'Ishi' passed on to academics at the University of California all he knew of the ancient crafts of the woods—crafts that had been handed from person to person since the Stone Age. He died of tuberculosis on 25 March, 1915.

Despite the stamping out of North

Raymond Mears teaches me how to use a fire drill. This is much harder than it looks. You spin the drill between the palms of your hands, exerting a constant (and considerable) downward pressure. After a few moments, spirals of smoke *should* begin to curl up from the foot of the drill. A bit more spinning and you should have a small pile of black embers which can be carefully scooped into your ball of 'old man's beard' and blown on until flames appear. These are then placed beneath a prepared 'tepee' of dry twigs. You have a fire for cooking, warmth, life (photo: Peter Inglis).

capote heavy coat with pointed hood, best made from the quality wool of a Hudson Bay blanket.
eshawana clematis wood; used for the base (**hearth**) of a hand-drill. Shoshone word.
hubu elderberry wood; used for the drill part of a fire drill. Paiute word.
shelter there are many different types, ranging from 'lean to' to 'bus'. The former does not require planning permission.
rawhide animal skin which has had the fat and the hair removed, and then dried.
sagwecio mistik wanahigan the second two words are a 'dead-fall trap'; a piece of balanced wood which kills an animal by falling onto it. **Sagwecio** is a mink.
strikealight a flint and steel firelighting set.
tabu-oo greater reedmace. Edible plant growing near water, good for carbohydrate. Paiute word.
wadub cordage made from young roots; the thin rootlets of spruce can for example be used for making laces, handy for constructing birch-bark canoes etc.
waginoogan a torch made from birch bark.
whangs thongs made from rawhide.
wickiup a lean-to shelter made from branches and leaves.
wigub cordage made from the bark of the bass tree.
zesub stinging nettles.

American culture, veins of knowledge have carried the traditions forward through the generations. One of the best-known documentors was Ernest Thompson Seton, originally from South Shields, Durham, who emigrated with his family to Canada in 1866 at the age of six. The young Ernest spent his days in the woods of Ontario, learning to track and sketch the plentiful wildlife. A gold medal for his sketching from Ontario Art School launched him on a trip to London to study at the Royal Academy School of Painting and Sculpture

and then back to Manitoba where he took up a position as naturalist for the provincial government. In 1898, his first book, *Animals I Have Known* was published. Seton's woodcraft tales and lively sketches had great appeal for youngsters, and 'tribes' of 'Woodcraft Indians' (or 'Seton's Indians') sprang up through America.

Seton published *Two Little Savages* and *How to Play Injun*, and in 1904 lectured in Britain on Indian woodcraft. It was while preparing for his second UK tour, in 1906, that he sent complimentary copies of his latest book, *The Birch-bark Roll of the Woodcraft Indians*, to various people whom he thought might be interested in his work. One of the recipients of *The Birch-bark Roll* was the Lieutenant General who had recently made his name at the Siege of Mafeking.

Robert Stephenson Smyth Baden-Powell had, by coincidence, been thinking along very similar lines to Ernest Thompson Seton. Like Seton, 'Stephe' had been hooked on the great outdoors from an early age. His school, Charterhouse, outside the Surrey town of Godalming, was blessed with several good copses: 'It was here that I

imagined myself a backwoodsman, a trapper, and an Indian scout. I used to creep about warily looking for "sign" and getting close-up observations of rabbits, squirrels, rats and birds.'

'B.P.' had already written a manual for boys called *Aids to Scouting*, but unlike Seton, B.P.'s boys were being groomed for military heroics in the colonies. Now searching for a formula that he could use to train boys for peace, B.P. had studied everyone from Epictetus to Pestalozzi and probed into the manhood-training methods of the Spartans, Zulus, Polynesians, Australian Aborigines and American Indians. Seton's book arrived out of the blue and the two men met at the Savoy in London to share ideas. Two years later Baden-Powell's *Scouting for Boys* was published, and the Scout movement was founded.

Little by little the wonderful wholeness—the 'Medicine Wheel'—of Indian life was being broken down into a series of specific techniques that could be illustrated in books or taught in lessons. A year after Ishi's death another expert, Horace Kephart, published his *Camping and Woodcraft*—a polyglot text-book which included traditional Indian techniques such as skinning and shelter-building, while suggesting for trips into country sparse of game that 'it is worth while to carry Worcestershire sauce and pure tomato catchup, to relieve the monotony of cured and canned meats or of too much fish'.

But in 1939 Bernard Mason's book *Woodcraft* began the long walk back to Stone Age roots. Where Kephart urged the use of woollen spiral puttees and secondhand military knapsacks, Mason provided plans for making buckskin bags. The wheel turned full circle with the publication from the late 1970s of a series of books by Tom Brown, a young white American who grew up among the wild woods and underscrub of the New Jersey Pine Barrens under the tutelage of an old Indian named Stalking Wolf. Among Brown's visitors to the Pine Barrens was Golden Fox.

Golden Fox grew up in Kenley, a suburb of semi-detached properties halfway between Croydon and the M25. His other name is Raymond Mears, and since the age of seven he has devoted himself to the woods. Now in his early twenties, Mears watches the present generation poison its own ecosystem with alarming resignation. 'Every piece of rubbish we kick into the atmosphere eventually comes back at us. Acid rain kills the trees, farmers in some parts of the world still use DDT and there is paraquat on these fields. In the outdoors you need shelter, water, fire, food and companionship . . . and that's really it for life. Shelter we've got, fire and food we make, companionship we have. But water is something we take for granted. We turn a tap on, and out it gushes. We don't appreciate where it comes from.'

'Now we need to look for a place to build a shelter' he said, changing the subject. We walked up to the skyline and then along a track wide-puddled with December rain. The conditions and time of year seemed far from ideal for camping without tent or sleeping bag.

Higher up, the wind sighed through the empty trees and the deep roar we'd heard earlier grew louder. We followed the track along the crest of the hill and round an angle in the wood to a blockage.

'What's this?' I asked.

Many of the techniques prized by Indians, aborigines and other nomadic peoples are being lost. It is only by learning these skills ourselves that they will be preserved for future generations. The skills of the woods, the firelighting, tracking, identification of birds and animals and edible plants are all enrichments that keep us in touch with the elements that are so fundamental to the survival of the human species (photo: Raymond Mears).

'Toyota Hiace. 1979.' A blue and white painted van lay on its side across the track. Bits of plastic, rubber strip, shards of ripped steel and broken glass mingled with the coppery mat of beech leaves. The front of the van had been blasted by a shotgun. The roar grew louder.

Where the track took a dip to the left, we climbed a bank. Below us clamoured a wide river of moving metal: a seamless stream of cars orbiting the M25 motorway. Even at a distance of two miles the smell was appalling; the noise engulfing any sound the wood might make.

'Because we're short of time we're going to build a quick shelter, a lean-to. We need to be out of the wind, on an east-facing slope where the morning sun will warm us. We'll build it from dead wood; never use anything that's living.'

Deft chops from a hatchet produced two verticals to support a ridgepole. From the ridgepole two supporting beams angled down to the ground. Across these we laid poles to form a roof.

'Now we need the insulation: make a rake from a beech branch and sweep leaves into piles. Then pack the leaves onto the roof.' In the descending gloom, Mears disappeared in search of fire-lighting materials. He returned with a handful of dry grass that he had found under a fallen log.

Gripping the grass in both fists he rubbed it vigorously until the fibres had separated into a ball of fine strands. Of the thirty or so ways of lighting a fire with natural materials, one of the simplest is the fire drill. Mears cut a socket and notch into a slice of sycamore. Laying this on the wad of dried grass he then produced a three-foot stick of elder, and shaved one end to fit the socket in the sycamore.

With the elder stick twirling between his palms it took only a minute or two for a curl of smoke to lift from the blackening socket in the sycamore. As the friction heated and scorched the wood, a tiny 'coal' dropped through the notch onto the grass.

Putting down the stick, Mears scooped up the grass as tenderly as if it were a nest of eggs and blew a tiny lance of air onto the glowing coal. Inside, the orange pinprick brightened and faded with every breath till suddenly it spread, fusing across the hairs of grass till it erupted into flame. Mears pushed the blazing wad beneath a tiny tepee of dry sticks that he had built previously.

'OK. Now you try' he said, handing me the sycamore and elder stick. I tried till the sycamore screeched, but produced little

more than blisters and the faint aroma of warm wood.

Our search for dead leaves took us up through the night-dark trees to the hill-crest that overlooks the part of the Home Counties fondly called 'The Garden of England'. Two conveyor-belts of headlights, twelve lights wide, drifted by in opposite directions like the flow of an

The hide bag of the woodsman, containing tools that include the knife, the piece of antler used for shaping flint tools and the 'noggin' – the drinking vessel shaped from the burl of a horse-chestnut tree, chosen because the grain of the burl follows the outline of the cup, thus making it completely watertight (photo: Peter Inglis).

electric current. Where the A22 met the M25 some of the current diverted into a whirlpool and eddied through a round-about. A helicopter chopped overhead; a jet bellowed over by the sodium glare of Gatwick Airport. Mears thought he detected a badger, or was it a fox? He couldn't hear.

Our bed for the night was a mattress of springy beech. Mears wrapped himself in a 'capote'—an Indian-style coat stitched from the thick acres of a Hudson Bay blanket. Capotes have a double back that can be stuffed with dry leaves and mosses to create a natural duvet-jacket.

The fire danced in the entrance of the lean-to, the heat bouncing off a 'reflector-wall' of logs we had built on the far side. Every three hours one of us would wake up and place more wood on the fire. Outside the wind had torn away the clouds, and the tree-tops swam beneath cold, bright stars. Inside, lying with feet to the flames, and covered by a single thin blanket to keep off the draughts, it was warm and peaceful.

I was woken an hour after dawn by long-tailed tits working their way up the wood, flitting from branch to branch chasing insects. A heavy mist hung in the now still trees. The fire glowed rosily in a bed of clean ash.

We walked the few yards up the hill to the footpath. Below us the motorway roared and spewed, a steel band slowly tightening

The wickiup in the morning. Behind the ashes of the night's fire, the lean-to tucks cosily into the hillside. Inside is a mattress made from springy birch twigs. At three-hour intervals through the night we woke and placed wood on the fire. Heat was 'bounced' into the front of the shelter by a 'reflector screen' behind the fire built from logs (photo: Peter Inglis).

around London. In the twenty-four hours since we had been in the wood, the Department of Transport estimated that 86,000 motor vehicles had passed by. Where on earth do they think they are going?

Action: *White Water Canoeing*

Executing an eskimo roll is not dissimilar to taking a turn inside a washing machine. It's wet, you go round and round, and it is somewhat disorientating. You grip the end of the paddle, hold your breath and plunge, looking for the moment in the cycle when a deft flick of the hips and sweep of the blade will spin you back to the surface. Miss the hip-flick and you roll far enough for one eye and half-a-nose to surface uncertainly before sinking again, bubbledy-bubble, like a timid hippo.

Hard though it is to master, successful rolling is as fundamental to white-water canoeing as a parallel turn is to downhill skiing. I took an hour's tuition in a heated swimming pool. The art of capsize recovery has been handed down from the seal-hunting Greenlanders. There are over thirty types of eskimo roll. Beginners are normally taught the Pawlata Roll before progressing onto the smoother Screw Roll; the trickier Storm Roll can be useful in water that is too churned up and aerated to provide natural buoyancy.

I had naively imagined that white-water canoeing would be fairly easy to pick up; I had, after all, been canoeing since the age of fourteen when my father Hol had led a family expedition down 11 miles of the River Dart in Devon—a river which had assumed at the time the awesome scale of the Grand Canyon. We had taken three vessels; there was a two-man folding canoe nicknamed 'Queen Mary' which was made from wood and canvas held together with string and wingnuts; there was a very solid fibreglass 'Merlin' touring canoe based on a design used by the Royal Marines in the marathon Devizes to Westminster race; and there was 'Eskimo Nell' a tiny surf canoe which could spin on a pinhead. By contrast, 'Queen Mary' wallowed through the waves like a geriatric walrus, and the Merlin cut the water—and any flotsam that floated before its sharp prow—with the indomitability of a Greek *tireme*.

With a crew compromising my father Hol, cousins Steven and Jeremy Spencer and sisters Elizabeth and Fiona, we floated past the back doors of Totnes and into the S-bends of the Dart as it zig-zagged round

headlands of hard igneous rock. Through Fleet Mill Reach, over The Gut, down Sharpham and Ham Reach and into Long Stream we floated, paddles dipping and flashing in sunlight bright enough to burn to black the woods at the water's edge. Past Pighole Point the Dart valley developed a late-middle-aged bulge; the current diluted and the town approached. Shortly before reaching the castle-crowned promontories that guard the river mouth we pulled the waterlogged canoes ashore. The West Country has been 'sinking' since the Stone Age, so that today the bed of the River Dart at its mouth is some thirty metres below sea level. Over the centuries the sea water has crept inland, flooding the main valley and its tributaries to give these lower reaches a sleepy well-fed feel; no hint of which is given by the boisterous antics of the youthful stream that plays its way down the peaty heights of Dartmoor far inland. It would be many years before I met the young Dart.

In the meantime my education as a canoeist took a catholic turn. With a schoolfriend I paddled the Merlin and another touring canoe through the reed-fringed waterways of the Norfolk Broads; for three days we sneaked along

White water canoeing is one of the thrill-sports: skill and danger are brought together in dramatic locations. True enjoyment comes when the fears created by unknown perils are overridden by the experience that turns each difficulty into an analysable challenge. Descending the River Dart, in Devon (photo: Rob Stratton).

One of the most important skills that a white water canoeist must learn is the eskimo roll (this is Martin Northcott, on the Dart). In serious rapids, capsizes can be frequent (and are often deliberate); the canoeist must be able to right the canoe without leaving the cockpit. Modern canoes are made from tough plastic which springs back to shape after colliding with rock (photo: Rob Stratton).

creeks out of sight of the motor-cruisers, freeboards submerged beneath a ballast of tents and tins of beans. Next came an attempt to shoot the rapids of Symonds Yat in the Merlin; I shot them all right, upside down. Years later, as part of a quadrathon I raced for 24 miles down the River Severn wedged in a kayak with a keel so effective that bends in the river had to be anticipated as if I was helming a supertanker. And on a lumpy river in Lapland I borrowed an open 'Canadian' canoe for long enough to discover how unnervingly unstable these wobbly buckets become when they ship

water. Most ignominious of all was the team quadrathon in Cumbria during which the speeding Canadian canoe containing the three members of 'Team Crane' managed to ram the central buttress of Workington railway bridge. The canoe folded in two then sprang apart catapulting its occupants like peas from a pod into the foaming water.

This was all scant preparation for the highly skilled world of white-water canoeing.

The swimming-pool rolling session was followed by a visit to a weir on the River Stour. My tutor for the afternoon was the photographer Rob Stratton, who also happens to be a canoe instructor. Dressing for white-water canoeing is marginally less involved than kitting up for a moon-shot. It being winter, I was recommended to start with a complete layer of thermal underwear. On top of this came a one-piece dry-suit tightly sealed at ankles, neck and wrists to keep the water out and heat in. You climb into this baggy membrane

through a slit between the shoulder-blades which is then zipped shut by your partner.

Next Stratton handed me a spraydeck, a neoprene skirt with a nine-inch rubber waistband which you pull up your legs. If you try and get it on over your shoulders it gets stuck. Then came a lightweight waterproof anorak and finally a slimline version of what most mortals call a life-jacket, but which for obvious reasons canoeists refer to as a 'buoyancy aid'. Even in icy weather gloves are frowned upon. 'It's important to *feel* and *grip* the paddle' urged Stratton; 'some people rub Vaseline on the backs of their hands, which helps the cold water run off. But if you get it on your palms . . .'

Dressed in our high-tech tutus we waddled like a pair of crusty old mallards down the muddy bank. So advanced is the technology of many of today's activities that walking while wearing the gear is virtually impossible; by the time you've dressed for rock-climbing, or sub-aqua diving, or canoeing, taking ten steps

assumes the difficulties of running a marathon in lead-lined clogs.

The canoes looked as light as balsa: tapered shiny lines modified by the odd ergonomic bulge. The early canoeists used the trunks of trees, painstakingly scraped with stone tools to form a dug-out. Later, lighter canoes were made by stretching the bark of birch or elm over thin ribs of wood or whalebone. Animal skins were also used for making the hulls. The Pyranha canoe I was using was made from CXL 9000 cross-linked polyethylene—a new type of plastic, which has a built-in 'memory' which allows the canoe hull to spring back to shape after the heaviest collisions.

It was an earlier version of the Pyranha that Mike Jones and his young team used on the Dudh Kosi in Nepal for their 'Canoeing down Everest' expedition in 1976. Jones had already made the newspapers when he shot 80 miles of rapids on Switzerland's River Inn, in 1969. Subsequently he led expeditions down the Grand Canyon (1971), the Blue Nile (1972) and the Orinoco (1977). He was killed trying to save a friend during his 1978 expedition to the Braldu River in Pakistan. Jones was one of the few to organise expeditions that explored white-water rivers using canoes; most often large rubber rafts are used. These unwieldy beasts are nearly unsinkable and demand little more of the occupants than brawn and nerve.

It was another Briton, John 'Rob Roy' MacGregor, who first popularised canoeing

as a means of travel and adventure. What appealed to MacGregor was the amphibious self-sufficiency of the canoe, here was a vessel that could be 'paddled or sailed, hauled or carried, over land or water to Rome, if I liked, or to Hong Kong.' MacGregor, who matched his eccentricity with a lifetime of philanthropy, paddled over the years through Europe, the Baltic and through Egypt the year before the Suez Canal was completed. His stories were presented (with appropriate embellishments) in hundreds of lectures he gave in aid of Britain's Working Men's Institutes. He tended to dress for lectures in a topi, turban or Arabian gelabiyeh and spoke from inside his canoe. It was after the publication of his bestseller *A Thousand Miles in the Rob Roy Canoe* that he founded the Canoe Club.

But to get back to the story . . . on the muddy banks of the River Stour, about to climb into a Pyranha 'Master'. A gang of schoolboy canoeists had turned up, and were charging through the mill-sluice's tongue of roaring water under the watchful eye of teacher Duncan Miller. ('The great thing about canoeing for schools is that it caters for the individual; we get the ones who are not so keen on team sports.') Why do children always make these things look so easy? Hermetically sealed into the canoe by the spraydeck, I pushed off from the bank. Compared to most other canoes I'd been in, this one behaved like a bicycle ridden no-hands: it was incredibly sensitive. Stratton took me through the various canoe

Essential clothing includes a helmet (in case your head strikes the river bed during a capsize), a watertight anorak (sealed at the neck and cuffs), a buoyancy aid which allows plenty of arm movement, and a spray-deck which effectively seals the canoe to your waist. You should never get separated from your canoe (photo: Rob Stratton).

strokes: forward, backward, the sweep stroke, bow rudder, high telemark, draw stroke and sculling. In the mainstream of the river we practised 'ferry-gliding': cutting across the river by pointing obliquely at the current. And we practised 'break-outs': turning from fast current into still water to rest and plan the route down the next section of river. 'Trees' warned Stratton 'are the most dangerous hazard. Never grab a tree: if you do, you'll stop dead and get pulled under. Barbed wire stretched across rivers can be nasty too. So can swans and undercut rocks.' Canoeing had suddenly become *very* complicated.

Next day we travelled to Dartmoor. Nearly twenty years after drifting down the lower Dart, I was going to get the chance to visit its more athletic middle reaches. I was in good company. Stratton had recently hurtled down the ferocious waters of the upper Dart; Martin Northcott (another instructor) had canoed in the Alps; Jamie Stewart and John Lyne run Torbay Outdoor Activities, whose specialities include white-water canoeing courses. We started at New Bridge, where an ancient stone arch rears over a gully of noisy water. The middle section of the Dart has three rapids of about Grade 3. The grades go downhill from 1, which is smooth moving water, to 6, which constitutes ultimate risk to life. On this basis, I seemed to have a 50/50 chance of emerging alive.

The chuckling current drew us downstream, rippled but hardly fierce. I felt almost secure: feet braced against the adjustable footrest and knees pressing hard on the hull. Water licked the deck as we swept round the first bend. The chuckle changed tenor; the river was about to clear its throat. The canoe in front disappeared from sight. I was pulled forward, paddling hard but not quite straight. The rules I'd

The 'pop-out' is a gymnastic trick in which the canoe is propelled backwards and upwards by the force of the water. Skilled canoeists are able to sustain ballet-like repetitions of pop-outs and rolls which often seem to bear no relation to the ferocity of the waters in which they play. Martin Northcott romping in 'Three Falls' near Holne Bridge, on the Dart (photo: Rob Stratton).

been taught raced chaotically through my mind: lean away from the current to keep the canoe deck from being pushed under; steer into the rapid at the right angle for the break-out. But the river was thinking faster than I was, and all of a sudden I was bucketing down an avalanche of water, sucked sideways and having to come to terms with an imminent ducking. To capsize so early in the day seemed unbecoming. After a small infusion of panic I managed to reach still water backwards but upright.

The first real rapid was called the 'Washing Machine'—a maelstrom of waves which I managed to survive by paddling the canoe so fast that I was airborne for most of the fall. Next came the 'Lover's Leap'—a sprightly little cataract sandwiched between the precipitous oak-laden walls of a sharp turn in the Dart. Lover's Leap is actually the eroded remains of an outcrop of schorl, a hard rock created by the combination of tourmaline and quartz. It was the meeting of a large lump of schorl with the underside of my canoe which came very close to providing me with a more intimate knowledge of riverbed geology. With water

creaming round my chest the canoe skated round a couple more rocks and down the fall. Three quick strokes through the frothy confusion below nudged the canoe into the gentle eddy of the 'break out'.

The final rapid was the biggest. 'Three Falls' is a little upstream from Holne Bridge. One by one the canoes ahead sank from sight, just the crazy waving of paddle tips to indicate the slalom route they were taking around rocks and 'stoppers'. I splashed water on my face (I had read that Mike Jones did this on the Dudh Kosi—he may have been doing a Grade 6 plus in Arctic temperatures, but that's what the Dart was beginning to feel like to me).

'Follow me' shouted Northcott above the din, 'head for that darker 'V'.' Following the bobbing stern of Northcott's canoe I dropped over the ledge that forms the first fall, swept round and down the second and poured through the third. I was flying and falling, in rocking, hysterical water-dashing fury, petrified of falling out, pleased as Punch to still be in. It was over: I was upright.

We carried the canoes back to do it again. Like a seal at play, Northcott slithered

through the falls then rolled his canoe onto its back, popping up for a breath of fresh air before catching another wave and disappearing again. Following Northcott, I fell over the ledge like a log, hit the second fall at the wrong angle and turned upside down.

My short session in the swimming pool the day before had taught me the first half of an eskimo roll, but not the second: I could roll till I was underwater, but had yet to master the hip-flick. Returning to the surface was still a stage beyond me. These thoughts, and several less rational ones, occurred in the peace, darkness and excruciatingly cold depths of the River Dart as I continued downstream beneath the canoe. For a short while, perhaps as long as it takes for a light-bulb to pop, I tried to remember whether it was the hip-flick that came first, or the downward paddle stroke. Being inverted did not help logical thought. Neither did the lack of air. Reluctantly I pulled off the spray deck and swam back to the daylight.

One day I'll be back on the Dart, and by then I'll be able to roll with the rest of them.

Like all Britain's white water rivers, the Dart is narrow, and depends on rainfall to keep it canoeable. Obstacles such as rocks and trees come thick and fast, demanding split-second reactions and considerable agility. Britain has produced some of the world's most adventurous canoeists. This is Martin Northcott on the Dart (photo: Rob Stratton).

65

Action: *Winter Mountaineering*

Climbing!' *came the warning shout from behind me. 'Dicky' Dickson, my third-form school chum, came slowly into sight. He was on all fours. On his right, the north side of the Aonach Eagach ridge tipped away for nine inches then abruptly disappeared into the sump of evening gloom. Dicky slowly lifted his ice axe. The axe was very heavy: it had started life as a roadman's pick. By sawing three foot off the wooden handle and by spending two terms hunched over a grindstone in the school metalwork shop, Dicky had whittled the pick into an approximation of an ice-axe. It was so heavy that its own momentum would frequently cause it to become so deeply embedded in ice that other axes had to be employed to free it.*

A dagger-cold wind cut in from the east. Most in the group—there were five of us I think—were clad in ex-WD fatigues that had been patched so many times that the seats were criss-crossed with seams as thick as railway sleepers. It had been raining lower on the mountain. Our absorbent clothing had soaked up several gallons of water, which had now frozen solid. Each of us was clad in a windproof suit of ice-armour. The only disadvantages of this organic, environmentally-sound weather-proofing was that if you stopped moving, your flesh froze to the inside of your clothes.

'How do I get round this block?' shouted Dicky. 'My trousers won't bend.' Slabs of ice the size of tectonic plates ground against each other on his thigh. I saw him struggle two-handed to lift his ice axe; watched the parabola of its fall. The axe collided with the ridge. Aonach Eagach trembled. Lumps of granite and ice mixed with shards of snow and tempered steel exploded in a white shrapnel haze then tinkled into oblivion.

Two hours later we were crossing Sgurr Nam Fiannaidh, the final summit on the ridge. Three thousand feet below, the street lights of Glencoe village flickered into life. We floated downwards towards the glen and a hot supper, each of us in a warm, contented bubble of achievement, success, relief, tiredness—all the things that have to be suspended till the goal is reached. To the north, beyond the big shoulders of the

Mamores, the white crown of Ben Nevis gleamed by the light of a slice of moon.

My father Hol, had been taking a small group of us to Scotland in January since our mid-teens. We would climb for ten days, whatever the weather. We ranged up and down the entire west highlands: from the big massifs of Skye, An Teallach and Torridon to the lonely northern monoliths of Foinaven and Arkle and Ben More Assynt. We ridge-walked; Hol's speciality was in taking us to peaks too remote for other mountaineers to bother with. We learned to lead; to navigate; to plan. The best days were the longest ones: up two hours before dawn we would walk through hard, moonshone snow, pull off boots to wade numbing rivers then tramp up a forgotten peak, to return 8 or 10 hours later through our own footsteps. This was adventuring on a grand scale, and the lessons learned in Scotland's winter mountains laid the foundations for trips like 'Running the Himalayas', 'Bicycles up Kilimanjaro' and 'Journey to the Centre of the Earth'.

But I was always in some awe of what we called 'real climbers'—those ice-corrie

Mountaineering is an all-rounder's activity: in winter it requires an ability to move on rock, snow or ice, a detailed knowledge of rope-work and belay systems, excellent navigation and a high level of fitness (Martin Moran on Tower Ridge, Ben Nevis).

Looking down on the Great Tower, from near the top of Tower Ridge. Immediately after the Tower, the route descends to teeter across an inches-wide ridge, then climbs up towards the summit cornices. Shortly after this, I dropped my Olympus OM1 camera. It fell 1,000 feet down Tower Gully. Amazingly, we not only found it later in the day, but the camera was still working, and has since been with me on all my major trips (photo: Martin Moran).

gladiators who, very occasionally, we would see at a distance, spattered onto translucent walls like flies on a windscreen, rows of alloy weapons chinking at their waists. These were the climbers who chose categorised routes; routes whose technical challenges were as important as the making of a mountain journey.

Winter climbing in Scotland requires three primary skills: the ability to move confidently over 'mixed ground'—snow, ice and rock; the ability to navigate accurately in 'white-out' conditions and the physical and psychological wherewithal to cope with winds that can top 100 mph and temperatures that can drop below minus 15 °C. Climbers wait for weeks for the perfect snow/ice conditions on a particular climb. The adversities of terrain and climate are more than matched by the challenge of the routes and the spectacle of the mountains themselves—many of which rise sheer for 3,500 feet from the lapping waters of sea lochs.

Scotland's winter peaks are not uncrowded; they are deserted. Here, a day's journey from some of Europe's biggest cities, you can discover true wilderness.

Martin Moran currently runs instruction courses and a guiding programme in Scottish winter mountaineering. He started climbing in 1972. After Cambridge University, he moved to Sheffield to practice as a chartered accountant.

'I became really keen, what you might call dedicated, climbing most evenings in the summer and every weekend. But winter climbing in Scotland I didn't do till 1979. I was really lucky; I picked a marvellous winter: it was the coldest freeze-up of the century and conditions were excellent. I used to hitch-hike up from Sheffield for weekends. Just getting to Scotland was quite a feat of endurance. It was a good forcing ground to learn winter climbing techniques, and we did some of the classic grade 3, 4 and 5 routes that year. After that I went on to the Alps and Mount McKinley in Alaska. Scotland is a good training ground. It gives you a miniature mountaineering experience, with conditions and weather that can be as bad as anywhere in the world.'

Moran went on to climb the North Face of the Eiger in 1981, and a year later, frustrated by the prospects of a career in an accountant's office, he began the training that would lead him to qualify for membership of the Association of British Mountain Guides. Having pulled out of desk work, 1983 and '84 saw him on expeditions to the Garwhal Himalaya in India.

In the winter of '84, Moran, supported by his wife Joy, embarked upon his biggest challenge to date. He planned to climb all the 3,000-foot mountains in Scotland (known as 'Munros') non-stop, in winter. There are 277 of them. It was an outrageous proposition. To speed him on his way across the smoother peaks, Moran planned to use skis; he also intended to raise money for the Third World charity Intermediate Technology. I.T.'s press officer, Steve Bonnist organised a press day for Moran. He invited journalists, and, to guarantee column-inches a major celebrity, Chris Bonington, to climb a mountain with Moran. Hamish Brown, the famous hill-walker, cousin Dick and myself would join in. I was doubly excited: at the prospect of joining Moran's epic adventure for a day, and at the thought that I would at last meet Chris Bonington.

Bonington has been the fugleman of

British mountaineering for as long as I can remember; as a boy I grew up on his siege-sagas in the high Himalaya and *Annapurna South Face* was the first hardback book I ever bought—back in the days when £3.25 wiped out weeks of pocket money. So it was with keen expectation that I pulled on my gaiters for a day's winter mountaineering with the great man.

He is fit. 'I'm in training', he said. 'Off to Everest soon.' Of course.

I was intrigued by Bonington's lunch-box. When we stopped at midday on the summit of Carn Liath he withdrew from his Berghaus pack a Tupperware container and prised off the lid to reveal a stack of neatly sliced sandwiches. I was mesmerised. Not just because I (and Dick, as usual) had brought no food with me and was (as usual) fainting with hunger, but because Bonington's food was so *ordered*. I think there may have been a perfect cube of cake too, but I'd had to look away by the time he moved on to pudding. To drink, he had one of those pocket-sized cardboard cartons of fruit drink, with a short, cellophane-wrapped straw attached to the side. As I ate as slowly as possible a currant that I'd found lodged in the pocket-fluff of my jacket, I reflected that the ultimate measure of mountaineering success must be the possession of such a lunch box.

The snow was knee-deep. Moran, on skis, was sliding briskly over the frozen crust. The Press, celebrity and hangers-on kept up with him for only three hours. Bonington had had his skis stolen the night before and was reduced to twice-normal walking speed; Brown peeled away having decided to return early to feed his dog; Dick was hampered by a pair of tennis-racquet -sized eskimo snowshoes he was experimenting with; Bonnist was slowed by his non-stop breathless commentary upon every step and every view; I just couldn't keep up.

Ultimately Moran became frustrated by the inability of his companions to keep up. He took off like a rocket and was soon a distant dot on the huge white lump of Creag Meagaidh. His last words to Dick and me that day were: 'Come up to Scotland again, and I'll take you on a *real* climb!'

Moran spent 14 hours climbing mountains that day. He finished all 277 peaks in 83 days, and raised £25,000 for Intermediate Technology.

Three years later, a chilly April day in London told me that it was worth a chance call to Moran's home in the Highlands.

'What's the weather like up there?' I asked.

'Excellent. Freezing and lots of snow. But it's only going to last one more day. Spring's nearly here. You'll have to come tonight.'

Just before noon the next day I tumbled from the Inverness train onto the single platform of Achintee station. We were in the car immediately, and that same evening were hiking up the trail towards the CIC

Moran traverses using the front points of his crampons and a droop-headed axe. Moran is a qualified mountain guide whose experience includes the North Face of the Eiger and his historic 'Munros in Winter' fund-raising feat for the Third World charity Intermediate Technology, in which he climbed non-stop over 277 3,000-foot mountains. It took him 83 days.

WINTER MOUNTAINEERING

bivvy bivouac: an emergency shelter for the night, typically consisting of huddling on an inches-wide snow shelf counting the seconds till dawn.

cornice an overhanging wave of hard snow at the top of a face which an ascending climber has to tunnel through.

crampons steel spikes which can be attached to the soles of boots for climbing on snow and ice.

crux the part of a climb where it is most acceptable to fall off.

dead-man a belay plate for use in snow, made from aluminium.

ice-axe *not* a walking stick, but a highly-developed hand-tool for use in steep climbing and for arresting a fall.

snarg a 'drive-in' ice screw, developed in the USA.

wart-hog a continental 'drive-in' ice belay.

whiteout typically created by the combination of a blizzard, nil visibility and a featureless snow surface. Perfect for compass work.

climbing hut at the foot of the north face of Ben Nevis.

Over tin mugs of tea in the hut, Moran talked of tomorrow.

'We'll try Tower Ridge. It's the most famous winter climb in Scotland, first climbed in March 1894 by Collie, Solly and Collier. They had no protection; no pitons; long axes. They cut steps to the top'.

I looked up Tower Ridge in the guide-book: '. . . a great expedition' it read '. . . the main difficulties are concentrated high up, and the whole route is exceptionally long and arduous.'

The Ridge is 1,900 feet high, an angled buttress splitting the north face of Ben Nevis. There were two others staying in the hut: Nick Harper and Kev Wilson, from Yorkshire. In January 1988 they had climbed Tower Ridge when it had been coated in heavy powder snow. It had taken them 8½ hours.

'Tower Ridge has everything,' announced Moran, 'steep snow, hands-on-rock, descents, traverses, a knife-edge snow-arete, crampon work and finally the problem of an overhanging cornice at the top.' In any other company I would have found the prospect chilling.

'That's the interesting thing about a winter climb,' concluded Moran, dunking a ginger biscuit in his tea, 'you never know the outcome till you get to the top. Tower Ridge is one of the most common Scottish winter routes to get benighted on. It's a route of Alpine length and scale. There was a party benighted last week on Tower Ridge. They had to be rescued.'

'But you told me to leave my sleeping-bag behind.'

'Yes. The only way to get up is by leaving it behind. You move faster that way!'

We woke early and sorted kit, arming ourselves for the climb with crampons, two ice axes each, a hard-hat, Gore-tex jacket and trousers, gloves, mittens, balaclava, and packs containing rope, slings, nuts, chocks, ice-screws, descendeur, head-torches and bars of fruit-and-nut.

There was so much snow that we could put on our crampons outside the hut. Moran mused into his straps: 'The Front Point Revolution changed winter climbing. It made it faster; more rhythmic. In the old days an ice pitch of 30 metres might take two hours, because you would have to cut steps all the way up. With front point crampons and drooped-head axes we can do that pitch in 20 minutes.'

We crunched over the corrie's chipped mirror floor towards the foot of Tower Ridge. The slope was thick with *névé*: snow that had melted then frozen again to provide a surface like crunchy icing sugar. The crampons bit sweetly and we began the steeper ascent into the little gully which leads up beside Douglas Boulder to the start point. Moran corrected me on crampon technique: 'Put your outside foot turned and parallel to the slope so that as many of the crampon points as possible sink into the snow; the other foot should be facing forward biting with the crampons' front-points. Your ice-axe should always be in the upper of your two hands. If you're zig-zagging up a slope, the axe should change hands.'

At the top of the gully we put on the rope. Moran edged up a 30-foot rock scramble, gloves and axe dangling from his wrists; crampons alternately biting ice and rock. The gully was filled with dribbles of ice and licks of snow, its walls bare rock. The sun pressed itself through the cloud. For a few moments the entire north face bathed in reflected radiance as every crystal and frozen waterdrop seemed to spark.

Apart from Harper and Wilson, who were planning fiendish things on an ice-wall to the left of Tower Ridge, we had the entire mountain to ourselves. The red, green and white rope snaked away from my waist towards the spiked soles of Moran's ascending boots. An enthused call wafted down the chilly slot:

'Nick! This is what we call mixed climbing: I've got one hand on rock, one hand on the axe and my crampons on hard ice.' He disappeared from view. Shortly, and a lot less elegantly, I followed. Moran was still talking when I caught up: 'I've done an awful lot of rock climbing, but over the years I've found that the adventure is to be found on big routes over snow and ice. Pure ice climbing is technically a lot easier than rock climbing; it's repetitive. But with ice climbing you may fall 60 feet instead of 6 feet. The ice climbers who get to the top are normally the ones who go for it.'

I pulled myself over the top of the gully. The ridge stretched ahead; a rickety ladder propped against the face. Moran continued: 'Half the fun in mountaineering is finding the balance between speed and safety. You can move in complete safety with a rope, but if you are always roped up you would never complete the climb before dark. Or you can move together, continuously, but if one of you slips, you've had it. You have to make a judgement.'

'Mmmmmm . . .'

'On an arete, if you're moving together, you both carry a couple of spare loops of rope in your hand, then when one slips, the other can jump down the opposite side of the arete. It's remarkably effective.'

'Yes, I imagine it is.'

'Of course a climber soloing—that is unroped—can climb much faster. I've soloed Tower Ridge in two hours. A roped party will take about 5 hours. A soloist never has to stop for any ropework, though in bad conditions you have to double the time. The longest ever recorded ascent of Tower Ridge was 18 hours. That was in 1907, when a party got into difficulties on the Ridge and had to traverse off it, then down a gully. 100 feet from the bottom, they found a vertical ice-fall and had to climb all the way back up to the summit plateau, by a new route. There were no rescue teams in those days.'

By now the adrenalin was all but squirting from my ears.

'Any more chirpy tales?' I enquired. We

seemed to be gaining height without recordable exertion. It was moderately relaxing.

'Tell me an Eiger story.'

'The friend that I did it with, Dave McDonald, had made three previous attempts. So he knew all about it. It was my first attempt, though of course I'd read all the history books. The Eiger involves 6,000 feet of vertical climbing, but it also involves a lot of traversing, and winding around cliffs, so that in fact you do about 9,000 feet of climbing. It is an inescapable route, so it can be very serious if you're caught by bad weather. Retreat is extremely difficult because the route is swept by stonefall, and in blizzards, by avalanches. It's the biggest wall in Europe. And it has a gruesome history; a lot of people have died on it. It's mixed climbing: pure ice, or iced rock. Scottish winter climbing is excellent preparation; although the Eiger is much bigger than Scottish mountains, here we have climbs which are technically far harder than anything you'd find on the Eiger.'

'We went up in good weather, and quickly reached 3/4 height on the face. We were at the bottom of the White Spider—that's the upper ice-field—when we were caught in a storm. We had to stay on a ledge known as the Traverse of the Gods for 31 hours. Just sitting there in our nylon bivvi sac waiting for the storm to finish. To retreat we reckoned it would have taken us 40 abseils. There was really no option but to wait for a break, and go for the top. On the third day we got a window of clear weather, and in 8 hours fought our way through very heavy snow to the summit. We got caught in another storm on the way down, and had to make a fourth bivouac.'

I looked down Tower Ridge. We appeared to be more than half way up already. Bivouacing is not one of my favourite hobbies; I once spent 5 hours of a January night sharing a plastic sack with my father Hol, moored by a rope to a snow-shelf at 2,000 feet on the back side of a mountain called An Teallach. It was not comfortable.

Ahead of me, Moran came to a feature known as the Little Tower. This was followed by the Great Tower, a 100-foot rock barrier. Moran led out along the side of the ridge. The steepness of the traverse was mildly awesome. With nothing more than the front points of his crampons and ice-picks in contact with the mountain, Moran appeared to be walking on air. Part way across the traverse, which appeared vertical from the small stance I occupied,

Moran paused and belayed himself to a wart of rocks protruding from the ice. He continued around the corner. This was the infamous Eastern traverse. Around the corner was a chimney which opened the way to the top of the Tower.

The most entertaining part of the route follows the Great Tower. A slight descent led to a perfect snow arete; its top maybe three inches wide.

'Here Nick, this is the test. Walk the arete.' It was one of those moments where the indignity of crawling for thirty feet on all fours was outweighed (just) by the optimistic illusion that, had this been a 3-inch wide white line painted on a pavement, it would have presented no problem at all. The urge to shut one's eyes in these situations is overwhelming.

Tower Gap is a parallel-sided notch in the ridge that has to be crossed in a single stride. I followed the rope over the edge of the notch, gingerly feeling for a foothold, then reversed myself until I was facing outwards. On each side, the abyss yawned. To reach the facing side of the notch meant launching out with a giant stride that would have to find purchase on a sloping lip of water-ice the width of a finger. I managed to get one crampon point onto the lip.

From there it was relatively straightforward. Moran led up to the cornice which hung, poised like a frozen wave, over the face. Head bowed against the cascade of

One of the great pleasures in mountaineering is the long walk home at the end of the day. In Scotland this can often mean a pleasant amble along a lake-filled glen, or a scramble down the crusted flank of a massif (this is a January day in Glen Nevis). The cocoon of satisfaction spun by summits reached is enough to keep you warm. Unless it's raining. In which case it is miserable.

tumbling snow, he chopped a slot through to the summit sky.

An hour later we lowered ourselves back through the cornice and began the long descent of Tower then Observatory Gully. Something in the air had changed; there was a slight wind; a warming. Ice began to clatter down the face like falling masonry. The cliffs each side of us began to fall apart. The face was dismantling itself; in days it would be bare.

'That's it then' said Moran, untying the rope. 'The end of another Scottish winter.'

Action: *Paragliding*

To step off a precipice and find yourself flying like a feather on the breeze is a sensation made all the more exhilarating by the thought that only your own skill and concentration separate this ecstasy of suspension from the reality of death. The preparations for take-off are methodical and absorbing: spread the canopy, check the lines, lay out the risers, buckle the body harness, clip the risers onto the harness . . . stage by meticulous stage until there is nothing left to check and it is time to face that infinite, formidable space that is to be your host for the next precarious seconds.

A few quick steps forward and the air rushes into the cell-mouths of the canopy, burrowing into the nylon tunnels until they tighten and rise from the ground. The pile of nylon is now a wing, high above your head, the risers tugging at your shoulders, urgent to be airborne. A look upward; head cricked back you scan the lines that fan out to reach each corner of the canopy. At this point is is quite reasonable—not at all sissy—to mutter to yourself 'This is quite frightening'. Because the next thing you must do is step over the edge.

Foot-launch paragliding—or 'parapente' as the French would have us call it—is in the ascendant. In the same way that windsurfing can be seen as back-to-basics sailing, so the rise of the paraglider is a return to the original dream of personal flight. The pilot hangs beneath a roughly rectangular canopy (it is wrong to call it a 'parachute', which is what you wear when you jump out of a plane) which can be steered from side to side and in varying angles of descent—sometimes ascent. Launching is achieved by walking off the windward side of ridges or hills. The joy in this new toy is derived from its portability: canopy and harness typically weigh a mere 5.5 kg, and can be stuffed into a medium-sized rucksack. You can walk, or bicycle, bus or train to the hills with your wings on your back. And it takes less time to prepare the canopy for take-off than it does to erect the average tent. It is the wing of which Daedalus dreamed.

Predictable weather, big mountains and an existing infrastructure of ski-lifts to reach the launch sites has encouraged an estimated 40,000 people on the continent to take up paragliding. In Britain, the mountains are still climbed by the traditional boot method, so for the growing band of 1,000 paragliders flying means humps-then-jumps and an endless quest for the perfect ridge, which should be flat-topped, long and smooth-faced, with a cross-section that is gentle at the bottom and top and about a 1:1 gradient in the middle. In good winds the layers of air which slide up such a slope are as smooth as the rise of an escalator.

Tracking to and fro across a ridge, a good pilot can tap rising thermals or even the crest of a 'wave' thrown up by adjacent mountains. Interestingly Britons are already acquiring a reputation as ridge-soarers, a testing discipline disregarded by many Alpine flyers, who tend to favour flights from top to bottom of a mountain, followed by a ski-lift to the top again. 'Fly-downs' are more thrill than skill and are not the main domain of the true paraglider pilot.

By the normal standards of air sports (motto: 'There's a fortune in flying, and I've

The moment of commitment; the canopy has been pulled up into the wind and is arching up to form a wing above the flyer's head. The next stage is to turn round, face to the wind, and take a few quick steps into the air. Action photographer David Higgs – who is normally on the other end of the lens – readies for a first flight from Lord's Seat in the Peak District.

PARAGLIDING

AGL above ground level; **ASL** above sea level.

canopy the nylon envelope composed of open-ended **cells** which fill with air when driven forward. Also known as the **sail**, **wing** or **glider**.

collapse partial deflation of the canopy in the air.

deep stall a stall in which the canopy has collapsed, but one which has yet to develop into a **tail-slide**; a plummet to earth. This is dangerous.

hook a thermal to catch or get into a rising column of air.

maillons small metal screw-gate links used to attach the **risers** to the **harness**.

risers the nylon tapes attached to the bottom of the rigging lines.

rotor the downdraught created by the 'breaking' of a wave of moving air, commonly on the lee side of a hill-crest. A very unsafe place for paragliders.

tuck the folding over of the leading edge of the canopy when the angle of attack becomes too small. A heartstopping moment.

spent it') paragliding is not expensive. Britain makes some of the best-value canopies. Brian Tripp began two years ago in a loft and is now turning out 40 or so of his 'Sportlite' range each week.

Tripp proudly points out that it was beneath one of his Sportlite 310s that in 1988 Swiss pilot Peter Donatsch snatched the prestigious Zugspitz Cup from an international flock of 84 flyers. He has also supplied canopies to a team who attempted to fly from the summit of 6,194-metre Denali, in Alaska.

Paragliding is descended from parascending, a sport of limited scope since the pilot relies on a winch, car or boat, to tow him into the sky on the end of a line. At a set altitiude, the line is released and the parascender flies down, sometimes to a target. Paragliding and parascending have much in common, but it is the British Association of Paragliding Clubs who can provide insurance cover for paragliding and the chance to take the first of several

paragliding qualifications, the F1. There are about twenty BAPC paraglider instructors in the U.K. I signed on for a four-day course with a young ex-climber called Steve Higham, who now runs Parapente Services.

Reading through the BAPC membership form, my eye stumbled over an italicised section which warned: 'National figures for injuries requiring more than first aid treatment are approx 1 in every 3000 flights'. I wasn't sure whether to be reassured or petrified. Over hot chocolate Higham ran through the theory of wind speed, air speed and ground speed ('if you add a 25 mph air speed to a 15 mph wind speed and you fly in the same direction as the wind, the speed relative to the ground is $25 + 15 = 40$; and that's how fast you will hit the ground if you try a downwind landing—which you will NEVER do!'). OK, so you land into the wind.

The canopy is made of nylon tubes ('cells'), closed at the back (the 'trailing edge') which fill with air when the canopy is drawn smartly forward. Fine polyester lines link the canopy to four nylon tapes (the 'risers') which are buckled to the pilot's body-harness using metal clasps ('maillons'). 'Got it?' To steer, and to determine the rate of descent, you hold in your hands two special lines (the 'controls') which run up to each side of the canopy's trailing edge; pulling these lines deforms the back corners of the wing, producing a braking effect similar to a plane's flaps; pull on the right line and you turn right; pull on the left line and you turn left. 'Simple.' Pull too far on them both and you stall the wing. A full-blooded stall will collapse the canopy and cause it to plummet like a shot pheasant.

We moved into the darkest Peak District, to the lower slopes of Lord's Seat, part of the whaleback ridge that runs above the stone walls of Edale valley. Under Higham's critical eye I spent the rest of the morning running into the wind towing the canopy. At first it felt as if I was trying to tow a sinking boat up a cataract: sudden gusts of wind would snatch at my balance. My feet had to pound like pistons to make any headway and, after running into a ditch, I learnt how to execute a turn.

Circling the ridge high above us was a gaggle of hang-gliders, and a solitary paraglider. 'Neil Slinger,' said Higham, 'he's the British duration record holder. He's stayed up for 3 hours 17 minutes.' It is a measure of how fast the sport has grown

that in 1986 the UK duration record stood at four minutes. In February 1989, the duration record was pushed beyond the limits of safety when Frenchman M. Styues stayed aloft for 11 hours 23 minutes over Hawaii. The F.A.I. have now put an end to this potentially lethal competition by refusing to record further duration records. (In the same month Frenchman André Bucher extended the paragliding distance record to 60 kilometres. It cannot be long before someone reaches the magic 100. The French lead the field in extraordinary paragliding exploits: in autumn 1988 Jean-Marc Boivin paraglided down the North Face of Everest in 12 minutes.

In the afternoon, we climbed further up the hill to a grassy level, spread the canopy and worked through the safety checks. Higham withdrew down the hill.

'When you're ready, go!' he shouted.

The slope fell away in a long, even ramp, tussocked with grass. I rocked forward. There was a loud rustle of nylon. Just five steps into my run the risers jerked hard at my shoulders; pulled me back a step. The canopy was up. I paused to check that all the cells were inflated and none of the lines tangled. Then forward again, running faster and faster till the ground began to lighten beneath my boots, leaping from tussock to tussock with giant's strides of seven, eight, ten, twelve feet till suddenly my legs whirred in the air. (For a human being there can be few more breathtaking acts of defiance than to unstick from gravity.) Boots, heart and brain were shed like a heavy overcoat; light and silent, stunned, I pendulummed beneath my bright arch. The Peak District, upturned faces, khaki grass, a rivulet slipped beneath my dangling boots. Then I was down. 'How far? How high?' I shouted. 'Twenty feet. Twenty-five maybe.'

I'd only hopped down a field but it felt as if I'd been up there with the sun.

That night I read *Skywalker* magazine— a rich seam of inspiration for both parascenders and paragliders. Each issue carries 'Incident Summaries' in which mishaps are

The purest, most economical form of flight. Swinging beneath your bright wing you can hover or swoop along ridge crests, hunting for the rising air; trying to read the invisible currents being deflected off the ground below. Paragliders are not as aerodynamic as hang-gliders, but they are a lot less fuss. The peat heights of Kinder Scout are in the distance (photo David Higgs).

Steve Higham, instructor of Parapente Services, scoops up his canopy after landing during a winter flight off Lord's Seat in the Peak District. All the equipment that you need for paragliding will fit into a medium-sized rucksack. It takes just a few minutes to lay out the gear, fit the harness, complete the safety checks and become airborne. Flying sites are strictly controlled by the BHGA.

reported with a view to deflecting recurrences.

'Student admits turning wrong way on downwind leg and landed on fast lane of motorway. Fortunately no vehicle problems.' 'Pilot released at 1,250 feet and after completing a 360° turn saw RAF Nimrod heading his way . . .' 'Target approach, stalled and fell 4 feet flat on edge of mat. Bit tongue.' 'Heavy pilot landed heavily on concrete with poor roll . . . Injury: buttock bruising'.

We caught up with Neil Slinger at his home near Manchester where he divides his time between making hand-crafted furniture and flying. Like many others, he's a migrant from the narrow world of target accuracy parascending. He's also an ex-aerobatic stunt parachutist.

'It's the power—it's a very visible thing,' says Slinger. 'You've got to be a bit of an exhibitionist; you're on show. When people watch, you play the game. We're lucky up here. This is the best area in the country. There must be hundreds of sites we haven't tried yet.'

What was it like to set the record?

'We had climbed up Mam Tor and I just knew it was a good day. The first ten minutes were like waiting for the kettle to boil. I was looking at my watch all the time, looking, looking. There were a lot of things to watch out for: a radio-controlled plane, a hang-glider and a rock-climber I know flying another paraglider. He flew in front of me and I got his dirty air. My canopy collapsed. It's the first time I've had that and the pants of my trousers fell out. I got reorganized and was getting phenomenal gains: half an inch of brake and I was shooting up. It's an amazing feeling when you've got height-gain without going back to the ridge; you've found the treasure you're looking for.'

While the conversation fluttered from thermals and lift-drag ratios to dynamic lift and laminar flows, to rotors and wing-aspect ratios, it occurred to me that this was a complicated sport.

Walter Neumark, the vice-president of the British Association of Parascending Clubs lives quite close to Slinger. Neumark (who is also a creative force in the hang gliding world) came to paragliding by a roundabout route which included test flying in the fifties a contraption called the ML-Cardington Inflated Wing. The 'Wing' looked like a cross between a boomerang and an air-bed, and had a wingspan of 32 feet. The pilot kneeled on the surface of the wing, and steered with a broomstick. Neumark's entry to parachuting was no less daring:

'In 1953 I came across a First World War patent of the Seehase parachute. I made a replica and my wife Ariane was the first to go up. The structure holding the parachute open collapsed. She wasn't wearing a helmet. We hadn't thought of that.' After a lifetime of experimenting with flying machines, Neumark finds himself a confirmed paraglider pilot: 'Soaring is wonderful, you're flying with your brain, *that's* the power point'.

Lord's Seat looks out across the peat-hagged heights of Kinder Scout. It felt very high up. A solid wind pressed up the slope. Higham watched me lay out the canopy, check the line risers, the buckles and straps. 'Fly straight out from the hill. When you're over the drystone wall in the valley, make a turn to the right, then at the end of the wall, turn left and land in the field.' Pretty straightforward.

The red and blue panels hung above, bulging with air, the lines looking thread-slender. My heart was running away like a motor whose flywheel had just dropped off. I looked down. A mistake. Fields the size of silicon chips lay side-by-side along Edale's floor. A train of centipede's thickness crawled towards Cowburn Tunnel.

'OK, Nick. Go when you're ready.'

(When is one *ever* ready to jump off a cliff?)

Three quick steps forward, boots scuffing grass. Then nothing.

I wish that I could find a way of describing the sensation that overwhelms a *terra-ferma*-based biped who runs off a hill top and goes up instead of down. It is a bit like hitting the down-button on a lift and going *up. UP.* But the view is a lot better than that from the average elevator and instead of talking to strangers about the weather you're wondering who'll water the umbrella plant if you don't come back.

It was all over in a matter of minutes, probably seconds. I remembered to cross my ankles ('It shows you're relaxed and enjoying yourself,' Higham had told me), and had time to twist my head and see the stick figures silhouetted against the late-day sun on Lord's Seat. So this is why birds always seem carefree; Jonathan Livingstone Journalist. Above the wall I pulled the right-hand control line and swung gently through a 90° turn, then on the left line to turn my back to the hill once again. There must have been the sound of wind but I don't remember it; just the invisible, quiet slide of exquisite smoothness. I felt the urge to shout about it, I did so, and felt rather foolish. Too soon the ground appeared (a loop-tape of Higham's last instruction ran round and round my head: 'Land into the

wind, flare just above the ground'). I touched the grass so softly that there wasn't even a footprint.

One week later I was back again. It had snowed in the meantime. Edale was white-washed and empty.

I felt confident: I'd been living and breathing paragliders for days. From high on the hillside I leapt outwards. The air felt different: heavy, soggy. Instead of lifting like a feather on the breeze, I toboganned downwards below a canopy that behaved as if it were filled with porridge. Clearing the stone wall at the hill bottom with a heartbeat to spare, I returned to earth with all the grace of a Barnes Wallis Bouncing Bomb.

By the time I had stopped moving, a large part of the field had been cleared of snow and I was up to my neck in the stuff: J. L. Snowman. Higham swooped out of the sky to land daintily beside my excavation.

'You know' he said, 'that's another thing to remember: the more time you spend paragliding, the less you find you know about it.'

Action: *Cycling*

On the counter of Catherine MacRae's post office in Ashnasheen stands a large glass jar marked 'Tablet'. It is full of small creamy-white cubes, tied up in 30p bags. On the basis of 20 miles to the bag, I bought four and pushed off along the sunny north shore of Loch a' Chroisg humming the theme to 'Local Hero' through a sugar-gummed mouth. Mountains crowded every angle, the valleys filled with flaming gorse.

I had a tailwind, and although I was unfit the bicycle felt as snug as an old armchair. This was a bike I used only for special journeys. The last time I had used it was two years ago, for a ride across the Himalayas, Tibet and deserts of north-west China. The tyres were still hard. I wondered whether anyone before me had cycled by Loch a' Chroisg on tyres filled with Chinese air.

After four miles of level pedalling by the water edge the road reared up and it took six minutes and another square of Mrs. MacRae's tablet to reach the radio mast at the top of the hill. Almost immediately the rocky slot at the head of Glen Docherty opened like a window onto distant Loch Maree, framing forests and islands. Among them was tiny Isle Maree, twelve miles away but clearly seen from the pass as a sharp black wedge in the centre of the loch. On this rocky islet the Irish saint Maol Rubha built his cell after crossing to Scotland in 671. He died on the Black Isle at the age of eighty, but was carried back to the west coast to be buried at Applecross.

So fast is the slope down Glen Docherty that the bike freewheeled until the bridge a mile before Kinlochewe. I stopped for a cup of tea in the Stag Grill Cafe but stayed for homemade lentil soup, cheeseburger ('it's beef from the Black Isle; the best' said Cathy Stewart, who cooks the food), apple pie and cream. And coffee. Then wobbled on towards Torridon.

Not far from Kinlochewe, the single track road crossed a bridge and from here I could look up through the trees to Beinn Eighe, a bulky mass of ridges, with spurs and fans of pewter screes that look decrepit compared to the clean-cut precipices of next-door Liatach. Burns with red pebble beds chattered at the verge and fields of heather swept towards distant peaks. This watershed separates the locked-in glens of inland Scotland from the cliffs and bays of the coastal Highlands.

A sign board at the edge of the climbers' car park pointed out the giant mole-hills of glacial moraine left along the valley side. The Lilliputian scale of the place is helped by Liatach striding up from the road for three thousand feet in a series of enormous sandstone steps. The triangular aspect of its southern face resembles a Mayan temple gone mad.

Dwarfed beneath this face is Glen Cottage. Cornelius Rieley was digging his garden as I came past. In the shed Cornelius showed me his big green bicycle, a roadster of the five-bar gate variety. 'Just the thing for getting to Torridon' he said, 'one turn of the pedals and this old bike doesn't stop till I reach the wood. Different on the way back of course.'

Torridon village is dotted across the pasture at the head of the sea loch. There are two places to see. A gate beside the Tourist Information cabin leads to the deer museum where, for 50p in the honesty box, you can browse through two rooms stuffed with skulls, antlers, an eagle trap,

My favourite bike country: the mountains and lochs of north-west Scotland. This is the view from the end of the track that leaves the village of Shieldaig and wends its way through bracken, heather and rock to the tip of the Camas-ruadh peninsula jutting into Upper Loch Torridon. The mountains are Beinn Alligin, Liatach and Beinn Eighe.

photographs of festering pelts (illustrating deer diseases) and the sad remains of a young stag who had died because his antlers got tangled in a discarded rucksack. The other place to call at is the last building on the right as you leave the village. Time hasn't disturbed the brown paint and bare boards of 'D. Mackenzie General Merchant' whose shelves carry—among other essential comestibles—boxes of original Scott's Porage Oats. I bought a can of Fanta and sat on the grass watching the tide come in.

Mackenzie's store marks the start of the serious hills. An unsympathetic climb took me up past the Ben Damph bar (the watering hole for local fishermen, gamekeepers and all) for a panoramic ride overlooking Upper Loch Torridon, the horned peaks of Alligin and Liatach and the matchbox crofts of Inveralligin on the far shore.

Shieldaig is half an hour from Torridon, its single line of squat pale crofts sitting above a curving beach looking west across the water to a small wooded island. Shieldaig's residents include three artists and a man who writes books about ley lines. It is the hardest place to leave. From the depths of one home I caught the echo of pipe music on a gramophone and next door a young man called Donald who wore a crucifix on one ear and oil company overalls was cleaning windows. 'It's something to do' he told me. Not far away, Tom Taylor was putting the roof on his new art gallery and round the corner an elderly lady was talking to Miss Macbeth of Carron House.

'Where are you going?' called Miss Macbeth's friend.

'Applecross' I replied, hoping to impress.

'Ooohh, I was in Applecross yesterday.'

'Did you cycle there?'

'No I jogged!'

Applecross is 25 miles from Shieldaig and is very remote. There are no shops or pubs between the two villages. Three hours to do the cycling I reckoned, plus an hour to create something unexpected.

One mile beyond Shieldaig a small side road dips down to the right, then zooms up to a bluff which looks back at Shieldaig. At the top, standing beside a shiny new Triumph Bonneville motorbike was a man in a plastic suit taking photographs. 'Hello' I called, 'I used to have one like that.' Randolph, who comes from Southampton, pulled his camera from his eye and said 'Everyone I meet says they used to have a Triumph Bonneville. It's so boring. It was much better when I used to collect dragonflies. Nobody else did that.'

The road rocked up and down like a roller-coaster ride. I whizzed by woods of oak and ash, above bays of absurd blues. My only interruptions on this idyllic road were the yak-sized Highland bull who stood squarely in the road and refused to budge until I threw grass in the opposite direction, and a hill of quite appalling steepness outside Ardheslaig. It has *three* black arrows on the Ordnance Survey map. Above it wheeled an eagle.

At Fearmore the road turned the corner of the peninsula and headed south. This is one of the most exposed parts of the ride and the wind seemed to be coming up the Sound from Skye in a solid mass. In bottom gear I winched myself south past the old crofting communities of Cuaig and Kalnakill, Lonbain and finally round the bend into the sheltered bay of Applecross.

With an almost indiscriminate hunger I fell through the door of the Applecross Tea Room and ordered seafood salad sandwiches made with baby scallops called 'queenies', drop scones and bramble jam, pink meringue and cream, chocolate crisp cakes and a pot of tea for two. Randolph, who had arrived an hour earlier, watched with some distress.

Since it wouldn't be dark till 10pm I now had several hours in which to find Saint Maol Rubha's grave. One of my panniers was filled with extremely heavy hardback books which gave clues to the grave's location. Seton Gordon, who looked for the grave in the thirties, said that it was in the old burial ground, marked by 'two rounded stones'. After zig-zagging through the long grass for twenty minutes, and re-reading the appropriate pages of Gordon's book, I found the two stones then returned to the Tea Room to report my find to Mrs Macrae, who serves the tea. 'No,' said Mrs Macrae (there are a lot of Macraes in Wester Ross) 'I don't think that's it. You should come to my house and meet Tommy Macdonald. He used to know Kenny Macrae and old Kenny knew the grave.'

I cycled the two miles to the tiny fishing hamlet of Camusterrach and in Mrs Macrae's sitting room met Mr Macdonald. He didn't know where the grave was 'but I can yell ye' he said 'that the two rounded stones are anterior to Maol Rubha.' Before Kenny Macrae had died he had written a history of Applecross which included an account of his own claim to have dug for, and found, Maol Rubha's stone coffin. But there was only one copy of the history, and it had been lent to Mrs Macrae's daughter, who lived in Strathcarron. Mrs Macrae's son Donald, who normally lives in a squat in London, where he works as a bicycle courier, offered to cycle with me the 18

miles to Strathcarron next morning.

After watching the sun set over Skye from a high rock above Ard-dhubh I rode back past the feathery reeds of little Loch a' Mhuilinn, and beneath the grand old beeches that line the Applecross waterfront, to the gravel track that leads up through the trees to the 'bed and breakfast' at Mr and Mrs Griffin's gamekeeper's house. On the dusky track I startled four deer.

Bealach na Ba—the Pass of the Cattle—is the longest, steepest hill in the British Isles. It climbs from sea level to 2,053 feet, then plummets back to sea level in a road distance of only 12 miles. It is the most spectacular piece of road in the country.

I met Donald at 8 am outside the Post Office. 'There's a funeral in Locharron today' he said. 'Half the village is going. They'll all be coming over the Bealach.' Donald led. He is very fit and has been

One of the great highpoints for cyclists in the UK is the summit of Bealach na Ba – the Pass of the Cattle. At an altitude of 2,053 feet, it comes at the top of the longest steep hill in the British Isles and separates the village of Kishorn from that of Applecross. On the eastern side you have to cycle down (or up) a series of switchback hairpins as grand as any in the Alps.

The end of the road comes at Ard-dhubh just south of the beautiful village of Applecross. Reaching the end of the road is rather like reaching a mountain summit. There is nowhere further to go; the goal is right before you. But it evaporates with the same mysteriousness with which it first appeared.

cycling to and fro over the pass since he was a boy. Later that morning the woman in Kishorn post office told me that she sometimes has to make tea for motorists too nervous to continue after surviving the Bealach's hairpins.

The gradient steepened as the road crossed the thousand-foot contour. Behind, the sea seemed full of islands: Rona, Raasay, spiky Skye and far away the grey shadow of the Hebrides. Near the top of the pass the first two mourners—two old gentlemen in tweeds and deerstalkers—shot past in a pick-up truck, closely followed by

and swipes to and fro across the corrie before tearing down towards the sea at Kishorn. Donald said that it was the only hill he knew that made his brakes smoke.

The hill between Kishorn and Locharron seems but a mild rise after Bealach na Ba. At Strathcarron I paused to read Kenny Macrae's story about his search for Saint Maol Rubha. The night before I must have been standing right on top of him. I pressed on alone round the windy shores of Loch Carron on a road that hiccoughed twice then rocketed up through the smashed forest above Stromeferry.

The moment I turned from the main road above Achmore the landscape lost its weather-blasted harshness. The tiny byway burrowed through a steamy funnel of rhododendrons and ferns. Leaning over the road, and soaring maybe 600 sheer feet from this jungle, was a long cliff like the prow of the Lost World. In Amazonia it would have been dripping with snakes. Just round the corner I came to a sign inviting passers by to stop to see the llama. At the same place, the Craig Highland Farm, there are pens with lop-eared rabbits, guinea fowl, peacocks and rare sheep. The owners, Mr and Mrs Heaviside, were not at home unfortunately, but I did catch sight of the llama.

With the end of the journey in sight I could feel myself beginning to procrastinate. Plockton offered the perfect opportunity to dally, and here, on the sea wall backed by palm trees (real ones; the Gulf Stream warms the bay) I spun out an hour watching boats bob to a backdrop of tree-rimmed cliffs and Duncraig Castle, then demolished a cream tea and sprinted for Kyle of Localsh convinced that I would now miss the train.

Through Duirinish I got my first glimpse of the islands and at Erbusaig the Cuillins on Skye began to solidify in the late afternoon haze. From the viewpoint on the hill called the Plock above Kyle I spent my last ten minutes watching the ferries churn across to Skye and counting islands. I reached sixteen, ate the last square of Mrs MacRae's tablet and rolled down to the train.

Donald's mother and father in a jeep, then Tommy Macdonald. Two more cars squealed upwards pursued by, faster than them all and spitting gravel on the corners, a lime-green Fiesta driven by the vicar.

From the summit of Bealach na Ba, the road slips giddily over the edge of the cliff

CYCLING

bit-and-bit taking turns at the front of a group of riders while the others shelter from the wind.

bonk historically used to define the moment when the body's blood sugar suddenly becomes exhausted; **sag** or **clapped** can also be used; a **bonk-bag** is carried on the back and contains Mars Bars.

cleats clamps attaching pedals to feet to prevent bicycle becoming lost during accident.

crank the metal arm onto which fits the pedal.

drop-out one of two slots at the end of a bicycle which take the wheel.

drum up to stop and make a pot of tea.

evens to ride a bicycle at 20mph.

hill a 15,000-foot pass.

honk to ride standing on the pedals.

skin-suit made from body-hugging ultra-thin stretch fabric to reduce wind resistance. Not to be worn without a bicycle.

Action: *Freefall Parachuting*

Britten Norman Islander G-ORED surged along the grass beside Queens' Avenue, lifted, then climbed steeply above the old Dakota parked in front of the Airborne Museum. Almost immediately, the twin-engined plane banked and began a lazy upward spiral. Inside, six of us sat on the floor of the fuselage, knees to chest, heads helmeted. In the pilot's seat, bright in the sunshine, Captain Mickey Munn MBE adjusted the trim, glanced over his shoulder and smiled encouragingly. The floor felt hot.

At three thousand feet the door in the side of the fuselage slid open. One of the red-suited figures shuffled forward and fell away, his upturned face as pale and round as a vanishing golf-ball. The plane circled. A second red body fell from view. Only four of us left now. My mouth was absolutely dry. The door slid closed; the floor tilted. The altimeter on my wrist read 5,000, then 6,000, the needle creeping round the white dial with appalling rapidity. Goggles on; 7,000, 8,000, 9,000, 10,000, 11,000, 12,000 . . . .

The door opened again. The plane was filled with the rough bluster of wind. I scooted on my backside the few feet to the square hole. Sergeant 'Sharky' Sheridan was standing on the sill, leaning into the slipstream. My legs went over the edge. I felt Greg Cox grip my suit. Between my knees Surrey looked like a dirty pub carpet. A small sign by the plane's wheel read 'Max Load'.

'Check in!' I shouted. Greg beamed back at me.

'Check out!' Sharky grinned.

'Up' I yelled. 'Down. Arch.' And pushed away from the plane.

Three days earlier, I had never worn a parachute; this was my first-ever jump and I was going to do it from a height three times that of Ben Nevis! Nothing I had ever done before had been so throat-chokingly terrifying. This for me was a real test; if you want to watch yourself face one of man's most primitive fears—falling—then try freefall parachuting.

When I first heard that it was possible to sign up for an 'accelerated freefall parachute course', I had assumed that the 'accelerated' bit referred to the velocity with which trainees were likely to hit the ground. But it actually refers to the intensity of the course: in the first two days of instruction (there are eight levels to complete before gaining certification) you can graduate from being a no-previous-experience, ground-based mortal, to throwing yourself from an aeroplane at 12,000 feet and free-falling for 60 seconds before pulling your own ripcord. Of all the hair-brained activities devised by man, this more than any—by a very, very long way—obliges the participant to re-define the meaning of 'sensation'.

The principle of the parachute is so simple that aerial descents have taken place for many centuries. It is said that the Chinese used them to leap from the Great Wall in the 1100s. Whether they were leaping for fun, to escape the enemy or because they couldn't be bothered to walk down the stairs, is not recorded. In 1485 Leonardo da Vinci drew a pyramid-shaped parachute which was held open by four wooden poles, but sensibly did not test his idea. And just over a hundred years later Fausio Veranzio (the 'para' part of 'parachute' is developed from the Italian

It is often remarked that expressions of extreme pleasure bear remarkable similarities to those of extreme fear. This photograph was taken at a height of around 9,000 feet, on the novice's first jump. On the right is instructor 'Sharky' Sheridan; on the left is instructor Greg Cox, both of the Parachute Regiment's freefall team, The Red Devils (photo: Graham Robertson/Red Devils).

After the words "Up, Down, Arch", the novice throws himself out of the plane door and into the slipstream. For a few seconds it's like diving headfirst into a washing machine. Instructors talk of novices suffering from several seconds of 'sensory overload'. This photograph was taken by L. Cpl 'Robbo' Robertson, who was hanging onto the outside of the plane's fuselage at the time.

word 'parare', meaning to shield: 'chute' is French for 'to fall') claimed to have leapt with a canvas-covered wooden frame from a tower in Venice.

But it was the French who provided the real impetus: first when a man called Louis-Sebastien Lenormand threw himself from a tree clutching two parasols, then, 14 years later in 1797, when Frenchman André Jacques Garnerin made the first successful parachute jump from a balloon above the Monceau park in Paris. Three years later,

Garnerin came to England, and from a height of 8,000 feet above London's North Audley Street, cut himself away from a balloon and made a wildly oscillating descent standing in a $2^1/4$-foot diameter wicker basket. He landed in a field behind St Pancras church with 'a few cuts and slight nausea'.

To this record of necky continental descents the British contributed one Robert Cocking. Realising that the next great problem to overcome was the oscillation characteristic of Garnerin's descents, Cocking built a parachute with the vertex pointing downwards to allow it to cut through the air in the manner of a blunt nose-cone. This it did very effectively. Cocking was found 'literally dashed to pieces' in a field in east London. His upside-down parachute was the original 'cock-up'.

Parachutes were used in the First World War to escape from shot-down observation

balloons, but it was not until the Second war that parachuting developed a strategic use. In April 1940 Hitler used a single parachute battalion for his surprise attacks on Denmark and Norway, then in June 1940 Winston Churchill called for 'the formation of at least five thousand parachute troops.' The Parachute Regiment campaigned through North Africa, Sicily and northern Europe, earning for itself the reputation of an elite fighting force—and its 'Red Devils' nickname.

Military parachuting usually involves mass-exits from large, low-flying aircraft, each man jumping with up to 80 or 90 lb of equipment and a 30 lb parachute. The parachutes open automatically using static lines hooked to the inside of the aircraft. Time spent in the air is minimised (around 40 seconds) and there is little opportunity or inclination for aerobatics. By contrast, jumping out of high-flying aeroplanes with self-activating parachutes (i.e. those fitted with ripcords) gives over a minute's worth of 'free time' before having to deploy the 'chute.

It was in 1962, when two members of the Parachute Regiment became the first British parachutists to pass a baton from one to the other while in free fall, that the idea of a display team took seed. A year later, the Parachute Regiment Free Fall Team was formed, and a year after that, the team officially became known as 'The Red Devils'.

Over the last 25 years the Red Devils have won a world championship; dropped in at countless public events; jumped out of a plane at 26,000 feet over Dover Castle then 'parachuted' across the Channel in 26 minutes to land in France; plummeted with Beaujolais Nouveau into the Thames; free-fallen for the Queen's 60th birthday and jumped into Wembley stadium for the '86 FA Milk Cup Final. The 'Red Freds' have a well-known soft-spot for charities (while I was with them they were refurbishing one of their team vans for 'Riding for the Disabled') and have developed a heart-stopping aerial repertoire. One of their specialities is the 'cutaway': having deliberately caused a dummy canopy to 'stream', the parachutist cuts free, falls, then—at the last moment—pulls open his main parachute.

The Red Devils perform for the Army (and the country) the kind of public relations act that has value beyond mere £s. The 24-strong team is composed of regular soldiers in the Regiment who sign on for a three year tour of duty. With the exception of manpower and accommodation, the team is mainly self financing; the costs are substantial: they bought their first aeroplane—an old de Havilland Rapide—for £1,000 in 1965; the Britten Norman Islander they run now cost them £650,000. In 1984 Coloroll (home fashions) became their primary sponsor.

It was with a sense of impending awe that I stared somewhat glumly from the window of the 7.12 from Waterloo to Aldershot too early one grey April day. It's one thing to say on the 'phone that you would *love* to come freefall parachuting; quite another when you realise that the next stop is Aldershot. Curiosity has a way of spoiling breakfast. Various military establishments slid by the window, among them a morbid hummocky field labelled 'Casualty Rescue & First Aid'. It was strewn with smashed Land Rovers, a rotting Bedford truck and the remnants of unidentifiable accidents.

I was met at the station by a staff car driven by a man wearing a red beret (the Parachute Regiment's famous berets are more maroon than red) who cheerfully countered my anticipatory terror by saying that it was 'all easy really and just playing with fresh air'.

'Yes' I said. Sergeant Hopper continued: 'People think that the higher you go up the more dangerous it is—but of course it's safer high up.'

'Yes.'

The Red Devils live in a modest office block in the centre of the Parachute Regiment's Depot. The entrance hall is lined with framed photographs of past team members who look across at more photographs of red parachutists piling out of planes, of falling in rings, trailing smoke and Union Jacks, of landings in improbably-small arenas; of handshakes with royalty. In the operations room Sergeant Major Kev Whittle was taking another Red Devils' booking; on the opposite side of the room Colour Sergeant Andy Sinclair was patiently talking a young trooper through the finer points of low-level turns. It was intensely busy and efficient. An outstretched hand burst through the door, followed by the compact ex-gymnast's form ('I fall like a bomb') of the team commander Captain Mickey Munn MBE, and his tail-wagging dog. We had time for a quick chat about the challenge of running the Red Devils ('I have had to become a businessman as well as a soldier') before I began work with the

FREEFALL PARACHUTING

CRW canopy relative work. Not for **kids** (see below).
chop to cut away from, or to jettison the main parachute.
dirt dive to practice a skydive on the ground.
dope rope a static line.
dump to open the main parachute, among other things.
hop and pop a freefall with a very short delay between leaving the aircraft and pulling the ripcord.
frap to die while skydiving. You can also use **bounce** or **go in**.
kids student parachutists.
mal a parachute that is malfunctioning, and from which you may decide to **chop**.
spud in a heavy landing.

first instructor.

Sergeant 'Sharky' Sheridan has a soothing Middlesbrough accent and an encouraging manner with cowards: 'The accelerated freefall course was started by an American, Ken Colman, in 1980. The idea was to train people faster; you learn 3 to 5 times faster than you can by static line jumping. You spend longer in the air, have longer freefall exposure so have more time to make mistakes—and to learn.'

(I heard my mother saying 'You *never* learn do you Nick'.)

'Of course, the safety factors on an AFF course are increased: before you can go on an AFF instructor's course you need to have done a minimum of 1,000 jumps and 10 hours of freefall.'

(Phew.)

'Mind you, the last bloke we had for AFF was a total zero. All over the place.'

(Oh.)

Sharky introduced me to the kit: overalls with hand-sized ribs on the arms and thighs so that the two 'jumpmasters' can grip the student during freefall, a lightweight helmet with radio earphones, gloves, a wrist-mounted altimeter, and the parachute backpack—a surprisingly small, black nylon pack fitted to a webbing body-harness. It weighed about 30 lb.

'The orange pad on the waist is the ripcord; on your chest you have the red cutaway pad, and the red handle is for the reserve parachute.'

We went through the drill for 'chopping' the main canopy in the event of a

malfunction, then: 'There are two built-in safety devices should you fail to pull the reserve handle: the AAD—Automatic Activation Device—works by barometric pressure and will deploy the reserve parachute at a set altitude, and the 'Stevens Lanyard' is a cord attached to the main canopy. It automatically pulls your reserve if you have to 'chop' your main canopy and forget to pull the handle.'

I could feel each fact being catalogued and shelved ready for instant recall in a way that I had never managed at school. Some of the facts were mind-boggling: during freefall you drop at a speed of 120 mph, and if you move your body into the 'Max Track' posture (like a missile) you can move horizontally at 60 mph.

But what of The Moment, the point at which you jump out of the door of a perfectly serviceable aircraft and begin to fall? 'The Americans call it 'sensory overload': the lights are on but there's nobody home. It happens on the exit and can last a few seconds. Your heart's doing ten to the dozen and your backside's the same. The challenge is to turn the shock into a buzz.'

Later that first morning, Lance Corporal Greg Cox took me outside and demonstrated the parachute landing fall (PLF). With the ram-air parachutes used by the Red Devils it is possible to 'flare' them on landing so that your feet touch the grass no heavier than falling goose-down. But novices make mistakes, one of the worst being to land *with* the wind: an error whose consequences can be likened to jumping off the platform of a fast-moving bus. 'The results' confirmed Greg 'can be reasonably unsatisfactory.'

Greg Cox then passed me on to Corporal Jim Scarratt. He spent the afternoon teaching me the theory of flying a ram-air parachute and achieving a landing without 'spudding in'.

Next morning, I spent the 50 minutes that it takes for the 7.12 to reach Aldershot mastering my rituals and mnemonics:

'Check in. Check out' I chanted breathlessly before a crowd of bemused schoolchildren.

'Up, In, Arch, G.A.S.P. (Ground, Altimeter, Secondary Jumpmaster, Primary Jumpmaster), Look, Reach, Pull (three times), G.A.S.P. again, freetime for photos, Regrip, Altitude, Look, Reach, Pull, (for real!), one thousand, two thousand . . . and so on, till one by one the children politely rose from their seats to move elsewhere in the carriage.

I noticed that the 'Casualty Rescue & First Aid' training ground beside the railway seemed to get bigger each time I passed it.

After a morning learning how to identify the various canopy malfunctions and an afternoon shared between plane emergency drills and the precise choreography that I'd be doing during the free fall, Jim Scarratt shot at me one of his surprise questions: 'What do you say when asked in the plane "Are you ready?".'

'Yes, sir!' It came as a ricochet; the last person I'd called 'Sir' had been my housemaster at school; amazing what the mind can do in two days.

On Day Three I was to make my jump. On the grass of Queen's Avenue the Red Devils were dressing a contingent from Farnham Art College ready for their static line jumps. The clouds hung at four thousand feet: too low for freefall. I walked up and down, tried jogging. 'It's all hurry up and wait isn't it' said Sharky sympathetically. Greg generously told me his theory of fear, of which he said there were two types: 'With recruits on their first jump there is an "I don't understand this" type of fear. And with people who have jumped already there is the "will I fuck it up" fear.' It is known (I have proof of this), that it is possible to suffer from both types of fear at the same time.

Also waiting for the clouds to clear was Chick Clayton. He was dressed in sun-bleached green overalls decked with badges and wings.

'I was with the Australian Air Force, did two jumps with the Air Ambulance Unit ten miles from Caen after the Normandy landings. Used to use Witleys then. Difficult things: they had a small hole in the floor: used to bang your head as you went out if you weren't careful. I've lost quite a few of my comrades now. I wanted to come over and pay my respects so I wrote to Mrs Thatcher. Then I got a phone call from Captain Munn. He said I could come and do a tandem jump, strapped to one of the team. I'm 82 years old.'

'You're not worried?' I asked hopefully.

'I'm exhilarated!'

On Day Four there were no clouds. Two miles up I was tumbling. I saw the earth above my head, then a horizon tilt like a see-saw; felt hands on my arms. A terrific roaring and a mind registering but not responding GASP! G.A.S.P. . . . Ground. I looked at the ground. There it was. Sort of khaki and basically in the right place: below.

Altitude. I looked across at my left wrist. It was waving about. Beyond it was Sharky's face, curiously out of shape. The needle on the altimeter appeared to be moving as I looked at it! Secondary Jumpmaster. I bawled at Sharky '11,000 feet'. He nodded. Primary Jumpmaster. I looked to my right. There was Greg. '11,000 feet' I yelled. He nodded.

A pair of fingers, hooked, slid in front of me. Hooked fingers meant move the legs in more. I did as I was told; thrust my crutch out, tensing the legs, felt steady. The hands let go of my arms. 'Robbo' Robertson, the Red Devils' photographer, floated in front, a few feet off, a camera perched like a pigeon on his white helmet. We all hung there. Just grinning.

I felt the 'regrip'. GASP again. Ground, altimeter . . . 5,000; the two nods. Any second now. Then the finger—the 'pull' command—from Greg. Look: eyes down to the waist and there was that lovely orange pad. Reach: right arm slowly down as left arm creeps round in front of head (the pad fits the hand so sweetly). Pull!

I yank the pad and count one thousand, two thousand, three thousand, four . . . and there's an almighty jerk that brings me up so tight I bounce like a marionette. Check canopy: there it is tight and taut as a bridge. Check airspace: three tiny white rectangles far below cutting across the grass—the parachutes of Sharky, Greg and Robbo. Roads and buildings are laid out as cleanly as a map; cars like pale flakes slide along the miniature conveyor belts. Control lines: I pull the two nylon toggle loops off their Velcro tabs. They feel light. Check slider. Looking up, I can see it safely down. Still looking up, I see the end-cells in the canopy are fluttering and only partly filled. Two 'pumps' on the control lines and the cells puff up and I'm flying and shouting at the top of my voice words one wouldn't normally use on the ground.

'Open and close your legs twice if you hear me.' Just for a moment I thought somebody had been lstening. But it was the radio in my ear.

'Pull the right toggle and turn to follow the three red, white and blue canopies below you.' Lance Corporal Chris Allen was 'talking me down'. I passed over the football stadium at three thousand feet. 'Pull the right toggle and do a 360 degree turn.' The canopy span me round. 'Pull the left toggle and steer away from the dropping zone.' I was starting to enjoy this (I couldn't exactly hear The Ride of the Valkyries, but the roaring in my ears had stopped—which was a start).

I was lined up for the downwind leg (my altimeter now read 1,000). 'Turn 90 degrees to the right.' I pivoted over the trees, then 'Turn again. Aim for the pit.' With the toggles up and the 'chute scooting along at maximum speed a gaggle of upturned faces whipped beneath me, cameras tilted.

Just above the grass I pulled deeply on the toggles. The canopy flared to a standstill, hung and sank gently so that I touched down with a slight knee-bend. As I coiled the lines and gathered up the airy billows of nylon, the radio crackled to life for a final time:

'We do hope that you enjoyed flying with the Red Devils. In-flight entertainment was provided by Sharky Sheridan and Greg Cox and your pilot today was Captain Mickey Munn MBE. Weather conditions in Aldershot tonight will be mild and beery. Please make sure that you leave none of your luggage behind and we look forward to flying with you again.'

At 3,000 feet you pull the ripcord. With a bang and a jerk big enough to push your heart into your boots, the main canopy is punched out of the backpack by a giant spring. You are flying, turning, gliding, steering with the control lines that run from your hands to the trailing edge of the canopy. There is *nothing* quite like it (photo: David Higgs).

Action: *Sea Canoeing*

The sea kayak twisted through the tide-race of humanity clogging Charing Cross Road. Jogging beneath the kayak were five people. At the prow was a young Scotsman called Brian Wilson who had just returned from paddling solo around the coast of Scotland. The others were cousin Richard, the dust of Kilimanjaro still on his boots, two school-leavers who had just run from Land's End to John o' Groats and myself. (As a cross-section of fund-raisers for the charity Intermediate Technology this quintet were fairly representative; money raisers for I.T. include Kate Benjamin, who rode a horse from Lands' End to John o' Groats, John Pilkington, who has trekked the Himalayas and Silk Route, the 4 Corners World Bike Ride . . .)

The kayak was over 17 feet long, tapered at each end to upswept tips, its deck patterned with lines and straps, watertight hatches, a spare paddle, compass and map-case. It was easy to imagine it nudging ice-floes under the glacier-snouts of Greenland. Through Trafalgar Square we padded, the slender vessel on our shoulders cutting like a harpoon across the currents of traffic. A taxi driver leant from his cab and shouted 'Put some wheels on it'!

Nearly an hour later, the canoe arrived at the BBC's 'Blue Peter' studios in Shepherd's Bush. We were asked to run round the garden with the canoe on our heads while Wilson described to the camera how he had paddled alone for days on end, pulling his canoe each evening up remote beaches on rollers made from collected drift wood and washed-up barrels.

Wilson's canoe was a 'Nordkapp', built by the British company Valley Canoe Products to a design perfected 13 years ago by VCP's director, Frank Goodman. In 1977 Goodman was one of a team of four who successfully rounded Cape Horn by canoe. The science of sea canoeing was developed by eskimo hunters who needed a boat that was fast and sea-worthy, and which made a stable platform for harpooning and carrying home the kill.

Sea canoes are much longer than river canoes and have a slender elegance that makes almost any other boat look like a clumsy bath toy. They are robust, and a full expedition canoe, kitted out for ocean paddling, will be capable of carrying up to 90 kilograms of equipment: food for several days, a freshwater still, spare paddles, sea charts, illuminated compass, rescue flares, survival bag, tent and a hundred and one other essential items will be stowed in watertight compartments beneath the deck. An expedition canoe such as the Nordkapp 'Cape Horn' (complete with an integral hand-pump for bailing out) will cost around one-eighth that of a good quality sailing dinghy. Over 10,000 Nordkapps have been built.

It was to join the annual Nordkapp Owners Meet that I took the 16.17 train from London Euston to Holyhead, on the island of Anglesey, off the coast of North Wales. The focus for this annual gathering

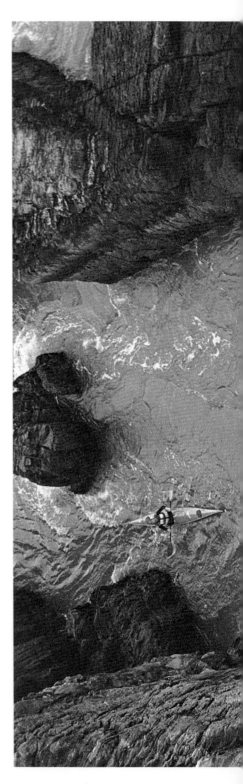

Sea canoes are one of the most versatile vessels ever invented: they can be used for poking around the lace-like frills of rocky coasts or for crossing surprisingly large tracts of water. Sea canoes have been used to cross the Baltic Sea, explore the coast of Greenland and (more than once) to round Cape Horn. With seals and sea-birds for companions, and the chance to land at beaches completely inaccessible to land-based bipeds, you have a unique opportunity to observe and explore; sea canoes are *sensitive*. This shot shows canoes on the annual Nordkapp Meet slithering through the gully between South Stack and the island of Anglesey, off the coast of North Wales (photo: David Higgs).

Canoe instructor Mick Devlin rides the surf as a Force Six gale pounds the bay of Porth Dafarch on Anglesey, North Wales. A slight misjudgement in conditions like this will lead to a forced roll. Sea canoes are much harder to turn quickly than white water canoes, so the canoeist has to be able to anticipate the forces of the water well in advance. The watertight deck hatches conceal storage areas used for carrying food, tent, spare clothes and so on, during longer trips (photo: David Higgs).

was the Anglesey School of Sea Canoeing (ASSC), based in sight of the sea at Treaddur Bay. I arrived minutes before closing time. The first person I met was Goodman—solid, bearded, clad in a Norwegian woolly, with an infectious enthusiasm.

'We'll probably have a group going round Holy Island tomorrow,' he told me over a recuperative pint. 'It's the classic trip, from Soldier's Point, past North Stack and South Stack, then Penryhn Mawr. There are two tide races.' I was dying to ask

about the Cape Horn trip.

'Nobody *really* knew what Cape Horn was like; all we knew was that it was a big cliff at the end of an island. The really difficult part is paddling down the west coast. There's a 15-foot swell reflecting off the cliff. It was a three-hour paddle, totally committing. The weather can change instantly: from 0 mph to full gale in 20 minutes. In fact we had 2 days of gales, 6 hours of calm then two more days of gales. We spent 5 hours of the calm weather paddling round the tip of Cape Horn. On the way back we did the equivalent of a Channel crossing—a 7-hour paddle. If the wind had gone wrong on us we'd have blown out to sea. We'd have had it. You can paddle in a gale—force 8—but only just; you're not going anywhere. There's a lot of spray coming off the waves, and the wind blows the paddle out of your hands. You can't see your friends because the troughs are long and shallow and the peaks are sharp and narrow; everyone is always in a trough, so you never see them.'

'Sea canoeing is all about the freedom

some of us have forgotten about: freedom *from* choice. What you do depends on the weather, the tides. If the weather is bad, you stay on the shore. It's also about escape routes. When Paul Caffyn did the Great Australian Bight, he had 114 miles of cliffs. That's very committing. He used to sit out in the swell counting the waves, and come in on the last of the big ones. The biggest problem with landing in surf is that you're unable to see because you're below the level of the waves.'

I went to bed dreaming of white horses in the south Atlantic and woke thinking about tide races: there is something slightly sinister about the boiling of a patch of sea where the invisibility of the bottom and the absence of any landform seem to place a human in a canoe beyond all means of reference.

Cloud the colour of tarnished lead sat above Soldier's Point. To our right, the Holyhead breakwater drew a ruler-straight line across the grey waves. To our left, beyond the knobbly headland protecting our small, sheltered cove, the tide would be sucking round the rocks of North Stack. Ahead of me, six canoes pulled away from the shore. I tugged the elasticated spray deck over the lip of the cockpit and, pushing with my hands on the pebbles, watched the bow of my kayak dip beneath an incoming wave. I was in a 'Selkie', a foot shorter than the 'Nordkapp' and slightly more stable. (A 'Selkie' is a mythical Shetland seal which comes ashore at night and takes a human form then dances till dawn. If you steal one of their seal-skins while they are dancing, you inherit their powers . . .).

Our little flotilla crept round Soldier's Point and into the grip of the ebb tide. Only by watching the shore can you gauge the strength of these tidal currents. It was as if we were washing down a giant river; the speed was quite startling. We slid across the broad bay of Porth Namarch. The canoes rose and fell in the swell, half-disappearing in each trough so that only the torsos of the canoeists could be seen, paddles cutting through air and water in a fluid figure-of-eight motion.

At first the tide race off North Stack was an almost inaudible muttering, but it grew by degree until the low roar of its agitated churnings seemed to fill every angle of the sea. A yelled 'Follow me' from Goodman and my 'Selkie' was knifing through the bulging shoulder of a wave then shooting downwards to burst through the next crest. Water creamed across the deck. In the confusion of colliding currents the canoe felt as if it was being punched at random by massive underwater knuckle. I paddled quickly, using the dipping blades for extra stability. Like leaves on a flood we bounced from the tail of the tide-race.

The tide-race had apparently been such good fun that half the group had paddled through the channel between Holy Island and the stack to shoot it again. Basking in the sensation of both being alive and dry, I spent a very content quarter of an hour exploring the nooks and crannies in the cliffs just south of the Stack. A paddle's length from the nose of my canoe a grey seal surfaced and turned his glistening football head, eyed me curiously and slid soundlessly beneath my yellow hull. With Aled Williams, an instructor from ASSC, I crept into the biggest cave of all. Its roof shone wetly in plum-reds and slime-greens and tapered as we eased into the darkness. As each wave rolled into the cave the water-level rose, lifting us to the ceiling. When there was no space left the wave

SEA CANOEING

baidarka the Russian word for an eskimo kayak from the Aleutian Islands.

clapotis the choppy confusion caused by waves bouncing off a cliff to meet incoming waves. Also known as **reflected waves**.

greenies big (green) waves that have yet to break, approaching a surf beach.

neap tide the season of the year when high tides are low and low tides are high, producing a minimum range of variation.

overfall a reef beneath the surface of the sea which causes rising currents to create **boils**.

pop-out when a canoe is propelled vertically into the air by the power of a breaking wave. Also known as a **sky-rocket**.

pump essential for serious sea canoeing; a hand operated deck-pump can remove up to 8 gallons of water in one minute.

retractable skeg the small hinged keel on a sea canoe.

seal launch/landing a launch or landing in which the canoeist stays in the canoe and uses the waves to move him. Hands are normally needed for extra propulsion.

strum box device to suck water from the bilges of a sea canoe.

detonated with a hollow boom at the back of the cave, flinging silver spray in our faces.

Out in the daylight the fleet was re-forming and the guillemots were lined up like hundreds of white candles on the ledges high above our heads. Hugging the rock walls we paddled across Gogarth Bay, pausing beneath a blank slab to watch a rope of rock climbers glued to a route called ' A Dream of White Horses'. Climbers and canoeists eyed each other with mutual incomprehension.

The great rock pedestal of South Stack is separated from Holy Island by a deep cleft. Fifty feet above the water a giddy bridge strides across to the lighthouse perched on top of the Stack. Cautiously, the canoes slid towards the neck of the cleft. The tide

poured through in continuous waves; the passage narrowed in the middle to an arm's span. 'Watch your bow' called Goodman, 'the angle to the current is critical.' I oozed into the tightening channel, drawn by the extraordinary force of water. The canoe held straight for a moment, then slithered past a huge rock and tried to pull sideways into a sickening boil of sucking, heaving water. Two hard strokes snatched the bow clear and I snaked back into the sunlight. One by one the other canoes shot from the rocky slot.

Still running with the tide we continued below the climbers' cliffs of Mousetrap Zawn and Red Wall. It became a game to sneak on the lift of a wave through the sinuous passages between cliff and rock. Out to sea I caught a momentary glimpse of three kayaks caught in a beam of sunshine, almost lost on the massive grey sea.

Behind Penlas Rock the canoes were hauled out of the water onto a rock ledge. Soup, tea and sandwiches appeared from watertight compartments. I borrowed a waterproof pad and wrote the words: 'Robinson Crusoe'.

'The Fangs' had been saved for the afternoon. This small group of rocks, and a larger set called 'Tide Rip Rocks', lie off the triple-tipped headland of Penrhyn Mawr. The tide-race that rips over these submerged reefs is—with North Stack—the most notorious (though not the biggest) of North Wales' offshore white water. Having made the long crossing of a bay called Abraham's Bosom we reached Penrhyn Mawr just as the tide was turning. Instead of being sucked inexorably southwards our little craft were now pushing against the solid weight of northward moving water. We hit the race at its most mellow, bumping through its building waves before they had begun to flex with the full strength of the flood tide.

'Reflected waves' called Goodman across the water. 'They bounce off the cliffs and mix with the incoming waves. Can be quite confusing.' It certainly was. Instead of rising and falling with the hypnotic regularity I had now adjusted to, the sea was cut up into a criss-cross of choppy waves that seemed to attack the canoe from all corners. We came to Porth Dafarch. I dallied a moment over the spot where lay the wreck of the *Missouri*, the four-masted steam-ship that struck these rocks in a snowstorm in 1886. A year earlier I had been 30 feet lower, breathing compressed air and watching a starfish twitch beside one of

The view from the sharp end. David Higgs took this photograph of Mick Devlin by mounting an Olympus OM2 camera inside a watertight casing lashed to the front of the canoe. The shutter was released by radio control from a cliff top overlooking the bay. Just after this shot was taken, a freak wave from the 15-foot swell rolled the canoe; camera, lens and radio unit were torn from the canoe. It was an expensive day (photo: David Higgs).

Missouri's decomposing ribs.

It seemed a long haul to Trearddur Bay. The paddle was beginning to weigh heavily; the sun nearly gone. For what seemed an age I had been watching a telegraph pole on shore creep with agonising slowness past a house. When finally we rounded the rocks into the shelter of the bay, the fight against the tide eased. 'I enjoyed that,' I said to Goodman. 'You have good kinetic balance'

he answered kindly. For someone whose ambitions for the day had been limited to not falling out of the canoe, this was a compliment to cherish.

The talk that night was of faraway places. A young couple called Anne and Andy Fleck had recently returned from canoeing among the Galapagos Islands. Nigel Dennis, the sea-bronzed 33-year old who runs ASSC, told me about the circum-

navigation (with Paul Caffyn) of Britain that he had made in 1980. In 85 days they had canoed 2,500 miles.

'We went through a physical barrier after two weeks. We had to stop and have a rest, purely because we were so tired. After that, the only rests we had were for bad weather. The biggest dangers were the firing ranges, bombing ranges and laser-beam ranges. At one point we had bullets whistling over our

heads. We wanted to get round the country quickly. If we'd had to wait for the ranges it would have taken ages. On our fastest week we averaged 45 miles a day. Also, what made it so fast was Paul: being the kind of person he is, we would quite often end up sprinting for land at the end of the day. I was damn sure he wasn't going to get away from me.'

'The biggest satisfaction for me, was deciding two years earlier to canoe round Britain. At that stage I hadn't sat in a canoe. Frank was the only person who didn't laugh at us. If you've got a bit of co-ordination, you can pick up most sports straight away.'

Eric Totty, from Kendal in Cumbria, favoured a less hurried approach.

'I've been attracted to canoeing for 70 years.' Eric told me. 'It's something indefinable. When I was young I was reading R.M. Ballantyne's adventure books for boys, *Hudson's Bay, The World of Ice, Ungava: a Tale of Eskimo Land, The Young Fur Traders*. Then I read about Gino Watkins who went by kayak with the eskimos and learnt how to roll. I canoed off the south-west corner of Greenland, in 1977 I think. We picked up an eskimo in a seal skin kayak and took him with us for a while. They've stopped making the seal-skin kayaks now. They make a replica out of canvas, which isn't the same thing at all. This one was made to his own measurements. We couldn't fit in it, the deck was so low. It fitted him like a glove.'

'Three years ago I crossed the Baltic from Sweden to Finland, via the Åland Islands. It was 220 miles. We had to take fresh water and food, because most of the islands are uninhabited. We camped on the islands each night. Conditions were beautiful to begin with, then a storm blew up and we were marooned on an island for six days. I wasn't worried, because I had plenty of time of course! I think I'm the oldest sea canoeist in the country. I'm eighty. And a bit.'

'My favourite area is the Holy Island stacks; it's the cliff scenery, and the tides of course. You don't get such strong tides in most places. This year I'm going down to the Bay of Biscay to do a circumnavigation of Isle de Ré. Then on the way home we'll probably paddle along the coast of Brittany.'

All through the night the waves grew, driven up the Irish Sea by a huge storm off Cornwall. By morning the height difference between the troughs and tips was 15 feet. Four canoes were launched into the surf of

Porth Dafarch. I joined a knot of awed spectators on the headland beside the bay. From the ocean marched dark walls of water, rising and leaning until momentum overtook gravity and each wall collapsed with a thundering, white, roar. Foam from the ripped-up water veined the bay. Smaller waves reeled off the rocks.

Into this cauldron paddled four tiny canoes. Waves crashed over them. For seconds at a time they disappeared, buried beneath the charging mountains of water. When it seemed as if they would never reappear, a figure cascading with foam would surface, then power the canoe into the next wall.

But this was sport, not travel: the idea was to batter a track through the surf, turn the canoe, then ride the waves back into the bay. 'Of course it's not what sea-canoeing is about really' said Goodman, almost apologetically. 'But this is the kind of surf that you need to be able to deal with if you're setting out on a serious sea journey.' As he finished his sentence a Nordkapp popped out of a wave top standing on its nose, then pirouetted to fall back to the water facing out to sea. Another Nordkapp shot backwards into the bay, its paddler leaning almost nonchalantly on the gigantic wave that was driving him towards land. Somebody was swimming for the shore.

That afternoon we put out to sea from the tiny port of Amlwch on the north coast of Anglesey. The waves here were but an echo of those bludgeoning the island's south coast. Having rounded the little island of East Mouse, we struck across Bull Bay, paused to explore the ruins of the old brick works of Porth Wen, and in a flurry of rain crept round the cliffs to Hell's Mouth. 'Hold on tight to your paddles,' called Goodman. 'There's a line squall coming.' Ahead, a large area of ruffled water was rushing straight towards us. It hit suddenly, trying to twist the paddle from my hands. I caught a side view of a canoeist hunched undeterred beneath the onslaught, paddle revolving with the smooth rhythm of bicycle pedals. Come to think of it, only a bicycle matches the pure simplicity of a sea canoe as a vehicle for *real* travelling. I licked the mixture of rain and sea trickling down my face and felt at home.

Action: *Hang Gliding*

As I write this, a 28-year-old woman from Camberley is waiting for light north-westerly winds and clear skies. Given such conditions she will rise at 2 am and, on the playing fields of the Civic Centre in Ashford, Kent, buckle herself into the harness of a hang glider. Shortly after 4 am the hang glider will rise, lifted on the end of 30 feet of nylon tape attached to the underneath of a hot air balloon. As the balloon climbs three miles into the sky, the temperature will slide down to minus 20 degrees centigrade. It will be so cold that her Himalayan clothing will feel as thin as cotton. To prevent her tear ducts freezing she will wear special insulated goggles, and in the thin air she will be breathing from an oxygen set.

For Judy Leden, who gave up her career as a nurse to concentrate on flying, this will be the most spectacular stunt in her short flying career. At the age of 22 she moved to Kitzbuhel, Austria, working in the ski resorts and cramming in as much mountain flying as she could. A year later, in 1983, she set a world record of 51 miles for the Women's 'Out and Return'; a month later, above the dusty trench of Owens Valley on the California border, she flew 146 miles—soaring at times to 18,000 feet—to establish a women's 'open-distance' record which has yet to be beaten. That same summer she won the British Women's Championship, and by 1986 had carried away the women's title for Europe and the World. Early in 1988 the car manufacturers Citroën contracted her to fly as a professional. With the new requirement to keep Citroën in the news, Leden's flying now tends to the ostentatious. Her current challenge is to become the first woman to fly a hang glider across the English Channel.

At 18,000 feet the balloon pilot will lean over the side of his wicker gondola and cut the nylon tape with a Stanley knife. For several seconds the hang glider will plummet nose first while Leden fights to

gain control. If anything goes wrong, she has to tear open the parachute pack strapped to her chest.

Without losing valuable height, Leden will set a course for France, and unless she is forced to ditch in the Channel, she will cover the 35 miles in about 45 minutes. The landing site is a golf course behind the village of Wimereux. Only one hang glider pilot has flown the Channel before. He suffered frostbite.

The extraordinary soars of top pilots like Judy Leden have been made possible by the application of modern materials to the first principles of manned flight. Long before the coming of aluminium, polycarbonates and Dacron, a German innovator called Otto Lilienthal (and his brother Gustav) began experiments with wings capable of lifting a man. Having discovered that arched, rather than flat, surfaces made superior wings, Lilienthal threw himself from hillsides hanging from contraptions not too dissimilar to the hang gliders of today. He achieved many successful flights until an unexpected gust of wind killed him in 1896. Others abroad were working along the same lines as Lilienthal: in the USA Octave Chanute was experimenting with moveable wing surfaces (he made over 100 successful flights) and in England, Percy Pilcher was flying an amended version of Lilienthal's weight-shift glider.

One man who has a unique insight into the perils faced by Pilcher and his peers is Walter Neumark, an ex-test-pilot who now

Judy Leden's, Britain's top hang-glider pilot, circles the take off point on Devil's Dyke, on the brink of the South Downs overlooking the the English Channel (photo: David Higgs).

lives outside Stockport, Cheshire. In 1961 Neumark flew a replica of Pilcher's glider for BBC TV.

'It was horrible . . .' he says, 'but it was good fun. You hung by your armpits and steered by weight-shift. You could move forward and back, and side-to-side. I wore heavy Alpine boots and swung them to left or right to steer. The replica wasn't as good as Pilcher's original, which had bamboo telescopic shock absorbers on the wheels. On my third flight the undercarriage broke.'

Pilcher was killed in 1899.

In 1903, two American brothers—Wilbur and Orville Wright of Dayton, Ohio—added a small petrol motor to their steerable glider. Focus shifted instantly from free flight to powered flight. Hang gliders were left on the shelf until Francis Rogallo, an American working for NASA in the 1960s, 're-discovered' them during his research into flexible-winged parachutes that could be used for steering space capsules during re-entry. By the 1970s hang gliding was established as a sport.

Noel Whittall is the chairman of the British Hang Gliding Association (3,500 regular members and 1,000 in training). He had read about hang gliders in a Sunday colour supplement in 1973. 'It looked like skiing in 3D', he says today with well-remembered relish. 'I fell for it!'

Britain consistently leads the world in competition flying. In 1987 John Pendry was World, European and British champion all at once—an extraordinary feat which was recognised by the Royal Aero Club, who presented him with one of their covetted gold medals (previous recipients have included the Wright brothers, Neil Armstrong and the crew of the non-stop-round-the-world superplane 'Voyager', Dick Rutan and Jeannie Yeager). More recently, at the European hand gliding championships held at Belluno, Italy in July 1988, Britain scooped first, second and third place, and the team championship too. So, what makes the British so good?

'Two factors,' says Whittall. 'In Britain we have to learn to fly in relatively hostile conditions: on a windswept isle with low hills. Secondly, we were fortunate about ten years ago in having set up a very effective competitive league in Britain which has meant that the top pilots are always flying together; always extending themselves. It's quite easy for us to pick good teams.'

Funsters and edge-players are

HANG GLIDING

angle of attack the angle between the glider and the oncoming airflow.

brainlock disconcerting condition which can strike prior to take-off. Also **clutch** or **twitch**.

drag various forces which resist the passage of the glider through the air. **Parasitic drag** is caused by the various appendages (wires, bars etc) on the glider.

mush the nasty state of unresponsiveness caused by flying at too high an angle of attack. Will be followed by a **stall** unless corrective action is taken.

pilot the part of the glider which hits the ground first.

stall caused when too high an angle of attack finally prevents the glider from flying. Recovery from stalls is an essential part of hang-glider training.

trail out occurs on the ground, when the glider travels faster than the pilot. Can be uncomfortable.

indistinguishable in the polymorphous world of hang gliding; it's a sport where sensuality and self-improvement (there is no such thing as a perfect take-off or landing) are threaded together. The hardware reflects the quest for more height; more distance; more agility. Pilots devour the 'specs' of new models, the sink rates, plane weights, the nose angles, with the avid delectation of train spotters apprised of a new brand of bogey. One of the country's leading builders, Airwave Gliders, is building 1,000 gliders a year. Their models range from the first-timer's 'Calypso' to the latest, race-tweaked 'Magic Kiss'.

With just a twinge of apprehension I took myself down to Brighton to sign on for a hang gliding course with the Sussex College of Hang Gliding. I was told to report at 9 am to an address which turned out to be a small workshop opposite the trading dock of 'T.G. Fruits' in Brighton Municipal Market. There were five others: Arkit Patel (draughtsman), Stewart McLeod (accountant), Bill Wallace (student), Simon Binner (computer sales-director) and Franklin Henson. I did not have to ask ages

to work out that I was the oldest student present. The others wore chilling expressions of confidence. 'Why are you doing this?' I asked Henson, who looked eighteen and moved as if he had been pushing weights from the cradle.

'I'm training to be a stunt man', he said. Simon's reason for being there was rather more heartening: 'My wife sent me,' he confessed, 'a birthday present. I think she's trying to get rid of me.'

Vince Hallam, instructor at the College, led us upstairs to a small office. Vince first flew in 1928 when he 'was a kid'. He started in Tiger Moths. After ten years in the Royal Air Force, as a ferry pilot, fighter pilot and then an instrument rating examiner, he joined the Bristol Aeroplane Company as a test pilot. Then he moved to commercial flying.

'I was flying the last of the scheduled bi-plane airliners—a Rapide to the Scillies', he said. After all that engine power, what's the attraction in hang gliders?

'It's back to basics isn't it? It's the most intimate form of flying! It's the simplest, most *real* form of flying; it's freer. OK so I'd like to fly Concorde. Or a Harrier jump jet. It's just that I like the extremes.'

We signed disclaimers and were issued with a sheaf of test papers and fact-sheets. It would have felt uneasily like a return to school had Hallam not been wearing on his head a hand-knitted tea-cosy of retina-melting colours.

On Devil's Dyke the mist swirled like smoke. Up here the South Downs fall away in computer-smooth curves. In the cafeteria we sat classroom-style round a formica table while Hallam took us through ground speed and wind speed: 'You can tell the air-speed by listening to the noise in your ears and feeling it on your face,' he said, folding a Kit-Kat wrapper into the delta-shape of a glider. He talked us through the anatomy of a glider (tubes, bolts, wires; every bit is vital), thermals, angles of drift, tracking, lift-drag ratios, turbulence, banks, rolls, yaws and stalls: 'If the angle of attack is too steep, the glider will stop supporting you. You will fall. (The Kit-Kat wrapper fluttered to the table.) We cannot afford to stall at any height above one foot.'

Outside the cafeteria hang gliders squatted on the grass like a flock of resting moths. One flew over our heads, whispering in the wind. Hallam led us to a long cocoon of tubes and cloth. It took twenty minutes to unfurl the wing, slide the battens into the sail, attach the wires and check all the fixings. For training purposes, two small wheels were attached to the ends of the control bar.

Hallam pointed to a bag of webbing and buckles: 'Put those on', he said. 'There should be one each.'

For someone who has never been able to get the twist out of car seat-belts; whose tie-knots regularly come out back-to-front; who has been known to wear his trousers inside-out without realising; the unfathomable loops and about-faces of a hang glider harness were nearly incomprehensible. Half strangled, I was rescued by Bill Wallace: 'I think you've got your head through the leg-holes', he pointed out. I was relieved when Arkit volunteered to make the first run with the glider. We all stood back. Raising the glider so that the triangle of the control frame rested on his shoulders, Arkit steadied himself then began to move forward.

'Faster, faster!' screamed Hallam. Arkit's feet pounded the turf. He left the ground for four—possibly five—feet. He was flying!

The afternoon was consumed with controlled hops, the glider tethered by rope to ground-crew running alongside. The next morning we drove over the South Downs to a hidden bowl called Bedingham on the seaward sides of Lewes.

'Vince, are we going to fly today?' asked Stewart McLeod.

'That depends on how much you've remembered from yesterday', replied Hallam.

After several leg-whirring hops beneath the training glider, we began to move back up the hill till we were 200 feet above the pin-like figure of Hallam. Arkit had emerged as the star pupil; I was nearly at the bottom of the class. My consistent error was to take my eyes off the 'target point' after take-off, a fault that led to erratic courses and unpredictable landings.

Stewart very nobly diverted attention from my own bumpy flights by managing to dive into the ground from the kind of altitude that seemed certain to break something in man or machine. It did.

'That's the end of flying for today', muttered Hallam as we sprinted towards the crumpled wreckage. Stewart lay prone beneath the twisted glider. Limb by limb, he pulled himself clear of the struts and cloth. He pushed his glasses back up his nose, looked thoughtful, and said: 'I think I did something wrong'.

Only one bar was broken. Hallam had a spare in the van. Half an hour later, Stewart was airborne again, soaring out from the hillside and touching down with a big grin.

With the afternoon closing, we carried the glider even higher up the hill. I ran through my checks: counting off the five quick-release points on the rigging; checking the 3 'Hs' (helmet, harness, hang point); then 'O.W.T.'—obstacles, wind, traffic. I slid my hands down the control frame and lifted; felt the wind inflate the wing; the straps tighten round my body. I located the target point: a barn on the hill opposite. Then I began to run, accelerating quickly to Olympian strides. The 'A' frame of the control bar began to lift, tugging at the straps. My feet scuffed the grass tops and suddenly I was running on air.

There was so much to think about: get the bar in; correct my hand position; search for the target point . . . it was over on the left. I shifted my weight then moved back to the centre of the control bar. The glider tilted into a gentle bank. I shifted the other way and centred again. The glider levelled out.

A voice on the helmet radio cackled urgently: 'Push out. Push out!' The ground was much closer than it should have been. I hit it hard with the piece of my anatomy least suitable for use as an undercarriage and was dragged face first across the part of

Landing at Bedingham deep in the South Downs with a training glider which has been temporarily fitted with wheels. Novice landings frequently end in 'trail-outs', in which the glider is slowed by the friction of every protuberance between chin and toes being scraped along the landing strip. Hang-gliders have a far greater range of flying capabilities than paragliders, but are more cumbersome (and expensive).

the field recently vacated by cows. Just in time, I closed my mouth.

'You're getting better', said Hallam.

POSTSCRIPT: Arkit, Stewart, Bill and Franklin all qualified at the end of the week with their 'F1' flying certificates. Arkit went on to buy his own glider, which he crashed at Rhossili in Wales, breaking two uprights (but not himself). He is now addicted to flying. When last heard of, Franklin was learning to joust and Judy Leden was looking at the possibilities of jumping off a 20,000-foot active volcano in Ecuador. I returned to flower-pressing.

Action: *Mountain Walking*

Just *downstream from the 'Jaws of Borrowdale' the village of Grange dozed beside a widening in the River Derwent while two boys in shorts re-enacted the Rhine crossings of '45 by hurling river shingle at each other to cries like 'It's war then is it!' and 'Don't you dare!'. Taking cover on the river's small island I dumped my rucksack on the still-damp grass and stowed away my jacket and the slice of fruit cake bought a few minutes earlier from Ron and Joan Norey's tea shop. In the distance between the bus-stop and Bridge Cottage tea shop—a matter of yards—I had been struck by the weight of my luggage.*

'You get people coming up here, over-weight or too old' Joan told me as I swayed unsteadily in the doorway. 'It's a lovely day and they race up the fell and when they get to the top they throw up their arms and say "I've done it" and a voice from the clouds says "Yes you have!" and bang! Over they fall and they wake up in a box wrapped in silk.'

I left Grange at a modest stride, walking south on a lane squeezed narrow by trees that quickly opened onto the walled fields of Hollows Farm. Ahead, the old volcanic plug of Castle Rock, 985 feet, all but blocked the way down Borrowdale. Around a Union Jack flicking idly from a tripod in the centre of a small sloping field, a large number of muddy-kneed teenagers were falling in and out of orange tents while a man wearing a Norwegian sweater shouted from the cab of a St Johns Ambulance Land Rover. Beneath the birches, in manicured glades, were other tents, the smell of cooking coming from little hissing stoves. The low bright sun sparked through the leaves like a solar short circuit.

I was up for the weekend, the plan being to tramp through the heart of the English Lake District in a gigantic letter 'C'. From Grange in the northern Lakes I would go to the south-west, crossing the mountains to spend Saturday night camping at Wasdale. On the Sunday I would turn east, past the high tarns to the deep sanctuary of Langdale where—if I arrived on time—I'd pick up a bus to the railway station at Windermere. The total distance I'd have to walk would be about 22 miles.

Where Borrowdale's jaws are clenched at their tightest, the riverside path is forced away from the water by a large sloping rock. A middle-aged couple in plimsolls were trying to reverse off this rock as I arrived. 'It's steep round there. We can't get round' said the woman.

'Do you know where the Bowder Stone is?' I asked.

'It's just over there. On the other side of the river.'

I began taking off my boots.

The water was cold, but not deep. It just covered my ankles. But the stones on the bed of the river were round and slippery like slimy cricket balls. On the far side a stile and path led up to a clearing. The Bowder Stone is an 'erratic' carried down from Scotland by the glaciers of the last Ice Age. It weighs about 2,000 tons and is 89 feet high. It rests improbably on one edge. In the late eighteenth century a Lake District landowner, Joseph Pocklington, drilled a small hole through the inches-thick base of the rock. He thought that it would be interesting for visitors to be able to shake hands through the hole. A wooden staircase has also been built to the top of the stone.

James Rees, eleven, from Porthcawl, offered to shake hands with me. Emerging from the mud-patch on which you have to lie to conduct this ritual, James hefted my rucksack, said 'Huh, nearly as heavy as mine' then scrambled to the top of the Bowder Stone by way of its steep upstream face. I used the staircase, which has 29 steps. From the top there is a view of cascading woodland and a distant brown curve of the Derwent.

I decided to recross the river where it was narrower, but deeper. The current tugged over my calves and the rucksack threatened to topple me backwards. To preserve my balance, I threw my boots towards the far bank. One of them hit the only overhanging branch in sight. The boot catapulted back into the river where it landed the right way up. It nodded off downstream trailing over its stern a limp sock like the body of a dying mariner. Images of trekking for two days across the Lake District mountains sharing one boot between two feet flashed before me as I ran as fast as is possible in thigh-deep water over slippery stones. After descending a minor cataract I overtook the boot, lunged, lost my footing and slid beneath the waters of the Derwent.

Sweating profusely I followed the path beside the wetly glittering river then turned into the crag to find Millican's cave. Between the wars Millican Dalton roamed the Lakes, rock climbing, floating across Derwent Water on his home-made raft and sleeping in his cave below Castle Crag. The mouth of the cave is very wide and low, like a monstrous fish mouth. Woodsmoke hung at its entrance and inside, sitting contemplatively on a rock, was a sixth former from Keswick School about to take 'A' levels.

Twenty minutes later I was on top of Castle Crag. The view from the Crag's bare pate embraces everything from the islets of Derwent water to the giants of the central fells like Glaramara, the two Scafells and Great Gable. My own path to the fells could be seen sneaking along the hillside towards Honister.

I followed the old trackway which

The early hours of a climb are always the most exciting: your legs and lungs are fresh and the rucksack still feels light. This shot was taken on the first day of the climb up Mount Whitney, the highest mountain in contiguous America (14,495 feet). In our packs were sleeping bags, a tent, and bags of food which we hung in the trees at night, out of reach of the bears.

The English Lake District on a spring morning; I took this photograph of Langdale Pikes (that's the Dungeon Ghyll hotel in the foreground) from the slopes of Side Pike during a quick scramble while waiting for the bus back to Windermere and the train. The Lakes are perhaps *the* favourite fells among English hill-walkers; despite their popularity, it is easy to find solitude with an Ordnance Survey (1:25,000) map.

wriggles from ghyll to ghyll, hugging the grassy contours, four hundred feet above the white pecks of Rosthwaite's cottages. Too soon it turned to the harder slopes of Honister Hause. I stamped up the steep quarry path to Fleetwith puffing to 'The British Grenadiers', then forked right to climb to the prow of Fleetwith Pike. Nearly dry, I flopped against the summit cairn and opened my eyes to see the twin lakes of Crummock and Buttermere receding towards the sea and three ravens turning on the updraught with a sliver of afternoon sun on their still wings.

The top of Haystacks is a confusion of crags and tarns, little becks and the odd

boot-sucking bog. It is a difficult place in mist. I tried first to find the 'perched boulder', one of Haystacks' curiosities. For ten minutes I tramped towards a small silhouette whose shape roughly corresponded with descriptions of the boulder. I kept losing it as I threaded my way through countless rocky knolls. When finally I stalked it to a hidden crest my 'perched boulder' presented itself with the smug grin peculiar to Herdwick sheep, then set off to dupe another walker.

Where Blackbeck Tarn lurks darkly beneath rock walls the track twists then rises to tickle the rim of a clear, rounded pool. The unshadowed surface of Innominate Tarn is saturated with sky; an adorable place.

Haystacks has two summits, a few steps apart, and separated by a knobbly rib. Below, the black acres of Ennerdale's dense conifers filled the valley floor. Sixty miles away where the sun was melting into the sea I could see a thin strip of Scotland tapering down to the Mull of Galloway. The wind had dropped. I pulled out my bars of Kendal Mint Cake. The traditional white

mint cake, which has the consistency of marble, is now facing competition from the softer 'brown' mint cake. Now there is even chocolate-covered mint cake. I had bought bars by Quiggins, Wilson's, Swarbrick & Dean and Romney's. Romney's was nibbled by Sir Edmund Hillary and Sherpa Tensing on the summit of Everest. It contains propylene glycol.

I followed the Scarth Gap path down to the isolated shepherd's hut that is now Black Sail youth hostel. Round a wooden table, nine or so sun-bleached heads were bowed over dinner. In a jersey whose shredded arms hung like seaweed, the warden, James Archibald, came outside and asked where I was going. 'Wasdale' I said. 'Camping?' he asked. 'Yes.' 'Nice evening.' He went back through the low door, and I crossed the River Liza.

Thirty minutes later, from the Black Sail Pass, the hut below was as small as a slate chip. The path down Mosedale undulates through beds of bracken then turns abruptly into Wasdale. In the quiet of evening the fields seemed frozen between their lines of old stone walls, walls built centuries ago by men who picked the rocks one by one from the valley floor. I put up my tent with the door facing east, and lay listening to the wind on the walls.

Michael Naylor was kicking a ball with his son in the yard as I came past in the morning. Joss Naylor, Michael's uncle, is well-established in Lakeland folk-lore as a champion fell-runner. The family have been sheep farming the fells here for generations. Michael was showing me his poems when a saloon car passed by. 'That's my father off on holiday' he said. 'First holiday for 60 years.'

'How old is he?' I asked.

'Sixty-one.' Two minutes later the car returned. It slowed at the farm gate.

'What's up?' shouted Michael.

'Forgot his jacket and wallet', the voice called back.

'Had his hand on his wallet all his life, then goes on holiday and forgets it,' said Michael.

I left Wasdale on the footpath that crosses a field to St Olaf's Church. Inside, seven rows of pews were crammed into its tiny interior and the beams were low enough to brush my hair. Birds were nesting in the yews outside.

The stony track followed the walls through to Burnthwaite Farm, then divided at Gable Beck. I took the left option, up Great Gable to join the climbers' track that traverses its southern crags. The path treads along boot-width terraces above 1,300 feet of scree that sweeps down to Lingmell Beck. Above is a jumble of contorted rock. The path is so narrow, and the consequences of stepping off it so obvious, that sightseeing is most safely done from the sitting position. The best-known landmark on this traverse is Napes Needle, a clean-cut spire standing free of the surrounding crags and rising sixty feet. It was first climbed in 1886 and has probably seen more hemp rope and hob-nailed boots than most other Lakeland rock. I was sitting beneath the Needle sucking on a piece of Quiggins (brown) when a man with celery tendons, nylon shorts and running shoes scampered down from the Needle. He was moving only slightly slower than a falling rock.

'Going far?' I called as he bounced past.

'The Gables, Great End, Scafell, Lingmell' he called back. 'Got to be down for lunch.'

Beyond the Needle the traverse scuttles across the loose stones of Great Hell Gate then creeps round the bottom of Kern Knotts Buttress. A pair of rock climbers

MOUNTAIN WALKING

balaclava a ridiculous-looking but incredibly efficient garment worn on the head.

billy an aluminium can used for camp cooking. **Billies** come in **nests.**

boot attaches to foot.

clag low altitude (knee level) cloud which is so wet that it feels like solid water. Accompanied by nil visibility. The best **clags** can be found in the Lake District, Wales, western Scotland and Tierra del Fuego.

dubbin revolting application used for waterproofing boots and hands.

rucksack also known as **pack** or **sac**. The **Sac Law** states: 1. that in any group yours will be the heaviest sac; 2. that any item you need from a sac will eventually be found right at the bottom; 3. that the weight of a sac increases exponentially with distance walked and height climbed.

were wedged into Kern Knotts Crack, and another was visible only by the soles of her feet and swaying hair from the top of hand-sized Innominate Crack.

High on the path beneath Great End, Sprinkling Tarn spreads beneath the wide skies. It is a peaceful spot. Behind the tarn I could see past Glaramara to the tiny pimple of Castle Crag, and beyond that Borrowdale, and I'm sure I saw the white flash of a sail on Derwent Water. Sprinkling Tarn is a good place for falling asleep on a sunny afternoon.

A frogman rose to the surface on the far side of the tarn, spouted from a snorkel, swam to the shore, and with some difficulty climbed from the water and waddled ponderously away with his flippers slapping the rock. I hurried after the figure.

'What are you doing? Did you find anything?' I asked. 'Are you looking for skeletons, Roman coins, stone axes?'

'No,' he replied. 'I just like doing really silly things. I was wondering how high I could do a dive. We're at 1,800 feet here.' His legs were a blur of shivers.

'Broad Crag Tarn's higher' I said.

'Yes. I saw a trout. Or I think it was. I'm not a fish person.'

Very odd. After a lap of the tarn I cut across watery grass to rejoin the track that now climbed with Ruddy Gill to meet the final aspect of my looping route. Ahead spread the eastern lakes and in the far mists, a smudge of the Pennines.

Past the inky disk of Angle Tarn I followed a track to Rossett Pike, and from a lichen-licked stone, peeked into the deep scoop of the Langdale valley. Pike of Stickle still looked a long way off. I ate a square of Romney's 'White'. Over Black Crags the boots plodded, then thudded the turf down to Stake Pass; the water came in on Martcrag Moor and they ran the last steps onto Pike of Stickle. When the last walker had disappeared, I started for the valley.

Mountain walking—in the Lake District in particular—has family connections for me. My cousins were brought up there: Richard, Adrian and Chris Crane. It was with Chris that I went to the Sierra Nevada to climb Mount Whitney, the highest mountain in contiguous America. We tried to do it in a weekend . . .

Round the edge of Mirror Lake lay the dried white trunks of trees, bleached like the bones of old whales. A fish flipped, silver in the sun, and plopped back into the black water, little ripples worrying the image of the mountain that lay on its surface with the clarity of a photograph. The only sound came from the trees behind us: a wistful sigh as the warming morning air rose from the dusty pan of Owens Valley far below to breathe its heat on the high cold granite.

Through half-closed eyes I could see the serrated teeth of Trail Crest, two thousand feet above. It looked a long way off. This was it: The Great American Wilderness. If I'd had the energy I would have pinched myself to make sure I wasn't dreaming. We were half way up Mount Whitney, the highest mountain in America's 'lower 48' states; the top of contiguous America. A cloud the shape of a drifting eagle slid into view. The air tasted like champagne.

Earlier, a Park Ranger had asked us if we knew about the bears. Bears! I'd known all about bears since I was old enough to look at a comic strip. Everyone knows that you climb a tree when chased by a bear. 'What sort of bears do you have round here?' I asked.

'We have two kinds of bears in the Rockies, the black bear which is actually brown, and the brown bear which is kinda brown.'

'So, how do we tell which is which?'

Mount Kenya in east Africa offers days of varied walking. This shot was taken on the 'normal' route which wanders up from the Naro Moru Lodge, through the 'Met Clearing' (where the dirt road ends) to Mackinder's Camp in the Teleki Valley. A rockier walk continues up to Point Lenana (4,985 metres), from where you can look across the shrinking Lewis glacier to the twin spires of Nelion and Batian – seen in the distance of this photograph.

'The black bear'll climb right up that tree after you . . .' I gulped.

'And the brown bear'll shake the tree till you fall out!'

Despite exercising a vigilance that would have picked up the flick of a whisker at a hundred paces we came across nothing more exciting during our morning's walk

than several tribes of marmots—gormless, hamster-coloured animals the size of a small cat that trundled about in a particularly aimless fashion beside the trail.

'A bit different to the Lake District, isn't it?' Cousin Christopher remarked as he rolled over and squinted at the towering mountains.

Mount Whitney lords over the thin saw-tooth Sierra Nevada range that separates the irrigated virility of California's San Joaquin valley from the inland deserts, plateaux and canyons of Nevada. The walk up Mount Whitney is one of the most popular in the U.S.A., largely because 8,367 feet of the 14,495-foot climb—over half—can be tackled by automobile.

For a walker brought up to believe that any hill worth walking up had to be at least half-a-day's march from the nearest tarmac,

the notion of driving to twice the height of Ben Nevis before taking the first step was, at first, a little disconcerting. For the four of us in our little group—used to the modest bog and rock of the Lake District, Wales and Scotland—the scale of the American Way seemed alien.

Our car, a hired Chrysler designed on the lines of a pre-war aircraft-carrier, reached 8,000 feet with little apparent effort, only to be baulked by a traffic jam just above the wooded gully where the stream from Lake Meysan runs into Lone Pine Creek. Faced by a steepening of the mountain gradient, the road engineers had been obliged to call a halt to their upward progress—though the crags above the car-parks were nothing that a few tons of dynamite wouldn't shift. Future technology ought to make possible a two-lane blacktop right to the summit of

Mount Whitney.

We berthed the Chrysler. At the snack bar, a Ranger told us that to walk on Mount Whitney, one had to have a Wilderness Permit. These were available at Lone Pine, a small town 13 miles back down in Owens Valley. Re-joining a glittering worm of hot cars, we drove back to the valley, and at the U.S. Forest Service office in Lone Pine ('The Little Town With Lots of Charm') were politely told that one had to apply in writing, in advance, to walk up Mount Whitney. Like the Acropolis, wear and tear on this national monument now calls for a degree of self-protection. There was a daily quota of 75, and one simply had to join the queue. I had a horrific vision of the Department of the Environment installing turnstiles at the bottom of Great Gable.

At dawn the next day, equipped with our Wilderness Permits, we were back at the road-head at 8,367 feet. We pulled on our boots and began walking.

The trail, a gravel path of easy gradient defined by a border of pebbles carefully laid like those in front gardens full of gnomes, picked a pretty path through stands of Jeffrey pine and red fir then crossed the north fork of Lone Pine creek and entered the John Muir Wilderness—California's largest official wilderness, covering 503,250 acres, and named after the man who, in the late 19th century dedicated himself to the preservation of his country's natural habitat. Muir led from the front, making headlines with his 'Thousand Mile Walk to the Gulf', an epic trans-American journey which finished in Georgia when he contracted malaria and typhoid. Thereafter he concentrated his efforts on the drier, higher airs of the Sierra Nevada and Rockies. 'In God's wilderness' he wrote 'lies the hope of the world—the great fresh, unblighted, unredeemed wilderness.'

As the sun rose, we stepped on from the trees into a dry zone dotted with dusty clumps of sagebrush and collapsed hikers. Up, we walked, through pockets of willow and pine that caressed our hot bodies with their cool shade, and tip-toed with outstretched arms across a rotting log that spanned the chuckling waters of Lone Pine Creek. The path switch-backed steeply, then eased. We paused in a yellow-flowered meadow busy with bees whose sounds were drowned by the urgent churning of the river, fiercer now as it cascaded through a cut in the rock-brow above us. A helicopter clattered up the valley on its way to collect garbage from one of the upper camps.

The urge to fall asleep on the shore of Mirror Lake was overwhelming—almost . . .

Shouldering our heavy packs, we resumed our upward progress, climbing a zig-zag rock path up the back-wall of the corrie above Mirror Lake, beyond the thinning trees and thence to Trail Camp, last resting place ('DO NOT throw trash in the toilet') of those who plan to press on into the thin, cool airs of the summit ridge. Beyond the camp reared a sheer 1,700-foot rock wall up which Nature offered no breach—not that Nature can stand in the way of a few judicious bangs. A hundred switch-backs had been blasted into that tortured pink rock.

On the crest of the ridge, at 13,777 feet, we scraped clear a stony platform, spread our sleeping bags, and with an orchestral light slanting from the west, over ridge, forest and peak from Farewell Mountain to Thunder Gap, we drifted off into a dreamless night.

At first, frozen light, we made our way in the raw early air along the deserted ridge to Whitney's summit, the peak untouched but for a small hut and 25 Californian hikers spread over the warm boulders like dirty washing. Someone flung a plastic frisbee into the void. It hung for a moment on the rising currents of warm valley air, then tilted on its long voyage down into the wilderness.

* * *

Conditions for frisbee flying on the British hills are not generally as good, though the walking is second-to-none. Hardly anywhere in Britain are you more than two hours' drive from a healthy-sized hill, and our rich inheritance of public rights-of-way provides easy access to wild country. Like Whitney, there are places where too many boots have caused serious erosion:—Clogwyn y Garnedd on the back of Snowdon now has flights of man-made steps, and on the Pennine Way, wooden footways now protect the more fragile parts. But much remains, and it is on the lesser-tramped hills that the greatest rewards are reaped.

If you prefer the simplicity of low-level walking along marked trails, Britain offers everything from the easy-going grass and woodland of the North Downs Way, South Downs Way and Ridgeway—all on London's doorstep, to quieter tracks like the historic Offa's Dyke Path through the

Welsh Borders or the much wilder West Highland Way, which scrambles from Glasgow to Fort William by way of the Trossachs and Glencoe. But for the free-style hill-walker in search of solitude, compiling a personal route from the Ordnance Survey 1:500,000 map series, there are thousands of miles of scope in these varied Isles. For cosiness, try the Cotswolds or Yorkshire Wolds, for an airy legstretch the Forest of Bowland or Berwyns, or for a damn good tramp Dartmoor, the northern Pennines or the slopes of North West Scotland. Little-trodden hill tracts across the water include northern Spain's Picos de Europa, much of France's Massif Central—and beyond the Arctic Circle, Norway's Lofoten Islands.

You can take hill-walking as seriously as you like; spend a fortune or very little. The essentials, a map and compass (and of course the knowledge and experience to use them safely), lightweight boots and bad weather gear need cost no more than a handful of CDs. For say four times as much as you can invest in a high-tech wardrobe which would include leather boots, socks, watertight gaiters, stretch breeches, windproof jacket, Gore-tex suit, thermal underwear, balaclava, gloves, small backpack, emergency bivouac bag, map and compass. Most of these items will last for many years, and most of them are appropriate for a range of outdoor activities: the same basic clothes can be used for hang-gliding, river-rafting or fishing.

And the actual process of perambulation costs nothing and gives all. Moving at the speed for which we were designed in a medium to which we fit, it is hard not to rejoice in the unique harmony that feet find in a hill.

Action: *Canoe Touring*

n the absence of a sponge, and at considerable personal
sacrifice' said Hol as we glided beneath Glasbury's bridge,
'I will empty the canoe of water with my handkerchief.'
   'Is the canoe leaking?' I asked, concerned that we might
sink before the first bend in our journey.
   'No,' came my father's patient response, 'the water is
being lifted in by your paddle.'

Our canoe was built to the Canadian pattern. Open-topped with upswept ends its aluminium hull rattled on shingle like stones thrown at tin. The great advantage of these open canoes is that they allow the paddlers plenty of space for moving about, stretching legs, giving lifts to pedestrians, snoozing during the siesta and so on. They are spacious; sedate. Accompanying us in a kayak was the British Canoe Union's access officer for the Wye, Chris Charters.

The plan was to make a journey by canoe down the River Wye—perhaps Britain's most loved touring river. We planned to complete the 24 miles over a leisurely weekend, with lots of time for exploring the historic riverbanks. Sealed in plastic bags, and lashed by rope into our canoe were spare clothes, washing gear and a large tin containing a camping gas stove, cooking pot and tin mug. 'In case we need a brew' argued Hol.

For once in my life I had put some planning into the journey, and had even gone to the trouble of booking us into a bed-and-breakfast at the halfway mark.

On emerging from Glasbury bridge, the river divided and we took the right-hand stream to rush by an island of blowing willows. Small waves slapped the hull, the water licking my arm with each paddle stroke. A swan slid serenely along the water margin, leading five frantic downy balls. Beyond the swan, a salmon jumped, a spark of silver followed by a soft 'plop'. Rains of the previous week had lifted the river over the shingle banks that in summer can ground a canoe. Ten feet above our heads the matted debris of past floods sat wedged in the forks of tree-trunks above the river cliff of terracotta-coloured earth. Hunting the current and sweeping wide on the bends

where the water ran deep and quick, the first hour was almost effortless.

Where a gurgling brook fell into the Wye beside a large, sunlit trunk we ran the canoes against the bank and stepped out to stretch our legs. Dovey Lewis was wrenching at a wall of weeds that looked ready to surge across his hard-won grass the moment he turned his back.

'I call him "boy" said Dovey, nodding at his white duck. 'He's just been out for a walk with me. He always knows what I'm talking about; you can tell by the way he cocks his head to one side. He's an Aylesbury, pure bred; just had eight ducklings. Course the drakes'll have to go. They'll be lovely on the table with a bit of sauce.' Dovey's jokes always end with an infectious gale of laughter. The duck pursued us back to the water, quacking at our ankles.

The two canoes swept gently past the mouth of Digedi Brook to meet a lozenge-shaped island. A heron turned its head as we approached, beat the air for what seemed an age, then finally became airborne, flapping like a pterodactyl across the river. As if to prove their aerobatic superiority a flight of sand martins stormed from their bunkers in the crumbly bank and darted about the canoes executing wing-tip turns, flips and dives, the air full of high-pitched 'cheek – cheeks'. We drifted by the lump-jawed profile of a rock the shape of a hippopotamus, while the heavy rump of the Black Mountains hovered transparently in the haze.

Shortly before Hay we heard the mutterings of Wyecliff Weir. An ivy-faced cottage slipped by. On the gravel spit inside the bend a family of five were spinning stones over the water. A striped deck-chair

stood in the sun behind them. Hol lined the canoe up for a gap in the Weir where the water poured through smooth and fast and the closer we got to the gap the stronger became the pull of the current until all we had to do was hold the canoe straight till it slithered down the fall into the small bouncing waves beyond.

Hay has a battered castle and over a million old books jammed into twenty or so shops. I wanted to find a copy of John MacGregor's *A Thousand Miles in the Rob Roy Canoe*. We browsed through Booths, the Cinema Bookshop and then Quintos. Buried in a cardboard box between *Babe Ruth's Own Book of Baseball* and E.W. Swanton's *Fungi and How to Know Them*, I found a copy of *Let's go Cycling* and forgot about MacGregor. Hol disappeared into a copy of Poucher's photographs of Scottish mountains; Chris found a book on French cooking. Quintos has a coffee dispenser for its long-stay customers.

Looking for a sponge, we were distracted by the window display at 'Sprog's Salvage' and poked our heads around the door to ask the price of an exotic blue and white Victorian under-glaze transfer-printed lavatory.

'£360' said the young man with the pony tail and brass-rimmed glasses.

'That seems expensive' said Hol.

'It's a lot for a bog' agreed the young man.

In 'The Bullring Foodstore', sharing a shelf with a row of 'Reckitts Bag Blue' and ranks of wooden scrubbing brushes, we found a large pink bath sponge.

The Wye escapes quickly from Hay, passing beneath the old Roman camp then running by the route of Offa's Dyke to

Dreaming down the Wye Valley in a 'Canadian' canoe; these canoes can take up to three people, and unlike a kayak (where you sit wedged into a narrow cockpit) open touring canoes such as this allow you to move around – within reason. There is plenty of space for picnics. Out of the water these canoes can easily be carried by two people (photo: David Reed).

elbow the ribs of the Radnorshire hills and Black Mountains that just for a while crowd almost too close for comfort. From water-level all you can see of Clifford Castle is a single, frayed rampart battling with the tree-tops. The castle was built by the Normans during their offensive against Wales, and destroyed by Owain Glyndŵr during his offensive against England. It is now owned by Betty and Charles Parkinson, who were given it as a wedding present. In 1949 Betty was one of a group of eight who rode from Land's End to John o'Groats for the Campaign Against Slaughter of Horses for Human Consumption.

Betty's husband Charles appeared from the garden. 'Thought you were from the council', he said cheerfully, pointing at our yellow life jackets.

'That's the barbican' Betty flung her arm towards a long slot in a grassy hummock beyond the house. 'Air Commodore Douglas Iron excavated it. Took him three years to move 300 tons in a wheelbarrow.'

Parts of the 700-year-old walls still stand thirty feet high, fringed by a sprouting of vegetation. Faint grazes made by the mason's tools still mark the blocks by the gateway. The windows in the keep have been eaten away but you can still look over the Wye with the eyes of Jane Clifford—adopted as 'Fair Rosamond' by generations of poets. Jane was born in the castle. Her beauty won the affections of many, but most fatefully those of Henry II. Some say that Fair Rosamond was poisoned by Henry's wife Eleanor of Aquitaine. Henry died unhappy in France, alone but for a faithful retainer and one of his sons by Rosamond, Geoffrey the Bastard.

From Clifford the river bounces back towards the bluffs on the far valley side beneath the village of Rhydspence and so to the toll bridge at Whitney. The old wooden bridge is built on stone piers which are clad on the upstream side with rusty iron sheeting. The bridge appeared to have been speared by an entire tree washed down the river by the last floods. Four canoeists from the 'Scrap Merchants Canoe Club' (potential members must provide proof of having destroyed a canoe) were setting up a barbecue on the grass by the bridge. They were taking a week to paddle down the Wye to Chepstow. They still had 90 miles to go. We had tea with 'Chris the Bridge', who used to be an investment manager for an offshore company before he bought Whitney toll bridge in 1981. When we walked up to the wooden gate that blocks

108

CANOE TOURING (these apply to a two-person canoe)

"Are you paddling?" The accusatory question that is thought ten times more often than it is voiced.

"back paddle" steerperson's command just before striking the bank/another canoe/sewage outfall.

BACK PADDLE! steerperson's command just before going over a weir.

"bail quickly" steerperson's command after canoe has sunk.

crocodile a log.

"I meant to do that" Steerperson's comment after folding the canoe round a bridge support in broad daylight on a still river.

passenger the person sitting in the front of a canoe doing all the work.

photography excuse for a rest.

river rat a keen canoeist.

"Why didn't you: back paddle/ stop paddling/part the water?" Post-sinking recrimination from steerperson to crew.

"We're nearly there" Steerperson's way of describing to a flagging crewperson a further 24 miles of canoeing, in the dark.

the road, he was a bit cross to find that someone had placed a white life-size inflatable skeleton in his toll-collector's chair.

As we left Whitney the sun broke through the clouds sending a fan of beams across the wooded folds above Clifford Castle. Now the Wye broke from the constraints of the Border mountains and began to meander lazily over a flat flood plain dotted with islands of trees. We stayed the night in a new farmhouse built by Milo and Sylvia Mason which looks across a dreamy loop of blue water known as Locksters Pool.

In the morning we paddled east through ruffled water which seemed to cup the sun in each wind-blown ripple. The wooded slab of Merbach Hill sidled towards us. Twice the river managed to turn through 180 degrees so that we found ourselves paddling hard into the same wind that minutes before had been helping us.

Just above some chuckling rapids we overtook a turquoise rowing boat. Two girls, one fair the other dark, beamed at the

sun while a young man in a baggy jersey pulled on the oars with the urgency that suggested either a leaking hull or the approach of closing time. Luke Chester-Masters confirmed that both were the case. We said that we hoped to see them later.

The bouncy little rapids helped us on our way to Bredwardine, where a high-arched red-brick bridge strides high across the water just upstream of the white-painted vicarage that was the last home of Francis Kilvert, the Victorian diarist. We pulled the canoes up onto the grass below the gardens of Brobury House Gallery. The house is Victorian, and on one corner has a turret with a roof like a rocket cone. From the terraced gardens you can look across a hammock of a valley to the fields and woods above Bredwardine's tiled roofs. It is a flawless English view.

In the converted coach block Eugene Okarma restores, colours and exhibits his enormous print collection. He emerged from the shrubbery dabbing his forehead with a white handkerchief. He had been gardening. Eugene was quickly joined by his wife, Margaret. They moved from Atlanta, Georgia to England in 1967. Eugene led us past a large water tray where stained prints are washed after being chemically cleaned.

'How many prints do you have here?' asked Hol.

'Around a hundred thousand' answered Eugene.

'I find that just mind boggling' said Margaret. 'I think Gene Okarma is the must unusual man I know. Being married to him has been *so* interesting. He nearly has a second degree in theology.'

We pushed the canoes back into the water; back to the secret world of shadows and eddies where eye-level is an arm's length from the water. Luminous weeds waved greenly beneath the shining hull.

One bend further we came to the 'Scar', where the river has slashed deep into the side of the hill to form a red cliff which leans over the river so that for a few seconds you could almost be descending the Grand Canyon. A dragonfly, its beating wings underlined in burning jade, overtook the canoe as we slowed to land beneath Moccas Court, a Georgian country house.

The chimney-piece in the Library of Moccas Court is made from scagliola which glows under an evening sun in the same shade of red as the Scar, which is framed in the facing window. Since the end of the 13th century Moccas has been owned by only

four families: the de Fresnes, Vaughans, Cornewalls and Chester-Masters. 'The only ghost story I know of' said Pam Saunders, whose husband Ivor is caretaker, 'was told me by a woman who used to work here as kennel maid and goose girl. Apparently Mary Jane Cornewall was drowned in the river here when she was seventeen, in about 1839, and it's said that her mother still walks the bank sometimes, looking for her daughter.'

We walked from the house to the tiny Norman church. On a sloping field beyond the church stood a circle of figures as crisp and white as origami cut-outs. The score was displayed on a school blackboard propped against the fence. Moccas village were batting against a team from the 'Glass House' pub in Mayfield. The hollow 'toc' of leather on willow followed us back to the river.

We climbed for a final time into the canoes. Our shadows stretched elastically across the calm water. 'Nobody's fallen in yet' observed Hol.

'Ah, but we still have Monnington Falls.'

My father Hol Crane beneath the bridge at Bredwardine, whose dozy cottages watch over the River Wye from a hillside that was once the site of a huge Iron Age hill fort. Bredwardine was also the home of the Victorian diarist Francis Kilvert.

'Oh good' he said.

As the paddles drew us into the current below the high terraces that climb up to Moccas Court, the silhouette of a girl moved from behind a tree and waved.

Action: *Ski-Mountaineering*

The conversation went something like this:
'*Magazine Editor: 'We would like you to go to Switzerland. Ski mountaineering is very popular there, especially at this time of year, in May. You use skins, which means you can go up as well as down.'*
NC: 'What are skins?'

Editor: 'And you must bring back beautiful photographs. Like this one (he flipped open an Italian magazine to present a double-spread showing a column of pin-like skiers set against a massive mountain wall). Can you ski?'

NC: 'Well . . .'

Editor: 'So, if you go for four days that will be long enough to ski up four mountains or complete some of the Haute Route.'

NC: 'Hot what?'

Editor: 'In Italy we do it a lot.'

NC: 'Yes.'

One plane, two trains and a bus later I was walking lopsidedly along the main street of Saas-Fee beneath two huge rucksacks. Saas-Fee is beyond the end of the road. It is so high—1,800 metres—that just a few handkerchief pastures separate the wooden buildings from the tumbling moraines and glacier that seem to hang above the roof tops. The tight confusion of alleys and cart-width streets are silent but for the hum of electric carts. Cars are prohibited from entering Saas-Fee; they rest redundant in a vast car-park by the bus station allowing pedestrians, free of intimidation, to wander the village breathing the pure, intoxicating Alpine air.

Saas-Fee is surrounded by glittering peaks (there are 14 of them of over 4,000 metres). I knew that because I'd seen a picture of them in 'Saas-Fee The Pearl of the Alps', the tourist brochure I'd been reading on the train.

But when I de-bussed it was clear that Saas-Fee was having an off-day. It was raining hard. I splashed through subfuscous streets towards the Bristol Hotel at the far end of the village. In the Bristol, Madame Bumann checked me in and agreed that the clouds would lift by the morning.

I had two calls to make: first to the ski

shop, where I was fitted out with boots, crampons, skis and poles. I was also handed the 'skins'; very sticky on one side; black and hairy on the other. They were about five feet long. Unrolled they looked like gigantic self-adhesive eyebrows. Then I telephoned Germain Derivaz, the *Bergführer und Skilehrer* who would accompany me during the next four days. We arranged to meet at the ski-lift at eight the next morning, unless the weather appeared unpromising.

Next morning the weather—at least by British standards—could have been worse. Water poured from the balcony rails in continuous streams; the cloud base was at about shoulder height. Germain said conditions were too bad for ski-mountaineering. This was a big disappointment. I took the Gondelbahn Spielboden from the village to a cloud-blown rock then changed gondolas and shot on upwards in the Luftseilbahn Langfluh to 2,870 metres.

Without the benefit of the guide I could not set off into the inviting white-out that lay beyond the steamy sanctuary of the Langfluh restaurant. But I could at least try out the equipment on some downhill runs. Hitching a lift on a caterpillar tractor I gained another few hundred metres and reached the foot of the Mittelallalin ski lift. Snow swirled and gusted. It was very cold. I seemed to be the only skier on the slopes.

Over the next three hours I reminded myself how much I'd forgotten. I do not enjoy downhill skiing because of the lifts:

A long column of ski-mountaineers make their way up the slope towards the foot of 4,027-metre Allalin. This all-purpose style of skiing makes it possible to travel uphill and across the broken ground of glaciers.

the idea of being pulled up a slope by a mechanical contrivance only to slide back to the bottom again seems pointless. And I *hate* chairlifts and ski-pulls. On ski-pulls I never seem to reach the top; my skis become derailed and I leave the piste to become wrapped around a pylon. Or I fall over and find myself being dragged face-first up the mountain. Once, on one of these horrible, single-person pulls the Swiss call a 'poma', the seat started with such a jerk that both my skis came off. On another occasion, mounting a twin-seated chairlift, the tip of my right ski caught on the ground. The leverage was so great that I was pulled forward from the seat. As the chair climbed higher and higher I slid beneath the restraining bar. The skier sharing the chair with me generously tried to save me by holding on to my arm. Locked together, we both plummetted from the chairlift. Having freefallen for ten feet then passed through a snowbank upside down, the other skier showed great restraint by limiting his reaction to a stream of swearwords and abuse which I recall finished on 'absolute pits.'

The second day was a washout too. Now I was beginning to worry: the prospect of returning home without *the story* is any journalists' ultimate nightmare. I opened my pad on the tiny table in room 204, dumped my glacier maps and skiing notes on the floor, and began writing an article called 'Rainy Days in Saas-Fee'.

Every hour, I checked the three dials attached to the outside wall of the 'Bristol'. On the third evening the hygrometer read 90%; the barograph 773 millibars and the temperature gauge 8° centigrade. Above the row of dials was a sign identifying it as a 'Wetterstation'.

Germain said the weather would soon change. Madame Bumann agreed.

On the morning of the third day, Germain gave me the green light. He was waiting for me at the ski-lift door. He wore a white peaked hat set at a rakish angle and a green, purple and yellow fleece jacket. In braced trousers borrowed from my 'Bicycles up Kilimanjaro' bag and a pair of cyclists' glasses with Elastoplast customising to reduce glare, I could not have looked less Swiss. I hoped fervently that he would not ask me how much skiing I had done. He did.

'A little.' I said. I could tell by his slight smile that he thought I was being modest. We chatted, knee-to-knee on the chilly seat. Germain had been a mountain guide for 20

112

SKI MOUNTAINEERING

avalanche one of the greatest dangers in the mountains, but one which is enormously reduced by a good understanding of the relation between types of snow and weather conditions. Avalanches can start on slopes as shallow as 30°.

crevasse a split (sometimes hundreds of feet deep) caused by movement in a glacier. Often disguised by new snow cover and therefore dangerous.

fall line the steepest angle on a slope.

harscheisen crampons which fit under the skis for use on hard, uphill snow.

ski-extreme not for ordinary mortals; pioneered by the French in the sixties, most routes are *twice* as steep as conventional red or black downhill runs. Slopes of 45-55° have regularly been descended.

skins artificial sticky-back fur strips which can be fixed to underneath of skis on uphills. Originally these were made from reindeer or seal skins.

snow-plough method of stopping by turning the tips of the skis towards each other if you have neither the space or ability to turn. Snow-ploughs are particularly efficient if you do them on your face.

years, taking clients rock-climbing in the summer, skiing in the winter. He skied up Allalin about ten times a year, though this was nothing compared to Saas-Fee's most famous guide, 73-year old Camille Supersaxo who was reckoned to have climbed Allalin one thousand times. Germain's longest standing clients were a German couple in their mid-fifties who returned each year. They had skied up 38 of Switzerland's 44 mountain peaks of over 4,000 metres. Once they have 'collected the set' they intend to start again.

The gondola up to Langfluh whispered through the mist. As a rocky ridge flicked beneath our feet, I caught sight of a family of marmots trundling like furry Morris Minors towards a patch of grass. I checked my pockets: gloves, scarf, balaclava, sunglasses, chocolate, compass, whistle. In

my pack was a thermal jacket and camera gear. The gondola jolted into the gaping mouth of the lift station, the attendant swung open the doors and we tottered on plastic boots out into the thin air.

What greeted us bore no relation to the Switzerland I'd grown to expect over the past two days. A light wind picked at the few remaining tatters of cloud clinging to the encircling mountains. Peaks crowded each other, shining shoulders of ice dropping to cracked glaciers and broad sweeps of snow that ran towards us in perfect sculpted curves. A few metres from the lift station the glacier tipped over the brink of the mountain bowl, to disappear from sight; a tortured, static cascade. Three inches of new snow lay on the packed ice beneath our feet. The echoey crunch of avalanches echoed through the sharp air like a giant chewing cornflakes. It was an enormous spectacle.

'Allalinhorn!' Germain woke me up. He was pointing towards the central peak on the skyline; the noblest peak. Allalin is 4,027 metres high. It was first climbed in 1856 by an Englishman called E.L. Ames in the company of two local guides, Franz Andenmatten and Joseph Imseng. Imseng became known as Switzerland's first skier. Its defences are breached by the ramp of a large glacier. I followed Germain's finger. We would ski up the glacier to the col that separates Allalin from its neighbouring peak, Feechopf, and there turn up the ridge to the summit.

Applying the skins is straightforward: The underneath of the ski must be dry. You then unroll the skin and hook the leading edge over the tip of the ski. Taking care not to create any wrinkles you then stretch the skin down the length of the ski and press it on. Because the hairs are angled rearwards, the ski will slide forward but not backwards.

The ascent was hard, physical fun. Ski-mountaineering bindings allow the boot to be locked to the ski for downhill runs, or they can be released at the heel so that you can 'walk' as if ski-touring. Mountaineering skis are generally shorter, lighter and more manoeuvrable than downhill skis. It is a versatile arrangement. The rhythmic swish of ski on snow had a somniferous effect in the bright morning light. Crystals danced and sparkled. By 11.30 am we were within sight of the col below Allalin. After a brief rest we started up the ridge. Here the steepness forced a zig-zag route. The Langfluh restaurant was now but a speck on the far side of the bowl. Gone were the sounds of the lifts; the presence of other skiers. To and fro we cut upwards, huffing hard in the thinning air.

Just after noon, we took off our skis and walked the last metres along the narrow ridge crest to the summit of Allalin.

With just one day left Germain arranged a grand tour of the valley's upper slopes. We began by skiing up the rump of brick-shaped Alphubel. At 4,206 metres, it is slightly higher than Allalin. Where Allalin's approaches had been even, Alphubel's were an exciting maze of crevasses and ice-cliffs. To demonstrate the perils of choosing the wrong route, Germain poked at a small depression beside our tracks. The snow caved in to reveal a gaping black slot; a crevasse big enough to take a body. It was lightly bridged by new snow.

Dwarfed by the stilled surf of the mountain's massive ice-sheet, we slid up, till we reached a vantage point below a sombre rock wall. We waited while two mountaineers swooped like swallows from the cliffs above, twisting and dipping, then disappearing over the bulge that led back to Langfluh. Without time to make the summit, we unpeeled our skins and descended sedately to the floor of the glacier, then contoured across the snow-bowl to pick up the 'Panorama piste'; a red run. We flew down, to pick up the trail that climbs to the Felskinn station. Here a foot-tunnel has been blasted through the mountain ridge to provide access to a long, level piste which heads for Egginerjoch and the Brittania Hut.

The trail leading to the Brittania Hut is part of the Haute Route. This, I had learned from Germain, was the high-level ski-route that runs for 130 kilometres from Saas-Fee to Chamonix via the glaciers of the Monte Rosa and the Matterhorn. It is a journey that on skis takes 7 days. It crosses eleven glacier passes and it is the most famous ski tour in Europe; some would say the world. The cumulative ascents and descents on the route add up to 20,000 metres. It was pioneered by British members of the Alpine Club in the 1860s.

The Brittania Hut crept slowly into view. Our skis rumbled over the foot of an avalanche cone and slid into the shade. Ice rattled beneath the skis. The Hut perches on a snowy shoulder with views back towards Saas-Fee in one direction, and an exciting panorama onwards to the Adler Pass. Beyond the Adler lies the way to Chamonix. Outside the hut, a man with a

handkerchief over his eyes lay dozing on a sledge in the last of the afternoon sun. He was wearing nothing but a pair of banana coloured Paisley underpants.

Our time was up. Skis off, we clumped up the stone steps to the warm, wooden room which has wrapped so many tired skiers in its cosy fug. Over beer and *kaffee fertig* (coffee, schnapps and sugar) I opened Germain's map and plotted a return: to the Haute Route.

Bergführer und Skilehrer Germain Derivaz demonstrates a ski-mountaineering binding in uphill mode. For downhills the heel can be locked to the ski giving the skier all the characteristics of a conventional downhill ski. Synthetic self-adhesive 'skins' can be attached to the underside of the skis for uphill sections; for very steep (or icy) sections, steel 'crampons' can be fitted to the skis.

Action: *Mountainbiking*

t was still dark when Ahmed Mansour slipped from beneath his blanket and padded across the room to make the tea. I ran my hand along the windowsill until it collided with the box of matches. The gas lamp flared and settled into a cosy hiss. My watch said 5.30 am.

On the seat opposite, Matt Dickinson was lying still. Asleep. Or pretending. I pulled the sleeping bag down to my waist; blinked at the room. For several neutral moments I distracted myself from the unpleasant prospect of leaving my sleeping bag by staring at the odd collection on the windowsill by my head; there was a wooden box filled with cassette tape boxes so scratched that the plastic was opaque; there was a huge radio-cassette with a broken handle; three dud batteries; some tourist brochures of Casablanca; a pile of postcards from clients Ahmed had taken into the mountains; several empty condensed milk cans (from the previous evening's binge); a plastic drinking bottle (mine), and four small, stamped posters from Mecca.

Matt grunted. I slopped out of my bag. There was no need to get dressed. The night had been so cold that we had slept in our clothes. Ahmed returned with a tall silver pot, a plate of unleavened bread and a bowl of olive oil. The three of us sat round the low round table. In silence, we tore pieces from the bread and dipped it in the oil. Ahmed was wearing the new maroon bobble hat that Matt had bought for him in the *soukh* last night.

Outside it was freezing. The bicycles felt cold, heavy, clumsy. Ahmed roped our two rucksacks onto the back of his mule. We carried the bikes down the stepped alleys separating the mud-walled houses of Toufrine. Below the village, we found the start of the track, lifted ourselves onto the saddles and began pedalling up towards the pass. This was our eleventh day; we only had nine days left to complete the journey.

One and a half weeks earlier three of us had rolled down the rippled flanks of Morocco's highest sand-dune and struck off across the desert towards the eastern end of the High Atlas. We were pedalling from the Sahara to the sea, a distance of 1,300 kilometres. On the way we planned to traverse the entire length of the Atlas mountains using mule tracks. Our expedition—and the name of the film that was being made of it—was called 'Blazing Pedals'. This journey had been intended to prove the versatility of mountainbikes: to cover the 1,300 kilometres in the 20 days available we would have to average 65 kilometres each day. The terrain would include sand, jeep-tracks, tarmac, stony mule tracks, river beds, snow, ice and the occasional rock face. The daily distances were too much for a horse or mule and the tracks impossible for a jeep or motorcycle. Apart from travelling on foot—which would have taken three times as long—mountainbikes were the only means of completing the journey.

A serious accident after five days reduced our number to two. Forty-eight hours travelling time from the nearest road, Chris Bradley had been thrown over the handlebars and landed on a rock. His knee was wrecked. With some difficulty, and an emergency bivouac on a high mountain, we had pressed on to rendezvous with the main film crew. Chris had pulled out. And because our map beat all known records of unreliability we had become lost for two days on the remote, arid plateaux of the eastern Atlas. We were well down on our schedule. Only the bicycles appeared to be performing predictably.

The madder side of mountainbiking: Matt Dickinson carries his bicycle to the summit of 4,176-metre Mount Toubkal, the highest mountain in North Africa. With him are Philip Millard and Stuart Bruce, part of the camera team led by director Alan Ravenscroft who filmed the event for the National Geographic/ Central TV 'Voyager' series broadcast in 1989.

Above: The legs of the self-propelled traveller are fuelled by curiosity; mountainbikes provide the ultimate in versatility: they are adaptable to tarmac, mud, snow and rock. During the Atlas Mountain traverse we covered 547 kilometres on dirt tracks, mostly of mule width or less. Here, Chris Bradley and Matt Dickinson pedal past the village of Mazal (though some people called it San Tet) on the fourth day of the journey. The large towered building is the *kasbah* used for defence when the village was threatened.

Left: The family of Said Amgoul, who provided us with a roof and a couscous meal in the village of Ouddidi at the start of our crossing of the mapless gorges and plateaux between Imilchil and Zaouat Ahansal. Amgoul's wife rose before dawn to make loaves of bread for breakfast. The loaves were torn and dipped in a communal bowl of warm melted cheese. The sweet tea was poured into tiny glasses from a slender, swan-necked metal teapot.

With its frankfurter tyres and cowhorn handlebars a mountainbike looks as generically distanced from the featherweight Tour de France racing machine as does *Equus asinus* from *caballus*. Yet the mountainbike, for all its clumsy appearance, is the most versatile of all human-powered vehicles. It can cross continents and climb mountains, is robust and can carry enormous loads.

Mountainbikes (or ATBs—all terrain bikes) can be traced back to a scrubby arrowhead or territory that tapers into the northern waters of the San Francisco Bay. Here, in Marin County USA in the late seventies, individuals such as Gary Fisher, Joe Breeze and Tom Ritchey could be found refining the fat-tyred bikes used till then for pedalling the boardwalks of coastal California into off-road hybrids capable of tackling the rugged trails that criss-cross the outlying folds of the Sierra Nevada mountains.

The boardwalk bikes—or 'clunkers' —were customised with lower gearing and better brakes. Month-by-month they mutated: stronger frame tubing was found, and the frame geometry was shortened to improve the handling. Up to fifteen gears were added, which gave the new bikes the climbing agility of mountain goats. Brakes became powerful enough to lock the wheels at 40 mph.

Before long a few mountainbikes arrived in Europe. They were copied by all the major manufacturers. In crowded countries like Britain, where a clear road is as treasured as an untramelled stretch of powder snow at the end of an Alpine season, the arrival of a vehicle that could be used to leave behind the mess and noise of motor traffic was seen as a heaven-sent opportunity to take to the trails.

In the same way that the invention of the motor-car encouraged a rash of madcap adventures—one thinks of Prince Scipione Borghese's dash in 1907 from Paris to

Right: The bikes we used on the journey from the Sahara to the sea were off-the-peg 'Ridgeback' mountainbikes, equipped with 21 gears. We each carried about 20 lb of luggage, though this increased on the sections where we were out of reach of the main film crew because we had to carry a TV camera, spare batteries, film magazines, clapper board and so on, in addition to our sleeping bags and waterproof clothing.

Peking in a 40 horsepower *Itala*—so the mountainbike has attracted eccentrics eager to explore the new diversion. Within months of mountainbikes arriving in Britain, two expatriate Australian lawyers (Tim Gartside and Peter Murphy) pedalled a pair of Ritchey bikes across the Sahara Desert. Since then, mountainbikes have been spotted in Antarctica, on the Tibetan Plateau, on the summit of Kilimanjaro, Chimbarazo, Mount Fiji and Mont Blanc and at Everest Base Camp. They have also been used to traverse the length of the Himalayas and the Andes. They are the chosen steed for the bicycle-couriers of Manhattan and London. The mountainbike seems to bring out a bit of the Borghese in all of us.

The hardware available is very seductive: mountainbikes come in a variety of styles from street-chic roadsters fitted with mudguards and carrying racks (the urban runaround) to fly-weight rock bikes with little more than a saddle, two wheels and a pair of brakes. Tyres are available in a variety of widths and tread patterns to suit mud, rock, tarmac or snow. The Finns, for whom a ride to the shops in temperatures of minus 20 is quite normal, produce a snow tyre embedded with tungsten steel studs. The better quality bikes are fitted with sealed bearings, which is useful if you plan to ford rivers or ride through deep bulldust. Gear levers (thumb-shifters) are mounted on the handlebars so that all the bike's controls can be operated without having to move your hands from the 'bars. When buying a mountainbike you need to choose a frame size about two inches smaller than you would normally use for a road bike.

In England and Wales, where our wildernesses are now so small that you don't see them if you miss the turning, the best off-road riding is to be found on bridleways and byways which are legally-defined rights of way. These are marked on Ordnance Survey 1:50,000 maps with red pecked lines. In Scotland there are

Day 13, near the ancient mountain stronghold of Telouet. The day before this photograph was taken, we had cycled and walked 98 kilometres over two high, snowy passes, sharing part of our journey with a muleteer/guide, Ahmed Mansour. Mansour left us at the summit of the Tizi-n-Timililt, to return to the village of Tamzrit, where he sheltered for the night. By this stage we had covered 700 kilometres since leaving the Sahara (photo: Annabel Huxley).

MOUNTAINBIKING

amazing boring.
death defying mildly hazardous.
incredibly steep nearly level.
foaming cataract a stream.
knobbly a tyre with big rubber knobs for gripping in mud or snow. Often seen in Oxford Street. **Studded knobblies** can be brought from Finland for use on ice.
mountain ledge a fenced footpath.
slick a treadless tyre for townies.
totally lost too dim to read a map.
absolute write-off a broken spoke.
uncharted wilderness a national park.

no rights of way and neither are there laws of trespass; mountains and moorlands are open for biking unless the landowner has imposed local restrictions. Everywhere, care should be taken to close field-gates and to leave no mark on the landscape. Even bicycle tyres can rip topsoil that can take months to heal.

Despite the individualistic nature of the British mountainbiking fraternity, organised events have been gaining in popularity. Events such as California's *Coastal Ranges Dirty Thirty* are being matched in Britain by excruciating races over the Pennines, Welsh forests and North Downs. The most famous is the annual *'Man v Bike v Horse'* held in the Welsh borders.

But this is leading us away from the important point: that the mountainbike is a uniquely useful tool for travel. It was on the strength of this that mountainbikes were chosen for the 'Blazing Pedals' expedition. The models which we used were

One of the problems particular to cycling in the eastern Atlas was the gradients, many of which were vertical. Typically we would spend three or more hours carrying the bicycles up trails which picked precipitous routes up the gorge walls (on more than one occasion traversing awesome drops on shelves a few feet wide). At the top would be a plateau of confusing topography. Having crossed each plateau, we would then have to find a way down more vertical cliffs. This photograph was taken on Day 5, beyond the village of N'Razzi about one hour before Chris Bradley was thrown over his handlebars, wrecking his knee.

off-the-shelf Ridgeback bikes, supplied by the London company Madison. They had 21 gears and the latest oval chainrings and self-tuning derailleur. Our luggage (which included a TV film camera, spare camera batteries, tape-recorder and a clapper board) was divided between panniers carried on the bikes and small backpacks.

The sand slalom in the Sahara; Chris Bradley tries to pedal down the flank of the highest sand-dune in Morocco, on the edge of the Erg Chebbi – the great sand sea two hours' pedalling south of the oasis of Rissani.

Later in the trip we compressed all the gear into backpacks alone, since the panniers proved too burdensome on the narrow rocky trails and rock-climbing sections of the route.

Anyway, to pick up the story again on Day 12: Dickinson and I were now about one third of the way along the Atlas mountains, with 9 days left to cover the 750 or so remaining kilometres. We still had 6 passes over 2,000 metres to cross and we were determined not to abandon our attempt to take mountainbikes up Mount Toubkal—the highest mountain in North Africa. But our immediate problem was to extract ourselves from the valley of the Tessaout and make the very long mountain crossing to the next valley west: Telouet.

We knew that this day had to be the turning point in the journey. We could not afford to lose any more time. Although Telouet was 100 kilometres away, and separated from Toufrine by two high passes, one of which was known to be snowbound and impassable to mules, we *had* to make it in one day. If we could not, then the chances of reaching the Atlantic within our 20-day deadline were nil.

The Tessaout was not a valley we wanted to linger in. The previous day we had been

forced to carry the bikes for six hours as we struggled to find a route along the sheer sided valley. The mule tracks were either washed away, obliterated by landslides or scrambled for hundreds of feet up the mountainside. We had been forced at the end of the day to take off our boots and wade through the deep and freezing river to reach the sanctuary of Toufrine on the far bank.

The mud-houses of Toufrine are plastered across a knoll of rock marking the confluence of the Tessaout river and the stream that runs down from the Tizi-n-Fedghat. Each house is two or three stories high, flat roofed and separated by narrow hay-strewn alleys. Ahmed Mansour, a muleteer and guide, lives in a large house at the top of the village. Our arrival coincided with the cooking of the evening *tagine*—the traditional Moroccan mutton and vegetable casserole. The meat, with carrots, potatoes, onions, olives and herbs is packed into a conical-lidded pot and left on the flames for up to two hours. The juices mingle; no flavour is wasted. When the host comes to lift the lid a volcanic cloud of mouth-watering steam erupts into the room. There are no plates; you pick at the pot with fingers and pieces of folded bread.

We left Toufrine before dawn. Initially, the track up the valley which led towards our first pass, the Tizi-n-Feghat, was wide enough for a jeep. Our tyres cracked through the frozen puddles of springs that had spilled and filled hoof-holes. Dickinson

sung 'Postman Pat' to himself. His young son is a Postman Pat fan.

Ahmed dropped out of sight, striding beside his mule. We pedalled in parallel, four wheels sneaking along the frozen track that unwound like a serpent up the pass. In one place a landslide had torn away the track, so that we had to teeter along in single file high above the river. Icicles as long as javelins hung from rock-walls. In our lowest gears we had to pedal delicately: too much torque and the rear wheel would spin, sending the rear of the bike skittering sideways. From the gloomy depths of our icy defile we could see ahead to the gleaming walls of Igrem-n-Iguioun and Mount Taouadja, their flat, snow-crusted flanks seeming to bar our way forward.

Just below the snow-line, we broke through into sunlight and sat on the grit to wait for Ahmed. Not a breath of wind nor cloud disturbed the sky. Ahmed arrived, grinning. Together we climbed the last yards to the summit of the Tizi-n-Fedghat. We were standing at a height 2,181 metres. Beyond the pass, the Atlas fell away, ridge spines tapering into the mustard haze of the desert. Squinting down into the lower layers of warm air we could see the huge puddle of the El-Mansour-Eddahbi reservoir 50 kilometres away beyond Ouarzazate. But we still had another pass to go—an even higher one. The Tizi-n-Timililt stands at 2,588 metres.

Ahmed led us off the main track. We headed towards the south-eastern ridge of

Igrem-n-Iguioun. Cutting across a mix of boulders, snow-patches and scrub, it became impossible to balance on the bikes.

Carrying mountainbikes is a very dull occupation. The least painful technique is to stick your head through the frame triangle and walk with the weight of the machine resting across your shoulders. For the first five minutes the carrying is almost restful compared to the effort of trying to pedal over rocky terrain. But thereafter the bike feels more and more like an instrument of torture and the desire to hurl it over the nearest cliff can become almost overwhelming.

We plodded beneath a cliff, then up a long, rocky ramp. We could hear the boom of wind sucking up from the Sahara. On the north side of the pass the air was uncannily quiet; almost warm in the sun. Ahmed stopped. He unloaded our two packs from his mule, shook our hands and departed. We watched the swaying rump of his mule pick a careful route through the crags. Ahmed would be back in Toufrine before nightfall. For Dickinson and me, Telouet was still a long way off. We chewed on a piece of bread Ahmed had given us, wriggling into gloves and overtrousers in the lee of a huge rock. We shouldered the bikes and clambered the last few feet to the top of the Tizi-n-Timililt.

We peered over the edge. A freezing gale of frightening intensity smashed into our faces. On the north side of the pass, the rock had been largely bare of snow; looking down the south side, all we could see was a vast, white wilderness. How could we possibly ride on that? Worse still, there was no apparent way down from the pass. The slope was very steep. Ahmed had waved his arm generously to the south west, but it was clear from the clean snow that no-one had passed this way for weeks.

We lowered ourselves over the edge. The snow was thigh deep. We were at the top of a 400-foot slope. Pieces of disturbed snow broke away and rolled in gathering balls out of sight. Very tentatively we began a traverse across the top of the snow slope. Slurries of snow avalanched away from the trench carved by our wallowing progress. The whole slope felt as if it might break away from the rock beneath and thunder down into the bowl below.

We floundered downwards, sliding the bikes across the snow surface, slithering and slipping until we reached the safety of the valley. Here the snow had formed an ice crust which gave way with every footstep. It

was impossible to ride; difficult to walk. Half an hour's labour brought us to the frozen shore of tiny Lake Tamda. We pushed on over a lip of rock and soon found that we could ride occasional sections. Here and there we picked up the traces of the summer mule track where it ran out from beneath the snow-banks.

With every kilometre gained we lost more altitude. The air warmed. Dickinson began singing 'Postman Pat' again. The track defined itself: a thin, wavering thread of darker brown. On the bikes again, we pedalled quickly, slipping beneath the bulk of Adrar Aglagal and entering the thin neck of the valley that runs down to the village of Anmiter. Near here are the salt mines from where long camel caravans used to set out across the Sahara. Terraced fields filled every nook and cranny of the valley. The track twisted between huge rocks and crept beneath cliffs. Children called from house doorways. With the afternoon drawing to a close we flew down the last few kilometres to Anmiter, bouncing down a jeep track that alternately shot through clumps of houses and skidded down the mountainside.

At Anmiter we had a shock. Instead of potholed gravel, the track changed to tarmac. It was the first tarmac that we had seen for 400 kilometres. Now the tyres hummed, deliriously smoothly. We had covered 90 kilometres since leaving Toufrine. Telouet was only ten away. As if to remind us that we were not home yet, an inky cloud spread like a stain across the sky and the first spots of rain splatted onto the road. Ten minutes later we were leaning into a gale, struggling to see the way through the premature dusk.

The battlements of Telouet stood silhouetted against a sky that seemed engaged in a frightful struggle between light and dark. We rolled down the hill, water creasing our faces, hearts lifted but minds too tired to speak. We had eaten two slices of bread all day, last drunk 12 hours earlier.

The tents were pitched in the lee of a hill beside the Kasbah. They had seen us coming. Arms reached from the darkness; caught the falling bikes. We were propelled beneath an awning, handed mugs of tea. A log fire hissed in the damp night.

'Well done chaps', said a dripping anorak. 'D'you think you'll make it now?'

'Of course . . .'

We did reach the Atlantic. We did climb Toubkal with the bikes. And we had another accident. But that's another story.

Mountainbiking down the back wall of the couloir just below the summit of Mt Toubkal at a height of 4,000 metres (photo: Annabel Huxley).

Action: *Taking Action*

You will find that for most sports there are four ways of becoming involved:

1. By joining a club.

2. By taking an approved course at a training school.

3. By going on an adventure holiday which involves the sport.

4. By teaming up with a friend who is already expert or qualified.

In the sections that follow, I have opened the doors to 1, 2 and 3.

Some considerations though:

Always check that instructors are fully qualified. Many of these sports can be extremely dangerous if proper safeguards and procedures are not observed.

Clubs tend to operate in evenings and weekends because their officials are donating their time voluntarily. So learning a sport this way can take longer (but is always less expensive).

In the UK there are a growing number of 'adventure centres' which provide multi-activity weeks; over several days you can combine for example, horse riding, caving, canoeing and so on. Before signing on for one of these courses check whether you can opt out or swap activities in case you find that some are more pleasurable than others.

Some training schools and activity centres will provide courses for small groups; this can be an opportunity for a group of friends to team up.

QUESTIONS TO ASK BEFORE JOINING A COURSE OR ADVENTURE HOLIDAY

1. Is it possible to change from one sport to another part way through a course?

2. On mixed-sport adventures, how much time will I be spending on a raft, trekking, sightseeing etc?

3. Are there any hidden costs in the course/adventure trip?

4. What special equipment/clothing do I need to bring? How much is provided?

5. What is the pre-sales and after-sales service like? Will the company organising the trip/course let me know in good time what equipment I need to acquire? Will they have the back-up to help me if I have to make insurance claims after the trip?

6. Who will be leading the trip/expedition/course?

7. What will be the accommodation?

8. Will there be children on the course/trip?

9. What kind of insurance cover (if any) is provided?

QUESTIONS TO ASK YOURSELF

1. Do I really want to spend seven days sitting on a horse?

2. Do I want to spend the time more on my own, or in the company of others?

3. I may want to learn to parachute, dive or climb, but am I prepared for the possibility that I may have to be shouted at by instructors?

4. Do I want a holiday, or a demanding learning exercise?

Action: *Initiatives*

The explosion of interest in outdoor activities in Britain has created the need for a network linking the hundreds of diverse outdoor groups. To date, networking organisations have been set up in four of Britain's cities, and plans are already laid to establish centres in a further six cities. They all run under the banner of Outdoor Activities Initiatives. Each O.A.I. acts as an information exchange which encourages better use of equipment, facilities and expertise. Members of the public can contact their local O.A.I. to find out where the nearest climbing wall is, or whether any clubs are canoeing at the weekend. O.A.I.s are also working to increase participation, especially among the Sports Council's target groups of youth, fifty-plus, women, disabled and ethnic groups. (Committed outdoorists should read the report by Lord Hunt's working party, 'In Search of Adventure: A Study of the Opportunities for Adventure and Challenge for Young People'.)

Outdoor Activities Initiative (London): 72 St John Street, Smithfield, London EC1M 4EX. Tel: (01) 490.4051. Fax 01-490.4186.

Outdoor Activities Initiative (Birmingham): The Ackers, Golden Hillock Road, Small Heath, Birmingham B11 2PY. Tel: (021) 722.3739.

Outdoor Activities Initiative (Greater Manchester): Miles Platting Centre, Manchester. Tel: (061) 203.4586.

Merseyside Outdoor Activities Association: Merseyside Outdoor Activity Centre, Queens Dock, Sefton Street, Liverpool L3 4AJ. Tel: (051) 708.6583.

Useful Addresses for Adventurers

The Adventure Sports and Travel Club: 565 Fulham Road, London SW6 1ES. Tel: (01) 385 4387/8/9. Publishes the *Worldwide Guide to Adventure Sports* and acts as a broker for small, specialist operators of adventure holidays.

British Activity Holiday Association: Rock Park, Llandrindod Wells, Powys LD1 6AE. Tel: (0597) 3902. Established to maintain standards of safety, instruction and quality of service among operators of activity holidays.

Central Council for Physical Recreation: Francis House, Francis Street, London SW1P 1DE. Tel: (01) 828.3163. The representative for Britain's sports and recreation bodies.

Royal Geographical Society: 1 Kensington Gore, London SW7 2AR. Tel: (01) 589.5466. The focal point for British geographical and exploration activity. Fellows have access to regular meetings with top explorers and travellers and to a library of exploration books. The RGS is a unique source of inspiration for adventurers and an important environmental forum.

Sports Council: 16 Upper Woburn Place, London WC1H 0QP. Tel: (01) 388.1277. The government quango charged with improving participation, quality of facilities and sports standards. A useful source of sports information too.

Stanfords: 12–14 Long Acre, Covent Garden, London WC2E 9LP. Tel: (01) 836.1321. Established in 1852 and billed as the world's largest map shop; sells maps, aeronautical charts, yachting charts (agents for Admiralty Charts) and guide books for most parts of the globe.

Meteorological Office Weather Reports

Free Met Office Weathercall cards, showing dialling codes and weather report regions can be obtained by dialling (01) 236.3500.

National forecast: (0898) 500400.

Five-day national forecast: (0898) 500430.

For your local forecast, dial (0898) 500, followed by your regional code:

Greater London	401
Kent, Surrey & Sussex	402
Dorset, Hants & Isle of Wight	403
Devon & Cornwall	404
Wiltshire, Gloucestershire, Avon & Somerset	405
Berkshire, Buckinghamshire & Oxfordshire	406
Bedfordshire, Hertfordshire & Essex	407
Norfolk, Suffolk & Cambridgeshire	408
West Midlands, South Glamorgan & Gwent	409
Shropshire, Herefordshire & Worcestershire	410
Centreal Midlands	411
East Midlands	412
Lincolnshire & Humberside	413
Dyfed & Powys	414
Gwynedd & Clwyd	415
North-west England	416
West & South Yorkshire & Yorkshire Dales	417
North-east England	418
Cumbria & Lake District	419
South-west Scotland	420
West-central Scotland	421
Edinburgh, South Fife, Lothian & Borders	422
East-central Scotland	423
Grampians & East Highlands	424
North-west Scotland	425
Caithness, Orkney & Shetland	426
Northern Ireland	427

Marinecall:

National 5-day Marinecall forecast: (0898) 500450.

For local coastal weather conditions, dial (0898) 500 followed by your regional code (refer to area map available from the Met Office):

Scotland North	451	Bristol Channel	459
Scotland East	452	Wales	460
North East	453	North West	461
East	454	Clyde	462
Anglia	455	Caledonia	463
Channel East	456	Minch	464
Mid-Channel	457	Ulster	465
South West	458		

Airmet: obtain Airmet card from the Met Office, showing forecast areas and dialling codes.

Mountaincall: twice-daily updated weather reports specifically for walkers and climbers using the Scottish Highlands: (0898) 500442.

For Scottish skiing conditions, dial (0898) 500440.

Action: *Sports Directory*

River Rafting

There are no 'schools' of rafting, but plenty of commercial organisations running journeys that vary from mild to extreme; learning the water skills forms a natural part of a first river-trip. On most raft trips the vessel is regarded as a means of enjoying the landscape and wildlife that border the river. On some trips you can spend up to two weeks with the same companions.

River rafting is a growing adventure activity, with new companies appearing each year; and a few sinking without trace. For addresses of current companies check with the tourist board of the country you're interested in, or start with the following:

Abercrombie & Kent Travel: Sloane Square House, Holbein Place, London SW1W 8NS. Tel: (01) 730.9600. Sun Khosi (Nepal). Zambezi (Zambia, Zimbabwe).

Acorn Travel Services: Acorn House, 172/174 Albert Road, Jarrow, Tyne & Wear NE32 5JA. Tel: (01) 483.6226. Colorado (USA).

American Round-up: 1 The Hawthorns, Box LA, Hemel Hempstead, Hertfordshire HP3 0AZ. Tel: (0442) 214621. Colorado, Grand Canyon, Green River (Colorado, Utah; USA).

Encounter Overland: 267 Old Brompton Road, London SW5 9JA. Tel: (01) 370.6845. Trisuli, Sun Khosi (Nepal).

Exodus Expeditions: All Saints Passage, 100 Wandsworth High Street, London SW18 4LE. Tel: (01) 870.0151. Trisuli (Nepal), Urubamba (Peru), Nenana (Alaska).

ExplorAsia: 13 Chapter Street, London SW1P 4NY. Tel: (01) 630.7102. Trisuli, Bheri (Nepal), Urubamba (Peru).

Explore Worldwide: 7 High Street, Aldershot, Hampshire GU11 1BH. Tel: (0252) 319448. Dunajec (Czechoslovakia).

Sporting Travel Services: 9 Teasdale Close, Royston, Hertfordshire SG8 5TD. Tel: (9763) 242867. Ammeran (near Östersund, Sweden), Kalix & Kaitum (near Kiruna, Sweden).

Twickers World Travel: 22 Church Street, Twickenham, Middlesex TW1 2NW.

Tel: (01) 892.7606. Trisuli (Nepal), Bio Bio (Chile), Fremri Emstrua & Markarfljót (Iceland), Zambesi (Zambia).

Reading

River Journeys edited by Russell Braddon. BBC Publications. 1984.

The Adventures of Tom Sawyer by Mark Twain. Penguin Classics, England, 1986 (first published 1876).

Kon Tiki by Thor Heyerdahl. Alan & Unwin, 1982 (first published 1950).

The Rage to Survive by Jacques Vignes. Adlard Coles, London 1976 (first published 1973).

Hot-air Ballooning

Starting

British Balloon and Airship Club, PO Box 1006, Birmingham B5 5RT. Tel: (021) 643.3224. (Information available by sending £1 plus s.a.e.).

Learning

The first step is to fly as a passenger on an 'air experience' flight. Flights can be arranged through the regional clubs of the BBAC (contact the BBAC to find out your nearest club) or with one of the commercial concerns listed below.

If you are going to take ballooning seriously, there are four different routes you can take: 1) buy your own balloon and invite qualified pilots to fly and instruct you (fabulously expensive); 2) buy a share in a syndicate which owns a balloon (quite expensive); 3) go to a commercial ballooning concern and pay for lessons by the hour (fairly expensive); 4) go to one of the few clubs which owns its own balloons (much less expensive).

Most people learn at clubs.

The names and addresses of the BBAC's regional ballooning officers can be obtained from the BBAC address above.

To fly your own balloon you need to hold a PPL (Private Pilot's Licence). A PPL requires you to have 15 hours flying time under instruction from any balloon pilot,

and a further 2 flights with an instructor. You must then take a written exam covering air law, principles of ballooning, meteorology and navigation, and then make a check flight with the examiner followed by a solo flight. You can then fly on your own, and take non-paying passengers.

A further 20 hours of flying and another check flight qualifies you for a restricted commercial licence; 75 hours and you can make a check flight for your full commercial licence (CPL). A full CPL allows you to fly with fare-paying passengers.

Air Experience Flying

Adventure Balloons: 3 Queens Terrace, Hanwell, London W7 3TS. Tel: (01) 840.0108. Farnborough (west of London), Somerset, France.

Ballooning World: 18 Linhope Street, London NW1 6HT. Tel: (01) 706.1021.

The Capital Balloon Club: same address as Ballooning World. Tel: (01) 724.2389.

Headland Hotel: Headland Road, Newquay, Cornwall TR7 1EW. Tel: (0637) 872211. Cornwall.

Mid-Bucks Farmers' Balloon Group: Mount Pleasant Farm, Stewkley, near Leighton Buzzard, Bedfordshire LU7 0LU. Tel: (0525) 240.451.

Skysales Ballooning Holidays Ltd: 249 Passage Road, Bristol BS10 7JB. Tel: (0272) 501196.

Instructional Flying

Adventure Balloons (see above for address).

The Capital Balloon Club (see above for address).

Balloon Holidays

Adventure Balloons. See above for address. Normandy, France.

Ballooning World. See above for address. Wye Valley, France.

Twickers World Travel. See River Rafting for address. Masi Mara (Kenya).

Reading

Aerostat The bi-monthly magazine of the BBAC (available to members only).

Ballooning: The Complete Guide to Riding the Winds by Dick Wirth and Jerry Young. Orbis Publishing Ltd, London. 1980.

Ballooning Handbook by Don Cameron. Pelham Books, 1980.

Sailing

Starting

Royal Yacht Association: RYA House, Romsey Road, Eastleigh, Hampshire S05 4YA. Tel: (0703) 629962.

Learning

Unless you have a friend or relation who has a boat and who is qualified to instruct, the simplest route to dinghy-skippering is through an RYA-recognised school, of which there are about 500 in the UK. All equipment is provided, and often accommodation too. Generally, estuaries and protected coastal waters offer a more exciting training ground than inland reservoirs.

The RYA runs a National Dinghy Certificate Scheme which has a set syllabus and five levels of qualification: Start Sailing (Level 1); Basic Skills (Level 2); Improving Techniques (Level 3); Racing Techniques (Level 4) and Advanced Skills (Level 5). The main areas covered are: rigging, ropework, launching and recovery, sailing techniques and manoeuvres, capsize recovery, racing, sailing theory and background, meteorology, clothing and equipment.

Below is a selection of RYA-recognised schools in the UK; all those listed run courses up to Level 3 and many can train to Level 4 and 5. Contact the RYA for additional addresses.

Achnamara Outdoor Centre: Achnamara House, by Lochgilphead, Argyll PA31 8PX, Scotland. Tel: (054685) 247. Loch Sween (sea loch).

Ardingly and Weir Wood Sailing School: Ardingly Reservoir, West Sussex RH17 6SQ. Tel: (0444) 892549. Ardingly Reservoir.

Banbury Sailing Centre: Greaves Pumping Station, North Circular Road, Ching-ford, London E4 8QB. Tel: (01) 531.1129. Banbury Reservoir.

Broxbourne Sailing School: St Julians Farmhouse, Roydon Road, Harlow, Essex CM19 5DT. Tel: (027) 979.3117. Inland lakes.

Calshot Activities Centre: Calshot Spit, Fawley, Southampton S04 1BR. Tel: (0703) 892077. The Solent and Southampton Water.

Club UK, Arctic Road: Cowes, Isle of Wight PO31 7PQ. Tel: (0983) 294941. Cowes, Isle of Wight, Solent.

Croft na Caber Watersports Centre: Kenmore, Loch Tay, Perthshire PH15 2HW. Tel: (08873) 236. Loch Tay (inland loch).

Cumbrae National Water Sports Centre: Inverclyde, Largs, Ayrshire KA30 8RW. Tel: (0475) 674666. Firth of Clyde.

Dover Water Sports Centre: 2 Cambridge Terrace, Dover CT16 1JU, Kent. Tel: (0304) 201348. Dover Harbour.

Emsworth Sailing School: The Port House, Port Solent, Portsmouth, Hampshire PO6 4TH. Tel: (0705) 210510. Chichester Harbour.

Exmouth Sailing School: 36 St Katherines Road, Exeter, Devon EX4 7JR. Tel: (0395) 265795. Exe estuary.

Fairlands Valley Park: Six Hills Way, Stevenage, Hertfordshire SG2 OBL. Tel: (0438) 353241. Fairlands Valley Park.

Glencoe Sailing School: Carnoch House, Carnoch Outdoor Centre, Glencoe, Argyll PA39 4HS. Tel: (08552) 350. Loch Leven (sea loch).

Grafham Water Residential Centre: Perry, Huntingdon, Cambridgeshire PE18 0BX. Tel: (0480) 810521. Grafham Water (reservoir).

Hatfield Marina Water Leisure Centre: Hatfield, Doncaster, South Yorkshire DN7 6EQ. Tel: (0302) 841572. Hatfield Marina.

Hillingdon Outdoor Activities Centre: Dews Farm, Harvil Road, Harefield, London UB9 6JN. Tel: (0895) 824171. River Colne Gravel Pit.

Instow Sailing Tuition Centre: Cross Trees, 9 Tavern Gardens, Weare Giffard, North Devon EX39 4QR. Tel: (02372) 21684. Taw Estuary, North Devon.

Island Cruising Club: 10 Island Street, Salcombe, South Devon TQ8 8DR. Tel: (054884) 3481. Salcombe Estuary (South Devon).

John Sharp Sailing (Fowey): Brockles Quay, St Veep, Lostwithiel, Cornwall PL22 0NT. Tel: (0208) 872470. Fowey estuary and Cornish coast.

Lakeside YMCA: YMCA National Centre, Lakeside, Ulverston, Cumbria LA12 8BD. Tel: (05395) 31758. Lake Windermere.

Laser School: Cornwall Activity Centre, Mylor Yacht Harbour, Falmouth, Cornwall TR11 5UF. Tel: (0326) 76191. Carrick Roads and Cornish coast (catamaran courses too).

Loch Insh Watersports: Insh Hall, Kincraig, Inverness-shire PH21 1NU. Tel: (05404) 272. Loch Insh (inland loch, near Aviemore).

Loch Rannoch Scottish School of Adventure: Loch Rannoch Estate, Kinloch Rannoch, Perthshire PH16 5PS. Tel: (08822) 201. Loch Rannoch (inland loch, near Glencoe).

Newton Ferrers Sailing School: Westerly, Yealm Road, Newton Ferrers, South Devon PL8 1BJ. Tel: (0752) 872375. River Yealm estuary and Wembury Bay (south Devon coast).

Oysterworld: 1 Wherry Lane, Wherry Quay, Ipswich, Suffolk IP4 1LG. Tel: (0473) 230109. Ipswich Wet Dock, Rivers Orwell, Stour and Deben.

Plas Menai National Watersports Centre: Llanfairisgaer, Caernarfon, Gwynedd LL55 1UE. Tel: (0248) 670964. Menai Straits.

Port Edgar Watersports Centre: Shore Road, South Queensferry, Edinburgh EH30 9SQ. Tel: (031) 331.3330. Firth of Forth.

Portsmouth Sailing and Outdoor Education Centre: Eastern Road, Portsmouth, Hampshire PO3 5LY. Tel: (0705) 663873. Langstone Harbour and Solent.

Pugneys Country Park: City of Wakefield MDC, Asdale Road, Wakefield. Tel: (0924) 386782. Pugneys Country Park.

Queen Mary Sailsports: Queen Mary Sailing Club, Ashford Road, Ashford, Middlesex TW15 1UA. Tel: (0784) 248881. Reservoir.

Rockley Point Sailing School: Rockley Sands, Hamworthy, Poole, Dorset. Tel: (0202) 677272. Poole Harbour.

Rother Valley Country Park: Mansfield Road, Wales Bar, Sheffield S31 8PE. Tel: (0742) 471453. Rother Valley Country Park.

Royal Victoria Dock Project: Victoria Docks, South Side, Off Silvertown Way, London E16 2BE. Tel: (01) 511.2326. Royal Victoria Docks.

Rutland Sailing School: Rutland Sailing Club, Gibbett Lane, Edith Weston, Oakham, Rutland LE15 8HJ. Tel: (0778) 343625. Rutland Water.

South Eastern Sailing Ltd: The Quay, Burnham on Crouch, Essex CM0 8AS. Tel: (0621) 782331. River Crouch.

Southmere Boating & Canoeing Centre: 63 Binsey Walk, Thamesmead, London SE2 9TU. Tel: (01) 310.2452. Southmere Lake.

Stoneywood Sailing School: 105 Stoneywood Road, Bucksburn, Aberdeen AB2 9HU. Tel: (0224) 712462. Loch of Skene (inland loch) and Findhorn (Moray Firth).

Surface Watersports: Ferry Meadows Watersports Centre, Ham Lane, Orton Waterville, Peterborough PE2 0UU. Tel: (0733) 234418. Ferry Meadows (Nene Park, near Peterborough) and Rutland Water.

Swanage Sailing School: 12 Grosvenor Road, Swanage, Dorset BH19 2DD. Tel: (0929) 423158. Swanage and Poole.

Tighnabruaich Sailing School: Tighnabruaich, Argyll PA21 2BD. Tel: (0700) 811396. Kyles of Bute.

Westminster Boating Base: 136 Grosvenor Road, London SW1V 3JY. Tel: (01) 821.7389. River Thames.

Wimbledon Park Sailing Centre: Home Park Road, London SW19 7HX. Tel: (01) 947.4894. Wimbledon Park Lake.

Learning to Sail Dinghies Abroad (not necessarily RYA courses)

Falcon Sailing: 33 Notting Hill Gate, London NW11 3JQ. Tel: (01) 727.0232. Paxos and Levkas, Ionian Sea (Greece), Bodrum (Turkey).

Greek Islands Sailing Club: 66 High Street, Walton on Thames, Surrey KT12 1BU. Tel: (0932) 220416. Paxos (Greece).

Minorca Sailing Holidays Ltd: 265 Green Lanes, Palmers Green, London N13 4XE.

Tel: (01) 886.7193. Fornells Bay, Minorca (Mediterranean).

Yacht Cruising Association: The Port House, Port Solent, Portsmouth, Hampshire PO6 4TH. Tel: (0705) 219844, Mediterranean.

Reading

The Pocket Oxford Guide to Sailing Terms (in waterproof cover) edited by Ian Dear and Peter Kemp. Oxford University Press. 1987.

Sailing: A Beginner's Manual by John Driscoll. Fernhurst.

Sea Stories by Joseph Conrad (a compilation), Grafton Books, London, 1986.

This is Sailing by Richard Creagh-Osborne, Fontana.

The RYA publish 3 hardbacks *(Beginners, Advanced* and *Racing)* to accompany their courses.

Cattle Driving

Believe it or not, in the UK there is no governing body of cattle-driving clubs. In fact there are no cattle-driving clubs. It is quite possible that there are not any practising cattle-drivers. If you want to do it, you have to go to America.

The qualifications required for cattle-driving (at participant rather than wrangler level) are no more than an ability to ride a horse safely over mixed terrain. The quarter-horses that are used on most ranches are agile and adaptable. The saddles are wide and padded and have horns; the stirrups are broader and deeper than those used in Britain. Wranglers will make sure that you are not saddled with a horse that is beyond your ability to handle, and rides are always graded so that you are not pushed into all-day epics right from your first morning. On all-day rides, packed lunches or picnics are provided, and there are often barbecues and dancing in the evenings.

If you want to join in with a genuine cattle round-up you have to coincide your trip with the farming programme of the ranch. There are generally only two round-ups a year on any ranch, each one lasting maybe a week.

The main UK operator for cattle driving holidays in the USA is: American Round-up: 1 The Hawthorns, Box LA, Hemel Hempstead, Hertfordshire, HP3 0AZ. Tel: (0442) 214621. Arizona, Colorado, Wyoming, Montana, Texas, Michigan.

Reading

Families That Take in Friends; An Informal History of Dude Ranching, by Joel H. Bernstein. Stoneydale Press Publishing Company, Stevensville, Montana. 1982.

Microlighting

British Microlight Aircraft Association: Bullring, Deddington, Oxford 0X5 4TT. Tel: (0869) 38888.

Learning

The first step is to take an 'air experience' flight with a qualified instructor. If you are still keen and would like to qualify to be a pilot, sign on for either a part time course, which takes several weeks, or the more intensive full-time course, most of which (weather permitting) can be compressed into a fortnight.

The basic qualification is the PPL (A) Group D and the curriculum includes aviation law, theory of flight, navigation, meteorology, and technical knowledge of your aircraft. The PPL (A) Group D has two levels: for the 'restricted' licence you need to have completed a total of 15 hours flying, 7 of them solo, and for the 'unrestricted' licence you need a total of 25 hours flying, 10 of them solo. You also need to have completed 5 hours of navigation instruction and 2 solo cross-country flights. On most courses you will be able to fly every day (weather permitting).

With an unrestricted licence you can either fly solo or with a non-paying passenger.

Either join one of the many microlight clubs (address list available from the BMAA) throughout the country, or take a course through one of the clubs and commercial concerns which instructs. A selection is listed below.

Aerolite Ltd: Long Marston Airfield, Stratford-upon-Avon, Warwickshire CV37 8RT. Tel: (0789) 299229. Long Marston Airfield.

Airborne Aviation: 3 Woodlinken Close, Verwood, Wimborne, Dorset BH21 6BP. Tel: (0202) 822486. Popham Airfield.

Air School Instruction: 2 King Edward Road, Chatteris, Cambridgeshire PE16 6NG. Tel: (03543) 5542. Lower Mt Pleasant Farm.

Baileys Yorkshire Microlight Centre: Woodall, 16 Gateland Drive, Shadwell, Leeds, West Yorkshire LS17 8HU. Tel: (0532) 738128. Rufforth Airfield.

Cambridge Microlight Club: 114 High Street, Sutton, Ely, Cambridgeshire CB6 2NW. Tel: (0487) 842360. Sutton Meadows airfield.

David Clarke Microlight Aircraft: NNAC RAF Swanton Morley, East Dereham, Norfolk NR20 4LW. Tel: (036283) 405. RAF Swanton Morley.

Devon and Somerset Microlight Flying Club: Barn Cottage, Westford, Wellington, Somerset. Tel: (082347) 6813. Smeathorpe Airfield.

Essex Airsports: 10 Dukes Avenue, Grays, Essex, RM17 5AQ. Tel: (0375) 371172. Damyns Hall Farm.

Lorton Aero Club: Whitestones, Under Skiddaw, Keswick, Cumbria CA12 4QD. Tel: (0596) 72762. Great Orton Airfield.

Medway Microlights: The Paddock, Burrows Lane, Middle Stoke, Rochester, Kent ME3 9RN. Tel: (0634) 270780. Middlestoke Strips.

Meridian Microlights Centre: 51 Wold Road, Pocklington, East Yorkshire. Tel: (0759) 304337.

Microflight: Shobdon Airfield, Hereford HR6 9NR. Tel: (056881) 8864. Shobdon Airfield.

The Microlight School: Enstone Airfield, Church Enstone, Oxford OX7 4NP. Tel: (060872) 8741. Enstone Airfield.

Midland Ultralights Ltd: 2 Tudor Cottage, North Kilworth, Lutterworth, Leicestershire LE7 6JB. Tel: (0858) 880627. Nazeby.

Moorland Flying Club: Davidstow Aerodrome, Davidstow, Near Camelford, Cornwall PL32 9YF. Tel: (08406) 517. Davidstow Aerodrome.

Northern Microlight School: 89a Croston Road, Garstang, Near Preston, Lancashire PR3 1HQ. Tel: (09952) 4694. Great Michael's Strip, Garstang.

Northwest Microflight Club: 9 Cannon Street, Eccles, Manchester M30 0FT. Tel: (061) 431 3407.

Pegasus Flight Training: Old Warden Aerodrome, Biggleswade, Bedfordshire SG18 9ER. Tel: (0048784) 2360. Old Warden Aerodrome.

Skyrider Aviation Ltd: Coventry Airport, Baginton, Coventry, Warwickshire CV8 3AZ. Tel: (0203) 307030.

South East Microlight Aircraft Centre: Gobery Hill Cottage, Sandwich Hill, Wingham, near Canterbury, Kent CT3 1JJ. Tel: (0227) 720400.

Southwest Airsports: Barton, Bolventor, Launceston, Cornwall PL15 7TZ. Tel: (056686) 514/ (0836) 760653. Woodlands Farm strip, near Bodmin.

Sussex Microlight Club: 16 Longcopse Lane, Emsworth, Emsworth, Hampshire PO10 7UL. Tel: (0243) 377356. Thorney Island.

Three Counties Microlight School: Hinton-in-the-Hedges Aerodrome, Steane, Brackley, Northamptonshire NN13 5NS. Tel: (0295) 811939.

The Wealden Microlight Club: The Mews, Shirley Hall, Langton Green, Kent TN3 0RQ. Tel: (089286) 3578.

Yorkshire Microlight Aircraft Club: 28 Carr Lane, Low Moor, Bradford, West Yorkshire BD12 0QS. Tel: (0274) 606193. Crossland Moor, Huddersfield.

Reading

Flightline Magazine. For address see BMAA. Official journal of the BMAA.
Travels with Pegasus by Christina Dodwell. Hodder & Stoughton, London, 1989.
The Microlight Pilot's Handbook by Brian Cosgrove, Airlife, Shrewsbury, 1986.

Sub-Aqua Diving

Starting

British Sub-Aqua Club: 16 Upper Woburn Place, London WC1H 0QW. Tel: (01) 387.9302.

Learning

It's essential to pass successfully through a sub-aqua course before diving independently. Sports divers have two main governing bodies: BSAC (British Sub-Aqua Club) and PADI (Professional Association of Diving Instructors).

BSAC have two basic qualifications: if you take the courses at a commercial agency, the Novice Diver course takes a total of about 10 hours tuition, and the Sports Diver course takes about 5 days full-time. Alternatively, these courses can be taken through one of BSAC's local clubs, which takes 3 to 6 months. With the Sports Diver qualification you can dive anywhere in the world with people of the equivalent (or higher) qualification. BSAC's Sports Diver course can be taken abroad (a list of addresses is available from BSAC head office). For the addresses of BSAC's local clubs, contact BSAC head office at the above address; the BSAC

commercial schools in the UK are listed below.

The basic PADI course is the 'Open Water Diver', which can be done in one week full time.

Schools Offering BSAC Courses

Andark Diving: 256 Bridge Road, Lower Swanwick, Southampton, Hampshire SO3 7FL. Tel: (04895) 81755.

Anglesey Diving Centre: Sea & Surf Centre, Trearddur Bay, Anglesey LL65 2UO. Tel: (007) 861122/861053.

Aquanautica: 26 Blackcap Close, Ayton, Washington, Tyne & Wear NE38 0DG. Tel: (091) 4177196.

Aquasport International: 80 Alcester Road, Moseley, Birmingham B13 8BB. Tel: (021) 449 4148.

Aquatic Leisure Pursuits: Maenporth Beach, Maenporth, near Falmouth, Cornwall TR11 5HN. Tel: (0326) 250852.

Aquaticus Diving School: 101 Huddersfield Road, Oldham, Lancashire OL1 3NQ. Tel: (061) 655 1370.

Barracuda Sports & Diving Centre: Unit 31, London Road Industrial Estate, London Road, Grantham, Lincolnshire NG31 1HP. Tel: (0476) 79200.

Bristol Diving School: 52 Old Market Street, Bristol BS2 0ER. Tel: (0272) 299544.

Current State Diving: 8 Kellaway Avenue, Redland, Bristol BS6 7XR. Tel: (0272) 247030.

Dive & Ski Sports: 3-5 Francis Street, St. Heller, Jersey, Channel Islands, Tel: Jersey 36209.

Diving and Marine Services (IOW): 75 Staplers Road, Newport, Isle of Wight P030 2DG. Tel: (0983) 525169.

Comdean Scuba Training Centre: 90 Waterfall Lane, Old Hill, Warley, West Midlands B64 6RJ. Tel: (021) 559 3659/ 8659.

The Diver Training College: Malt Kiln Lane, Appleton Roebuck, York, North Yorkshire YO5 7DT. Tel: (0904) 84424.

Diver Training School: The Quayside, Exmouth, Devon EX8 1ER. Tel: (0395) 266300.

Durrington Marine Centre: 5a Lakeside Business Park, Pinfold Road, Thurmaston, Leicester LE4 8AS. Tel: (0533) 6402222.

Fort Bovisand Underwater Centre: Fort Bovisand, Plymouth PL9 0AB. Tel: (0752) 408021.

Gildenburgh Water: Eastrea Road, Whittlesey, Peterborough PE7 2AR. Tel: (0733) 202867.

Guernsey School of Diving: Les Quatre Vents, Rue des Monts, Delancey, St Sampson, Guernsey, Channel Islands. Tel: (0481) 47664/49524.

Hull Dive Centre: Unit 9, Factory Estate, English Street, Hull HU3 2BE. Tel: (0482) 25772.

Isles of Scilly Diving School: Highertown, St Martins, Isles of Scilly TR25 0QL. Tel: (0720) 22848.

Just Divin': 20 Westfield Avenue, Hooe, Plymouth, Devon P19 9PF. Tel: (0752) 408200.

London Underwater Centre: 13 Glendower Road, London SW14 8NY. Tel: (01) 876 0735.

Mermaid Diving Centre: 152 Pomeroy Street, London SE14 5BT. Tel: (01) 708 1945.

The Poole Dive Centre: Sunseeker International Marina, West Quay Road, Poole, Dorset BH15 1HX. Tel: (0202) 677427.

Robin Hood Dive School: 152 Leeds Road, Heckmondwike, West Yorkshire WF16 9BJ. Tel: (0924) 443843.

Scuba Dive Instruction: Adonis Court, Northfield Avenue, Ealing, London W13 9RJ. Tel: (01) 840 7772.

Scuba-Tech Dive School: 8 Owen Road, Skerton, Lancaster LA1 2AR. Tel: (0524) 381831.

Scuba Techniques: Elmsworth Lane, Porchfield, Isle of Wight P030 4LR. Tel: (0983) 523655.

Scuba Training Ltd: 44 Lansdowne Crescent, London W11 2NN. Tel: (01) 221.8272.

Scuba World Diver Training: Piccadilly Service Station, Chelston, Wellington, Somerset TA21 9HY. Tel: (0823) 4760085.

Shadwell Basin Project: Shadwell Pierhead, 1 Glamis Road, London E1 9TD. Tel: (01) 481.4210. Shadwell Basin.

Slater's Aqua Sports: 111 Black Bull Lane, Fulwood, Preston, Lancashire PR2 3PA. Tel: (0772) 715281.

Solent Sub Aqua School of Diving: Solent & Wight Diving Services, Duver Road, Seaview, Isle of Wight PO34 5AJ. Tel: (0983) 612442.

South East Diving Centre: 140 Richmond Road, Gillingham, Kent ME7 1LS. Tel: (0634) 579624.

Southern Sports Lodge: 4 Athol Street, Port of Mary, Isle of Man. Tel: (064) 832943.

Stoney Cove Diver Training Ltd: Stoney Cove, Stoney Stanton, Leicestershire LE9 6DW. Tel: (0455) 272768.

Sub Action: 90 Harbut Road, London SW11 2RE. Tel: (01) 585.2589.

Treasure Island Diving School: The Promenade, Aberavon, Port Talbot, West Glamorgan SA12 6QR. Tel: (0639) 884108.

Truro Diving Services: 38 Lemon Street, Truro, Cornwall TR1 2NS. Tel: (0872) 77652.

The Watersports Centre: All Seasons House, Park Road, Oldham, Lancashire OL8 1DB. Tel: (061) 626 0274.

Lewis Aqua Sports: 64 Commercial Road, Port Talbot, West Glamorgan SA13 1LG. Tel: (0693) 882312.

Swindon Dive School: 51 Devizes Road, Old Town, Swindon, Wiltshire SN1 4BJ. Tel: (0793) 481804.

Waterways Diving Centre: South Pier, Waterways, Ellesmere Port, South Wirral, Cheshire L65 4EF. Tel: (051) 356 4286.

West Wales Diving School: Hasguard Cross, Haverfordwest, Dyfed SA62 3SJ. Tel: (0437) 781457.

Schools Offering PADI Courses

Andark Diver Training. Tel: (042) 121 5558. (See Sub Aqua for address.)

Aqua Sport International: see above for address.

Chester School of Diving: Dee Sports, 67 Brook Street, Chester, Cheshire. Tel: (0244) 314204.

Divers Down: The Pier, The High Street, Swanage, Dorset BH19 2AN. Tel: (0929) 423565.

Diving Leisure: The Tropicana Pool, Rockley Sands Holiday Estate, Hanworthy, Poole, Dorset BH15 4LZ. Tel: (0202) 680898.

Diver Training School: see above for address.

Fort Bovisand Underwater Centre: see above for address.

London Underwater Centre: see above for address.

Treasure Island Diving Services: see above for address.

Truro Diving Services: see above for address.

Watersports: First Tower, St Helier, Jersey. Tel: (0534) 32813.

Diving Holidays (courses available at some locations)

Twickers World Travel: see above for address. Ireland, Malta, Red Sea, Cayman Islands, (Bonaire) Caribbean, Thailand, Maldives, Galapagos, Truk (West Pacific), Comores (Mozambique Channel).

Reading

Skin Diver Magazine, Petersen Publishing Company, 8490 Sunset Boulevard, Los Angeles, California 90069. Tel: (213) 854.2470. US monthly magazine: available in the UK.

Subaqua Scene Magazine, Skyline Publications, Sunseeker House, West Quay Road, Poole, Dorset BH15 1JF. Tel: (0202) 665616. Monthly magazine. Official magazine of the Sub Aqua Association.

The Silent World by Jacques Cousteau. Elm Tree Books, London. 1988 (First published 1953).

Underwater Diving: Basic Techniques by Peter Dick and David Sisman. Pelham Books, London. 1986.

The Great Diving Adventure by Horace Dobbs, Oxford Illustrated Press, Oxford 1986.

Sport Diving: The British Sub Aqua Club Diving Manual multiple contributors. Stanley Paul 1987 (First published 1959).

Classic Dives of the World by Horace Dobbs. Oxford Illustrated Press, Oxford.

Caving

Starting

National Caving Association, General Secretary, White Lion House, Ynys Uchaf, Ystradgynlais, Swansea SA9 1RW. Tel: (0639) 849519, or Information Secretary: 3 Vallertort Road, Stoke, Plymouth PL1 5PH.

Learning

Either join one of the 400 or so local caving clubs which are affiliated to the NCA (contact the NCA to find which club is operating in the areas in which you are interested) or take a paid holiday/course with one of the commercial concerns listed below. Many local clubs run training courses. Some local education authorities run caving courses; contact the National Caving Association at White Hall Centre, Long Hill, Buxton, Derbyshire SK17 6SX (Tel: 0298 23260).

The main caving areas in Britain are the northern Pennines, Derbyshire Peak District, South Wales and the Mendip Hills (Somerset). Caves are also scattered through South Devon, North Wales, Cumbria (Furness area) and in north-west Scotland.

Adventure Balloons: See Ballooning for address. Cheddar Gorge (Somerset).

Dartmoor Expedition Centre: Rowden, Widecombe in the Moor, Newton Abbot, Devon TQ13 7TX. Tel: (036 42) 249. Buckfastleigh, Ashburton (Devon).

Freetime Activities: East Mostards, Garsdale, Sedburgh, Cumbria LA10 5NT. Tel: (05396) 20828. Yorkshire Dales.

Seal Guides: Rock Lea Activity Centre, Station Road, Hathersage, Peak National Park, Derbyshire S30 1DD. Tel: (0433) 50345. Peak District.

Reading

Caving Practice & Equipment ed: David Judson, David & Charles, Newton Abbot, Devon. 1984.

The Darkness Beckons: The History and Development of Cave Diving by Martyn Farr, Diadem Books (Hodder & (Stoughton), London, 1989 (first published 1980).

The Great Caving Adventure by Martyn Farr. Oxford Illustrated Press, Oxford. 1984.

Underground Britain: A Guide to the Wild Caves and Show Caves of England, Scotland & Wales by Bruce Bedford. Willow Books, Collins, London. 1985.

Horse Riding

Starting

British Horse Society. British Equestrian Centre, Stoneleigh, Kenilworth, Warwickshire CV8 2LR. Tel: (0203) 696697.

Learning

The BHS 'Horse Knowledge and Riding Examination' is taken in three stages, after the initial Road Safety Test. By the end of Stage III you will have covered horse physiology and health, daily routines, watering and feeding, saddlery, shoeing, clipping and trimming and a range of riding techniques from trotting to jumping.

The BHS annually-revised guide to over 600 approved riding schools in the UK is called *Where to Ride* and is available in large bookshops, or direct from the BHA.

Trail-riding for Experienced Riders

Arctic Experience: 29 Nork Way, Banstead, Surrey SM17 1PB. Tel: (0737) 362321. Iceland, Canada.

Ferniehirst Mill: Jedburgh, Roxburghshire TD8 6PQ. Tel: (0835) 63279. Cheviot Hills.

Flanders Farm Riding Centre: Silver Street, Hordle, Lymington, Hampshire SO4 6FD. Tel: (0590) 682207.

Kidlandlee Trail Riding: Kidlandlee, Harbottle, Morpeth, Northumberland NE65 7DA. Tel: (0669) 50254. Cheviot Hills.

Loch Ness Log Cabins: Drummond Farm, Dores, Inverness-shire IV1 2TX. Tel: (046 375) 251. Loch Ness.

North Wheddon Farm Riding Holidays: Wheddon Cross, Minehead, Somerset TA24 7EX. Tel: (064 384) 224. Exmoor.

Northumbria Horse Holidays: East Castle, Annfield Plain, Stanley, Co. Durham. Tel: (0207) 235354/230555. Northumbria.

Twickers World Travel: as for Arctic Experience.

Reading

Horse Keeper's Encyclopaedia by H.W. Walter, Eliot Right Way Books, Surrey, 1988 (first edition 1950).

Tschiffely's Ride (10,000 miles in the saddle through the Americas from Argentina to Washington) by A.F. Tschiffely. Hodder and Stoughton, London. 1952.

Saddletramp: from Ottoman Hills to Offa's Dyke by Jeremy James. Pelham Books. 1989.

Viewing

Horse Thief (film), directed by Tian Zhuangzhuang, set in Tibet in 1923.

Rock Climbing

Starting

British Mountaineering Council: Crawford House, Precinct Centre, Booth Street East, Manchester M13 9RZ. Tel: (061) 273.5835.

Learning

The most enjoyable route into rock climbing is through a friend who is already experienced enough to lead you safely up the beginning routes. It's a bug that, once caught, forces a steep and cerebral learning curve. There are a multitude of climbing clubs through the land which always encourage newcomers as well as providing regular 'meets' at which you can team up with other climbers. It is a sociable sport. The BMC can provide a list of UK clubs.

There are two types of climbing instructor in the UK: those who hold the Mountain Instructor's Certificate (MIC)

and those who have qualified to belong to the prestigious British Association of Mountain Guides (BAMG). The BAMG is recognised worldwide. Both qualifications are administered by the BMC. Members of the BAMG choose to instruct or lead in some or all of the following: rock climbing, snow and ice climbing, expeditions, ski mountaineering, wilderness skiing and off-piste skiing. Guides can be hired at a fixed rate by the day (rates are higher for the Alps than for the UK).

An address list of current British guides is available from the BMC.

Below is a selection of activity centres and climbing schools which offer rock-climbing instruction.

BMC see above.

Bowles Outdoor Centre: Eridge Green, Tunbridge Wells, Kent TN3 9LW. Tel: (0892) 665665. Bowles Rocks.

Brede Arkless: Buarth, Deiniolen, Gwynedd LL55 3NA. Tel: (0286) 870518. (Includes courses for women run by women).

Calshot Activities Centre: Calshot Spit, Fawley, near Southampton SO4 1BR. Tel: (0703) 892077/891380. Swanage cliffs, Dorset coast.

Cuillin Guides: Stac Lee, Glenbrittle, Isle of Skye IV47 8TA. Tel: (047 842) 289. Cuillin Mountains.

Dartmoor Expedition Centre: See Caving.

Geoff Arkless Mountaineering: Riverside Restaurant, Betwys y Coed, Gwynedd, Wales. Tel: (06902) 650.

Alan Kimber, Professional Mountaineering Services: 15 Annat View, Corpach, Fort William, Inverness-shire PH33 7BR. Tel: (03977) 726. Scotland. Alps.

Mountain Adventure Guides: Stuart Miller, Eel Crag, Melbecks, Braithwaite, Keswick, Cumbria CA12 5TL. Tel: (0596) 82517. Alps, Nepal.

Mountaincraft: Glenfinnan, Fort William, Scotland PH37 4LT. Tel: (039 783) 213. Fort William and Glenfinnan area.

Nevis Guides: Bohuntin, Roy Bridge, Inverness-shire PH31 4AH. Tel: (039781) 356. Scottish Highlands.

Roger Payne: 24 Aylmer Road, London W12 9LQ. Tel: (01) 749.5544.

Plas y Brenin, The National Centre for Mountain Activities: Capel Curig, Gwynedd LL24 0ET. Tel: (069 04) 280. Snowdonia.

Polaris Mountaineering: The Old Telegraph, Llaneilian, Amlwch, Gwynedd LL68 9NN. Tel: (0407) 830069. Snowdonia.

Rowland Edwards: Compass West, International School of Rock Climbing, Sennen, Cornwall TR19 7AR. Tel: (0736) 871447.

Seal Guides: see Caving for address.

Solid Summit: Admin: Oaklands Guest House, Llangollen Road, Trevor, Llangollen, Clwyd LL20 7TG. Tel: (0978) 820152. Bookings: Kirby Avenue, Prestatyn, Clwyd LL19 9HR. Snowdonia, Lake District, Scotland.

Association for Adventure Sports: Tiglin Adventure Centre, Ashford, County Wicklow, Ireland. Tel: 010 35 3404 40169.

Learning to Climb Abroad

Alpine Guides: Bron Fuches, Dinorwic, Caernarfon, Gwynedd LL55 3ET. Tel: (0286) 870215. Alps.

Austrian Alpine Club: 13 Longcroft House, Fretherne Road, Welwyn Garden City, Hertfordshire AL8 6PQ. Correspondence: PO Box 43, Welwyn Garden City, Hertfordshire AL8 6PQ. Tel: (0707) 324835, Austrian Alps.

Brian Hall, Mountain Experience: The Cottage, Whitehough Head, Stockport. Tel: (0663) 42114. French Alps.

International School of Mountaineering: Club Vagabond, 1854 Leysin, Switzerland. Tel: (01041) 25 34 13 21. Alps.

Spanish Rock: Waymann and Barnicott, Bryn Eryr, Bryn Refail, Caernarfon, Gwynedd. Tel: (0286) 870330/870742. Spanish sierras.

Climbing Walls (London)

Brunel University: Kingston Lane, Uxbridge, London UB8 3PH. Tel: (0895) 52361.

Jubilee Hall: 30 The Piazza, Covent Garden, London WC2E 8BE. Tel: (01) 836.4835.

North London Reserve Commando: Cordova Road, Mile End Park, Bow, London E3 5BE. Tel: (01) 980.0289.

Sobell Centre: Hornsey Road, Finsbury Park, London N7 7NY. Tel: (01) 609.2166. A list of about 150 climbing walls is available from the B.M.C.

Reading

Climber and Hill Walker magazine. Holmes McDougall Ltd, The Plaza Tower, East Kilbride, Glasgow G74 1LW. Tel: (03552) 46444.

High Magazine, Springfield House, The Parade, Oadby, Leicester LE2 5BF. Tel: (0533) 716111 (monthly).

Feeding the Rat: Profile of a Climber by Al Alvarez, Bloomsbury, London, 1988. Flamingo p/b, London, 1989.

The Games Climbers Play: A Selection of 100 Mountaineering Articles edited by Ken Wilson. Diadem Books, London. 1978.

I Chose to Climb by Chris Bonington. Victor Gollancz, London, 1966.

On and Off the Rocks by Jim Perrin. Victor Gollancz, London, 1986. Paperback 1988.

Nordic Skiing

Starting

British Mountaineering Council see above for address.

The Ski Club of Great Britain: 118 Eaton Square, London SW1 W 9AF. Tel: (01) 245.1033.

Learning

The techniques used in nordic skiing are best learnt from an expert, particularly the tricky telemark turn.

The Guides Carnet of the British Association of Mountain Guides is the main British qualification a guide can obtain (see 'Rock Climbing'). It does not however entitle you to lead ski-touring trips.

Highland Adventure Nordic Ski School: Knockshannoch Lodge, Glenisla, by Alyth, Perthshire PH11 8PE. Tel: (057 582) 238. Glenisla and Glenshee.

Highland Guides: Nordic Ski Centre, Rothiemurchus, Aviemore, Inverness-shire PH22 1QH. Tel: (0479) 810729. Cairngorms, Strath Spey.

Learning Abroad

Ramblers Holidays: Box 43, Welwyn Garden City, Hertfordshire AL8 6PQ. Tel: (0707) 331133. Austria, France and Switzerland.

Ski Club of Great Britain: address above. Switzerland, France, Austria, Pakistan . . . worldwide.

Reading

Mountain Skiing by Vic Bein. The Mountaineers, Seattle. 1982.

Woodlore

There is no governing body for woodlore; it is one of the most individualistic activities ever invented. Woodlore is best learnt first hand from an expert—if you can find a genuine one—and from books and personal

experience. Note that woodlore has been partly re-interpreted as 'Survival', so that many of the techniques practiced by the north American Indians and encouraged by Kephart, Thompson Seton, Baden-Powell *et al* are now taught by some of the new-generation survival schools.

The addresses below are mainly those of schools teaching survival skills rather than woodlore specifically.

Breakaway Survival School: Mick Tyler, 17 Hugh Thomas Avenue, Holmer, Hereford HR4 9RB. Tel: (0432) 267097.

Dartmoor Survival and Safety School: Freepost, Plymouth PL1 1BR Tel: (0752) 605380.

EAST (Executive and Staff Training): 4 Mornington Terrace, Harrogate HG1 5DH. Tel: (0423) 531083. UK.

Sporting Travel Services: See River Rafting. Sweden.

WEST. Wilderness Expeditions and Skills Training: Arrina, Shieldaig, Ross-shire IV54 8XU. Tel: (05205) 213. Scotland.

Reading

Camping and Woodcraft, A Handbook for Vacation Campers and Travellers in the Wilderness by Horace Kephart. The Macmillan Company, New York. 1931.

Woodcraft by Ernest Thompson Seton. 1910.

Woodcraft and Camping by Bernard S. Mason. Dover Books, New York, 1974 (originally published by A S Barnes & Co, New York, in 1939).

The Survival Handbook by Raymond Mears, Oxford Illustrated Press, Oxford 1989.

White water Canoeing

Starting

British Canoe Union: Mapperley Hall, Lucknow Avenue, Nottingham NG3 5FA. Tel: (0602) 691944.

Learning

You should take instruction from a qualified instructor before venturing onto any white water. The BCU run a number of kayak proficiency tests which take the beginner from elementary aspects of canoe control through to completing the eskimo roll. Either join one of the BCU's Members' affiliated clubs (a full list of addresses are in the BCU's Members' Year Book) or take a course at a commercially-run centre (see below).

Abernethy Outdoor Centre: Nethy Bridge, Inverness-shire PH25 3ED. Tel: (047 982) 279. Loch Morlich and the River Spey.

Association for Adventure Sports: Tiglin Adventure Centre. See above for address. Lake and rivers near Dublin.

Bowles Outdoor Centre: see above for address. Swimming pool. River Medway and Sussex coast.

Current Trends Canoe School: Adbolton Lane, West Bridgeford, Nottingham NG2 5AS. Tel: (0602) 818844. Nottingham, Wales, Scotland, Scandinavia, Continent.

Loch Insh Watersports Centre: Insh Hall, Kincraig, Invernessshire PH21 1NG. Tel: (054 04) 272. River Spey.

Sporting Travel Services: see River Rafting for address. River Are (Sweden), Rivers Trisuli, Tamba Kosi (Nepal). Experienced canoeists only.

Artificial Slalom Course

Holme Pierrepont National Watersports Centre: Adbolton Lane, Holme Pierrepont, Nottingham. Tel: (0602) 821212.

Abroad

Sporting Travel Services: 9 Teasdale Close, Royston, Hertfordshire SG8 5TD. Tel: (0763) 242867. Nepal.

Reading

Canoeist magazine: 4 Sinodun Row, Appleford, Oxfordshire, OX14 4PE. Monthly.

Canoeing Down Everest by Mike Jones. Hodder & Stoughton, London. 1979.

Canoeing and Kayaking by Gordon Richards. B.T. Batsford. London. 1981.

Start Canoeing by Anne Williams and Debbie Piercey. Stanley Paul, London. 1980.

White Water Canoeing by Ray Rowe. Salamander Books, London. 1988.

Raging Rivers Stormy Seas by Terry Storry. Oxford Illustrated Press, 1989.

Winter Mountaineering

British Mountaineering Council (see Rock Climbing).

Learning

Mountaineers are more individualistic than most; few belong to clubs, or feel a need to, and most learn the ropes by going to the hills with friends whose experience they know and trust.

Winter mountaineering is not safe unless you are a confident rock, snow and ice climber and can move happily over mixed ground. Equally important, you must understand the fundamentals of survival in sub-zero conditions. See Rock Climbing for details of qualifications and courses available through the BMC. The BMC can also provide a list of qualified winter mountaineering guides who operate in the UK and Europe.

The organisations below run courses and holidays.

Alpine guides: See Rock Climbing. Alps.

Association for Adventure Sports: Tiglin Adventure Centre. See above for address. Ben Nevis, Glencoe, and the Alps.

BMC: See above for address.

Cuillin Guides: see Rock Climbing. Cuillin Mountains. Isle of Skye and the Alps.

Mal Duff: 20 Mid Causeway, Culross, Fife KY12 8HS. Tel: (0383) 880432.

ExplorAsia: See above for address. Himalayas.

Brian Hall: See Rock Climbing. French Alps.

International School of Mountaineering: See Rock Climbing for address. Alps.

Alan Kimber: See Rock Climbing.

Stuart Miller: See Rock Climbing for address.

Martin Moran: Park Cottage, Achintee, Strathcarron. Ross-shire IV54 8YX. Tel: (052 02) 361.

Mountain Craft: See Rock Climbing for address. Glenfinnan and Fort William.

Nevis Guides: See Rock Climbing for address.

Roger Payne: See Rock Climbing for address.

Solid Summit: See above for address. Snowdonia and Scottish Highlands.

Travellers Waterside: Kent's View, Kendal, Cumbria LA9 4HE. Tel: (0539) 28334. Himalayas.

Reading

Mountaincraft and Leadership (A Hand book for Mountaineers and Hillwalking Leaders in the British Isles) by Eric Langmuir. The Scottish Sports Council/The Mountainwalking Leader Training Board, 1984.

Everest The Hard Way by Chris Bonington. Hodder & Stoughton, London, 1976.

Everest: Kangchung Face by Stephen Venables, Hodder & Stoughton, 1989.

Scotland's Winter Mountains: The Challenge and the Skills by Martin Moran. David & Charles. London. 1988.

One Man's Mountains (Essays and Verses) by Tom Patey. Victor Gollancz, London. 1987 (first published 1971).

Touching the Void by Joe Simpson. Jonathan Cape. 1988.

Paragliding

Starting

British Association of Paragliding Clubs, 18 Talbot Lane, Leicester LE1 4LR. Tel: (0533) 513007.

Fédération Aéronautique Internationale (F.A.I.), 6 rue Galilée, 75782 Paris, Cedex 16, France. Tel: 4720-91-85 or 4720-01-64; telex: AEROFRA 611580F. The F.A.I. promotes paragliding as a sport, and has established the rules for national and world records, and medals for world championships.

Learning

There are two grades of basic paragliding qualification. The F1 course takes about 4 days of intensive instruction, by which time the budding pilot should be able to launch the canopy, control the canopy in the air, and land safely. Pilots who only hold an F1 certificate should only fly under supervision of F2 pilots. B.A.P.C. insurance for F1 pilots is only valid if they are flying under the supervision of F2 pilots.

The F2 qualification involves completing a number of tasks (including 1 1/4 hours of soaring), some of which have to be done under the eye of an instructor; others can be supervised by an F2 pilot. There is also a written exam. By flying regularly, it is possible to qualify for the F2 in about 6 months. F2 pilots are covered by B.A.P.C. membership insurance and need not be supervised.

The length of time needed to qualify for both F1 and F2 will naturally depend on weather conditions; it is best not to assume that by setting aside four days for an F1 that you will automatically qualify *after* four days. Schools will not instruct pupils under 16 years old. Schools will provide the canopy, harness and helmet; generally, all you need are ankle boots (which should have lace holes not hooks—which can catch in the rigging), strong trousers and weather clothing.

Five of the most popular areas for paragliding in the UK are: Mam Tor area

(Pennines), Devil's Dyke (Brighton), South Wales (Hay Bluff and Rhosili), the Lake District and Scotland.

Before flying abroad, paraglider pilots should contact the appropriate national body:

American Paragliding Association (A.P.A.), PO Box 177, Riverton, UT84065, USA. Tel: 801 254 7455.

F.F.V.O. 54 bis rue de la Buffa, 0600 Nice, France. Tel: 93886289.

S.H.V., Zurcherstrasse 47, 8620 Wetzikon, Switzerland. Tel: 01 932 4353.

D.H.V. Schaftlachersha 23, 8184 Gmund, West Germany. Tel: 080 2181 81.

F.I.V.L., via S. Sebastiano 42, 13062 Candelo, Italy.

Austin Aero Club, Prinz Eugen Shasse, Vienna.

The following schools have qualified instructors:

Michel Carnet: Sky Systems, Knoll Business Centre, Bellingham Crescent. Old Shoreham Road, Hove, BN3 7GS. Tel: (0273) 423650.

Parapente Services: Hyde Bank Mill, Hyde Bank Road, New Mills, near Stockport SK12 4BP. Tel: (0663) 43438 (daytime); (0663) 47513 (eves, weekends).

Welsh Hang Gliding Centre: 1E High Street, Crickhowell, Powys NP8 1BD. Tel: (0873) 810019.

Reading
Sky Wings magazine. The bi-monthly journal of the BAPC, serving British parascenders, hang gliders and paragliders.

Drachenflieger Magajin, Ringier Verlag, Ortlerstrasse 8, D-8000 Munchen 70, West Germany. Tel: 089 76992118. (Best paragliding magazine—includes international site guides.)

Vol Libre 3 rue Ampere, 94200 Ivry-sur-Seine, France. Tel: 46727460.

Parapente News Newsletter published by Parapente Services (see above).

The ABC of Paragliding by Hubert Aupetit. Retiné, Vol Libre. 1989 (first published 1986). Available in English and French.

Cycling

Starting
The Cyclists' Touring Club: Cotterell House, 69 Meadrow, Godalming, Surrey GU7 3HS. Tel: (04868) 7217.

Doing
There are no 'schools' of cycling: you simply get on your bike and *do it*. But for those unsure of the type of bike best suited to a particular trip, or the best kind of roads to use, it might be worth joining one of the CTC's local branches (District Associations). Alternatively pick through the books listed below for relevant tips.

Joining an organised cycle tour (addresses below) is one way of meeting companions and learning the basics.

Adventure Cycles: 2 Snow's Cottages, Mamhead, Kenton, Exeter, Devon EX6 8HW. Tel: (0626) 864786. Devon.

Anglia Cycling Holidays: Ballintuim, near Blairgowrie, Perthshire PH10 7NJ. Tel: (025086) 201. Suffolk (Constable Country), Norfolk, Cambridgeshire, Scotland, East Anglia.

Anglo-Dutch Sports: 30a Foxgrove Road, Beckenham, Kent BR3 2BD. Tel: (01) 650.2347. Netherlands, Austria.

Bent's Bicycle Tours: 65 Grove Road, Harpenden, Hertfordshire AL5 1EN. Tel: (05827) 69782. Bavaria.

Belle France: Bayham Abbey, Lamberhurst, Kent TN3 8BG. Tel: (0892) 980885. In the tracks of R.L. Stevenson (Cevennes, France), Massif Centrale (France).

Bicycle Beano: 59 Birch Hill Road, Clemonger, Hereford HR2 9RF. Tel: (0981) 251087. Shropshire and the Welsh Marches.

Bike Events: PO Box 75, Bath BA1 1BX. Tel: (0225) 310859. Europe.

Cyclists' Touring Club: See above for address. Worldwide.

Cyclorama Holidays: The Grange Hotel, Grange-over-Sands, Cumbria LA11 6EV. Tel: (05395) 33666. Lake District.

Flatford Mill Field Centre: East Bergholt, Colchester CO7 6UL. Tel: (0206) 298283. Suffolk's Constable Country.

Headwater Holidays: 62a Beech Road, Hartford, Northwich, Cheshire CW8 3AB. Tel: (0606) 782011. Lot Valley. Loire Valley and Jura mountains, France.

Highland Cycle Tours Highland Guides: Aviemore, Invernessshire PH22 1QH. Tel: (0479) 810729. Scottish Highlands.

Intasun, Intasun House: 2 Cromwell Avenue, Bromley, Kent BR2 9AQ. Tel: (01) 290.0511 ext 339. Danube.

Susi Madron's Holidays: Lloyd House, 22 Lloyd Street, Manchester M25 W4. Tel: (061) 834.6800. France.

SVP France: 122 High Street, Billingshurst, West Sussex RH14 8EP. Tel: (040 381) 5165. Western Loire, Auvergne (France).

Twickers World: see River Rafting for address. Southern China.

Reading
Bicycle Action Magazine: 331 Athlon Road, Wembley, Middlesex HA0 1BY. Tel: (01) 997.811.

Bicycle Magazine: The Northern & Shell Building, PO Box 381, Mill Harbour London E14 9TW. Tel: (01) 987.5090. Monthly.

Cycle Touring and Campaigning: The official magazine of the Cyclists' Touring Club (see above) Bi-monthly.

Cycling Weekly Magazine: Surrey House, 1 Throwley Way, Sutton, Surrey SM1 4QQ. Tel: (01) 643.8040. Weekly.

OCD Cycloclimbing: 37 Acacia Avenue, Hale, Altrincham, Cheshire WA15 8QY. The official magazine of the pass-climbing club, L'Ordre des Cols Dur.

Around the World on a Bicycle by Thomas Stevens. Century Hutchinson, London. 1988. (First published 1888).

Full Tilt: Ireland to India with a Bicycle by Dervla Murphy (first published 1965 by John Murray).

The Great Bicycle Adventure by Nicholas Crane. Oxford Illustrated Press. Oxford. 1987.

Journey to the Centre of the Earth by Richard & Nicholas Crane, Bantam Press, London, 1987, Corgi Books, 1988.

Richard's New Bicycle Book by Richard Ballantine. Oxford Illustrated Press, Oxford. 1988.

Freefall Parachuting

Starting
British Parachute Association: 5 Wharf Way, Glen Parva, Leicester LE2 9TF. Tel (0533) 785271.

Learning
Freefall Parachuting in the UK is tightly regulated; every UK skydiver belongs to the BPA.

There are three ways of making a first jump:

Static Line: after training for at least 6 hours you jump from a height of 2,000 to 3,500 feet. Your parachute opens automatically.

Tandem Freefall: minimal training is required. You jump from 12,000 feet attached to an instructor who opens the parachute and controls the landing. Tandem skydiving allows handicapped people to experience parachuting.

Accelerated Freefall (AFF): after eight hours training you make a first jump from 12,000 feet accompanied by two instructors. You pull your own ripcord and land independently.

Assuming that the first jump has not turned you back to flower-pressing you can embark on freefall training by working your way through Levels 1 to 8 of the Accelerated Freefall system. This takes 7-10 days if you are a fast learner and have good weather. You can also sign on for a ram-air conversion course (converting you from static line jumps on a round 'chute, to freefall on a rectangular, steerable ram-air chute).

A first jump can be made at the centres and clubs listed below.

Al Skydiving Centre: Rectory Farm, High Street, Cambridgeshire PE19 4UE. Tel: (076 77) 7065.

Black Knights Parachute Centre: Patty's Farm, Hilliam Lane, Cockerham, near Lancaster. Tel: (0524) 791820 weekends; (0510924) 5560 midweek.

British Parachute School: The Control Tower, Langar Airfield, Langar, Nottingham. Tel: (0949) 60878.

Doncaster Parachute Club: Doncaster Airfield, Doncaster, South Yorkshire. Tel: (0302) 532922 weekends; (0532) 505600.

Flying Tigers Skydiving Centre: Goodwood Airfield, Chichester, West Sussex PO18 0OH. Tel: (0243) 780333.

Halfpenny Green Skydiving Centre: The Airfield, Bobbington, near Stourbridge, West Midlands. Tel: (038) 488293.

Headcorn Parachute Centre: The Airfield, Headcorn, Kent, Tel: (0622) 890862.

London Skydiving Centre: Cranfield Airport, Cranfield, Bedford MK43 0AP. Tel. (0234) 751866.

Manchester Free Fall Club: 9 St Andrews Road, Stretford, Manchester M32 9JE. Tel: (061) 865 3912. Whitchurch, Shropshire.

Peterborough Parachute Centre: Sibson Airfield, Wansford, Peterborough. Tel: (08324) 490.

Slipstream Adventures: The Airfield, Headcorn, Kent TN27 9HX. Tel: (0622) 890641/890862.

The Sport Parachute Centre: Tilstock Airfield, Whitchurch, Shropshire. Tel: (0948) 841111.

Swansea Parachute Club, Swansea Airport: Fairwood Common, Swansea, West Glamorgan SA2 7JU. Tel: (0792) 296464. Gower Peninsula, South Wales.

Thruxton Parachute Club: Thruxton Airfield, Andover, Hampshire SP11 8PW. Tel: (0264) 772124.

Wild Geese School of Adventure: Training 27 Drumeil Road, Aghadowey, Coleraine, County Londonderry, N. Ireland BP51 4BB. Tel: (0265) 818669.

Reading

The Complete Sport Parachuting Guide by Charles Shea-Simonds. A & C Black, London. 1986.

Sky Diving in 8 Days by Miles Clark, Osprey, London, 1989.

The Sport Parachutist Magazine The official magazine of the B.P.A. Bi-monthly.

Sea Canoeing

Starting

British Canoe Union see White Water Canoeing for address.

Learning

You should learn with a qualified instructor before venturing out to sea in a canoe. Some canoe schools run residential courses lasting one week, during which time you can master skills ranging from launch and control through to compass navigation, tides, currents, beaching, surf, meteorology and so on. The BCU run a number of kayak proficiency tests. Either join one of the BCU's affiliated clubs (a full list of addresses is in the BCU Members' Year Book) or take a course at a commercially-run centre (see below).

Anglesey School of Sea Canoeing: Trearddur Bay, Anglesey, Gwynnedd. Tel: (0407) 86020.

Calshot Activities Centre: see Sailing for address.

Current Trends Canoe School: see White Water Canoeing for address.

Overseas

Arctic Experience see Horse Riding for address. Greenland, Canada.

Nigel Foster Canoeing Ventures: 5 Tan-y-bwych, Myndd Llandegai, near Bethesda, Gwynneth LL57 4DX. Tel: (0248) 602058. Scottish Islands, Iceland.

Twickers World Travel: see River Rafting for address. Glacier Bay (Alaska).

Reading

Canoeist magazine: S T & R J Fisher, 4 Sinodun Row, Appleford, Oxfordshire OX14 4PE. Monthly.

Blazing Paddles: A Solo Journey around Scotland by Kayak by Brian Wilson. Oxford Illustrated Press, Oxford. 1988.
Keep it Moving: Baja by Canoe by Valerie Fons. The Mountaineers, Seattle. 1986.
Sea Canoeing by Derek Hutchinson. A & C Black, London, 1976.
Start Canoeing by Anne Williams & Debbie Piercey. Stanley Paul, London 1980.

Hang Gliding

Starting

British Hang Gliding Association, Cranfield Airfield, Cranfield, Bedfordshire MK43 0YR. Tel: (0234) 751688.

Learning

Book a course at a BHGA registered school (see below) and spend 4 or 5 days to complete the Elementary Pilot Certificate. You will be able to fly off the ground on the second or third day. The next stage is to take the Club Pilot Certificate, either with your registered school or with a club. Total tuition time is reduced if there is no break between the two courses. The Club Pilot Certificate takes 8 or 9 days and includes glider control movements, theory of flight, glider handling and soaring. Next comes the Cross Country Pilot Certificate, and finally the Advanced Pilot Certificate—the highest level awarded by the BHGA.

The hang-gliding schools listed below are registering with the BHGA.

Cairnwell Hang Gliding School: Cairnwell Mountain, Braemar, Aberdeenshire AB3 5XS. Tel: (03383) 331.

Devon School of Hang Gliding: 1 Dovedale Road, Beacon Park, Plymouth, Devon PL2 2RR. Tel: (0752) 564408. Dartmoor.

Free Flight: 274 New Church Road, Hove, Sussex BN3 4EB. Tel: (0273) 411239.

High Adventure: Tapnell Farm, Afton, Yarmouth, Isle of Wight PO41 0YJ. Tel: (0983) 754042.

Hiway Flight Training: Longtown, Hereford HR2 0LE. Tel: (0873) 87266. Military training only.

Lomond Hang Gliding: 48a Garscube Terrace, Ravelston, Edinburgh, Scotland. Tel: (031) 313 2808.

Mercia Hang Gliding School: Charter House, 45 High Street, Alcester, Warwickshire. Tel: (0527) 501489.

The Northern Hang Gliding Centre: Dunvegan Lodge Front Street, Barmby Moor, York Y04 5EB. Tel: (0759) 304404.

Northern School of Hang Gliding: Hey End Farm, Luddenden Foot, near Shipley, West Yorkshire HX2 6JN. Tel: (0422) 834989.

Peak Flight Ltd, 4 Abbey Units, Macclesfield Road, Leek, Staffordshire ST13 8LD. Tel: (0538) 383659.

Pennine Hang Gliding School: 1 Maplin Avenue, Salendine Nook, Huddersfield, West Yorkshire HD3 3GP. Tel: (0484) 641306.

Skyriders British Hang Gliding Schools: 15 St Mary's Green, Biggin Hill, Kent TN16 2RB. Tel: (0959) 73996.

Skysports: 36 Hatherleigh Road, Abergavenny, Gwent. Tel: (0873) 6112.

Skywing Sports: 59 Chelsfield Road, Orpington, Kent BR5 4DS. Tel: (0689) 73873 or 55932.

Sussex College of Hang Gliding: 49 Church Street, Brighton, Sussex BN1 3LF. Tel: (0273) 609925. South Downs and Wales.

Welsh Hang Gliding Centre: 1E High Street, Crickhowell, Powys, South Wales NP8 1BD. Tel: (0873) 810019.

Wiltshire Hang Gliding Centre: The Old Barn, Rhyls Lane, Lockeridge, Marlborough, Wiltshire SN8 4EE. Tel: (0672) 86554. Wiltshire Downs.

Windlord: 2/3 Home Farm Cotttages, Swarland, Morpeth, Northumberland. Tel: (0670) 87774.

Reading

Sky Wings magazine: The official magazine of the BHGA includes parascending.

The Complete Hang Gliding Guide by Noel Whittall. A & C Black. 1984.

The Student Handbook & The Pilot Handbook. Both published by the BHGA.

Mountain Walking

Starting

British Mountaineering Council (see Rock Climbing for address).

Learning

Largely self-taught, but there are courses and qualifications available through the BMC (see Rock Climbing). The Mountain-walking Leader Training Scheme (Summer) trains and assesses the technical and leadership skills required by those wishing to lead groups of young people in the British mountains. The course is composed of training and assessment, which must be separated by one year. During this year

134

candidates are expected to gain experience in three different mountain regions and climb a minimum of 30 peaks over 600 metres. The syllabus itself covers navigation, walking skills, equipment, camp craft, security on steep ground, mountain hazards and emergency procedures, meteorology and conservation.

An MLTB winter scheme is run by the Scottish Winter Mountain Leader Board (1 St. Colme Street, Edinburgh EH3 6AA. Tel: (031) 255.8411.

The organisations listed below run trekking holidays (sometimes with instruction).

C-N-DO: Scotland Howlands Cottage, Sauchieburn, Sterling FK7 9PZ. Tel: (0786) 812355. Scotland.

Cuillin Guides: see Rock Climbing for address.

Dartmoor Expedition Centre: see Caving for address.

Exodus Expeditions: see above for address. Atlas Mountains (Morocco), Alps, Sierra Nevada (Spain), Cragus and Taurus Mountains (Turkey), Kenyan Highlands, Malawi mountains, Himalayas, Karakorum, Andes, Korean mountains, Indonesian mountains.

ExplorAsia: 13 Chapter Street, London SW1P 4NY. Tel: (01) 630.7102. Himalayas, Andes.

Brian Hall: see Rock Climbing for address. French Alps.

International School of Mountaineering: see Rock Climbing for address. Alps.

Alan Kimber: see Rock Climbing for address.

Martin Moran: see Winter Mountaineering for address.

Nevis Guides: see Rock Climbing for address.

Outward Bound Eskdale: Eskdale Green, Holmbrook, Cumbria CA19 1TE. Tel. (09403) 287.

Roger Payne: see Rock Climbing for address.

Polaris Mountaineering: see above for address. Snowdonia.

Sporting Travel Services: see River Rafting for address. Connemara (Eire).

SVP France: see Cycling for address. Auvergne.

Twickers World Travel: see above for address. Alps, Pyrenees, Pindos and Taygetos Mountains (Greece), Corsica, Iceland, Atlas Mountains (Morocco), Himalayas, Thai Hills (Thailand), Mount Kenya, Mount Kilimanjaro, Andes, Patagonia.

WEST: see Woodlore for address.

Reading

Trekking: Great Walks of the World, ed: John Cleare. Unwin Hyman, London, 1988.

A Short Walk in the Hindu Kush by Eric Newby, Picador, London. 1981 (first published in 1958 by Secker and Warburg).

Mountainbiking

Starting

Mountain Bike Club Albert Street: St Georges, Telford TF2 9AS. Tel: (0952) 610158.

Like road cycling, mountainbiking is self-taught. There are two rules: 1. to take great care not to damage the countryside 2. to treat mountains with the same respect that a climber or walker would; in wild places you need bad weather clothing, food, map and compass. And commonsense.

Mountainbike Courses

Outdoor Adventure: Atlantic Court, Widemouth Bay, Cornwall EX23 0DF. Tel: (028885) 312.

Mountain Bike Club: see above for address. East Anglia, Cornwall, Shropshire.

Mountainbike Tours

Adventure Balloons: see Ballooning chapter for address. Somerset.

Ancient Treks: North Lodge, Whitchurch, Pangbourne, Berkshire RG8 7NU. Tel: (0735) 72762. Chilterns, Ridgeway, Downs, Wessex.

Beics Betwys: Tan Lan, Betwys-y-Coed, Gwynedd LL24 0AB. Tel: (06902) 766. Snowdonia.

Breckland Bicycle Breaks: Tom Sillis, Santon House, Santon Downham, Suffolk IP27 0TT. Thetford Forest.

Clive Powell Mountain Bikes: The Mount, East Street, Rhayader, Powys LD6 5DN. Tel: (0597) 810585. Wales.

Mountain Bike Club: see above for address. Tenerife. Majorca.

Mountain Bike Dales Tours: 39 Rowan Court, Catterick Village, Richmond, North Yorkshire DL10 7RS. Tel: (0748) 811885. Yorkshire Dales.

Neuadd Arms Hotel: The Square, Llanwrtyd Wells, Powys. Tel: (05913) 236.

Seal Guides: see Caving for address. Pennines.

Reading

Mountain Biking UK magazine, Pacificon

Limited, Woodstock House, Luton Road, Faversham, Kent ME13 8HQ. Tel: (0795) 538903. Monthly.

Bicycles up Kilimanjaro, by Nicholas and Richard Crane, Oxford Illustrated Press, Oxford. 1985.

The Mountain Biking Handbook by Barry Ricketts.

Canoe Touring

British Canoe Union see White Water Canoeing for address.

Learning
The BCU run a range of touring kayak and Canadian canoe tests which can be taken if you need confirmation of your canoeing skills. Either learn through one of the BCU's affiliated clubs (a full list of addresses is in the BCU's Members' Year Book) or take a course at a commercially-run centre (see below; contact BCU for list of approved centres). Inland waterways in Britain are subject to access restrictions and many are private. In some places, licences are required. Contact the BCU for information.

Calshot Activities Centre (see Sailing for address).

Current Trends Canoe School (see White Water Canoeing for address).

See also all schools listed in White Water Canoeing section.

Canoe Tours
Abercrombie & Kent Travel: Sloane Square House, Holbein Place, London SW1W 8NS. Tel: (01) 730.9600. Zimbabwe and Okavango Swamp, Botswana.

Association for Adventure Sports: see above for address. River Barrow, Eire.

Headwater Holidays: see above for address. Loire Valley, Creuse and Jura Mountains (France).

Mobile Adventure Training: Bridge Works, Knighton Fields Road West, Leicester LE2 6LG. Tel: (0533) 440165. Scotland, Lake District.

Sporting Travel Services: see River Rafting for address. Scandinavia, France, Canada.

Reading
Canoeist magazine, S T & R J Fisher, 4 Sinodun Row, Appleford, Oxfordshire OX14 4PE. Monthly.

Start Canoeing by Anne Williams & Debbie Piercey. Stanley Paul, London, 1980.

Path of the Paddle: An Illustrated Guide to the Art of Canoeing by Bill Mason. Key Roster Books, Toronto, 1984.

Deliverance by James Dickey. Pan Books, London. 1971. (first published in UK by Hamish Hamilton, London, 1970). John Boorman's film of the book stars Jon Voight and Burt Reynolds.

Ski-Mountaineering

Austrian Alpine Club (UK branch): 13 Longcroft House, Fretherne Road, Welwyn Garden City, Herts AL8 6PQ. Tel: (0707) 324835.

Starting
British Mountaineering Council (see Rock Climbing for address).

Ski Club of Great Britain: 118 Eaton Square, London SW1W 9AF. Tel: (01) 245.1033.

Learning
The only ski-mountaineering qualification in Britain is the Guides Carnet, held by instructors who have graduated into the British Association of Mountain Guides (see 'Rock Climbing').

Skiing
BMC. See Rock Climbing for address.

International School of Mountaineering: see Rock Climbing for address.

Mountain Guides: Nevisport, High Street, Fort William. Tel: (0397) 4767.

Roger Payne: see Rock Climbing for address.

Scottish Mountain Guides: Airleywight, The Crescent, Kingussie, Inverness-shire PH21 1JZ. Tel: (05402) 532.

Ski Club of Great Britain: see above for address. Alps.

Stuart Miller: see Winter Mountaineering for address.

Reading
Ski Mountaineering by Peter Cliff, Unwin Hyman, London, 1987.

Ski Mountaineering in Scotland edited by Donald Bennet and Bill Wallace. Scottish Mountaineering Trust. 1987.

A Little Walk on Skis: from the Mediterranean to Austria along the Alps off piste by Peter and Beryl Wilberforce Smith. Dickerson, Norfolk. 1987.